Working with
Self-Harming Adolescents

A NORTON PROFESSIONAL BOOK

Working with Self-Harming Adolescents

A Collaborative Strengths-Based Therapy Approach

Matthew D. Selekman

W. W. Norton & Company
New York • London

Originally published under the title LIVING ON THE RAZOR'S EDGE: Solution-Oriented Brief Family Therapy with Self-Harming Adolescents

Production Manager: Leeann Graham
Manufacturing by Haddon Craftsmen

Library of Congress Cataloging-in-Publication Data

Selekman, Matthew D., 1957-
Working with self-harming adolescents : a collaborative, strengths-based therapy
approach / Matthew D. Selekman. – [2nd ed.].
       p. ; cm.
"A Norton professional book."
Rev. ed. of: Living on the razor's edge. 1st ed. c2002.
ISBN 0-393-70499-8 (pbk)
1. Adolescent psychotherapy. 2. Solution-focused brief therapy. 3. Self-injurious
behavior. 4. Psychotherapy. I. Selekman, Matthew D., 1957- Living on the razor's edge.
II. Title.

RJ503.S447 2006
616.89'14'0835—dc22   2005052345

W. W. Norton & Company, Inc., 500 Fifth Avenue, New York, N. Y. 10110
www.wwnorton.com

W. W. Norton & Company Ltd., Castle House, 75/76 Wells St., London W1T 3QT

1 3 5 7 9 0 8 6 4 2

Contents

Foreword

In 1985 I heard a story from Bruno Bettleheim. While living in Europe during his younger years, he was receiving a training analysis. He regularly shared the waiting room with a disturbed 10-year-old boy who was also in analysis. In those days, the rules of analysis were very strict and Bettleheim knew that conversation and interaction between anaylsands was taboo. But, on occasion, the boy would walk over to the window planter, pluck a bud off the cactus, and chew on it. Blood would pour from his mouth and it was all Bettleheim could do to restrain himself from intervening. Finally, after about a year, when the boy again went over and began chewing the cactus, Bettleheim could no longer restrain himself and demanded that the boy stop this horrible behavior and explain why in the world he did such a thing to himself.

The boy turned to Bettleheim, pointed to his mouth, and said flatly, "The pain here is nothing compared to the pain here," this time pointing to his heart. Bettleheim was stunned into silence by the profound lucidity of the boy's words.

Self-mutilation, like anorexia, is perplexing and difficult for medical personnel, loved ones, and many therapists to understand. It is also challenging to treat. This book helps readers understand the experience and motivations of adolescents who harm themselves. Additionally, it gives practical methods for treating this bewildering, challenging problem.

I once had a client who exclaimed during a session, "I know what you are doing! You are looking for the jewel under the garbage." I liked that description and it came to mind again when I read this book. In order to work effectively with this tough problem, you have to believe that there is, indeed, a jewel under the garbage. That there is a living, breathing, healthy human being beneath the disturbing behavior and feelings that accompany self-harming.

I have heard many times over the 23 years I have been teaching solution-based therapies that they surely can't work with difficult, serious pathologies. This book debunks that myth, and this is what makes it unique. Most other literature on the subject of self-harming is grounded in pathology-based approaches. This book is the first to take a solution-oriented, competence-based, nonpathology approach to self-mutilation.

What is admirable about Matthew Selekman's last two books is that he strives to be flexible and nondogmatic. I came across a bumper sticker some time ago that said, *I'm sorry, but my karma just ran over your dogma.* It seems to be Matthew's karma to push the boundaries of solution-focused therapy (and perhaps the buttons of dogmatic solution-focused purists) by including ideas from various therapy approaches that can expand the rather narrow guidelines of the solution-focused approach while still remaining true to its spirit. He works under the rather unusual guideline of *Use whatever works, as long as it is respectful.*

So, read this book for its many clear and helpful techniques and methods, but also read it to absorb its spirit: flexibility and faith in the underlying competence and health of the people with whom we work. This book is not only on the razor's edge of innovative, effective therapy—it is a cut above.

—Bill O'Hanlon

Practical Guidelines for Parents on How To Prevent and Constructively Manage Self-Harming Behavior with Their Adolescents

"Why is my daughter cutting herself? Does she want to die?" "Is my son trying to get even with me about something? What should I do?" Often, I am asked these questions by parents of self-harming adolescents who are both perplexed by this behavior and at a loss for what to do. Although there are many causes of self-harming behavior, some of the most common ones have to do with extremes in the quality of the parents' attachments to their adolescents (that is, a lack of boundaries or too much emotional distance), the adolescent's difficulty with self-regulation, which has to do with their inability to adequately soothe themself or manage their moods when experiencing emotional distress, and the adolescent's struggles with fitting in with peers or affiliating with negative peer groups. Many adolescents learn how to cut or burn themselves from their peers. In order to be accepted by and bond with them, they feel compelled to engage in this behavior. However, when adolescents have secure and positive attachment bonds with their parents, they are less likely to fall prey to this strong peer pressure to self harm or engage in other self-destructive behaviors like substance abuse or bulimia.

Most parents, once they discover that their son or daughter is self harming, become quite anxious and fearful for his or her safety. In response to this fear, parents regularly look through their adolescent's bedroom and personal belongings for sharp objects, greatly restricting the adolescent's opportunities for autonomy, and in extreme situations, a parent might move into the adolescent's bedroom to try and prevent him or her from self-harming. Other parents respond in the opposite way. Rather than increasing their emotional support and protective behaviors with their adolescents, they react with anger, lecture at them about the dangers of this behavior, minimize the seriousness of this behavior, treat this behavior as "attention-seeking," or become so emotionally disconnected from their adolescents that they do not respond at all to their self-harming behavior. This latter response may especially occur among parents who are too wedded to their professional careers and do not provide enough boundaries between their work and family lives, or among parents who are struggling with severe marital and post-divorce conflicts or other unresolved personal issues.

All of these difficulties can fuel invalidating interactions and emotional disconnection between the adolescent and his or her parents. The different types of parenting responses described above can either trigger or maintain the adolescent's self-harming behavior. In addition, adolescents are more likely to affiliate with negative peer groups when they feel like their personal boundaries and autonomy are being prevented or they feel repeatedly invalidated by or emotionally disconnected from their parents.

Ideally, parents should respond to their adolescent's self-harming behavior by remaining calm, trying to comfort or soothe him or her, and trying to secure a good understanding of what prompted this behavior. Furthermore, the parents should invite their adolescent to share with them how they can assist in better managing the current stressors in the adolescent's life. The more parents can consistently make themselves available for emotional connection, support their adolescent's strivings for more independence, and provide and enforce rules and their consequences, the less likely their son or daughter will be to engage in self-harming and similar behaviors. Research indicates that the stronger and more secure the parents' attachments are with their adolescents, the less likely adolescents are to gravitate toward a negative peer group (Henggeler, Schoenwald, Borduin, Rowland, & Cunningham, 1998). Researchers who have studied resilient children and adolescents (that is, kids who have consistently been able to quickly rebound from painful life events) found that their secure attachments with parents or key caretakers had a "steeling" effect on them, which served as a protective function in helping them cope with these adverse life stressors (Haggerty, Sherrod, Garmezy, & Rutter, 1994; Anthony & Cohler, 1987).

afbct + page 3

RESEARCH ON SELF-HARMING ADOLESCENTS

There is very little research on adolescent self-harming behavior. Those studies that have been conducted include adults in the samples, making it unclear how adolescents who self harm are different from adults. In an effort to expand my knowledge base in the area of adolescent self-harm, I conducted an exploratory study with 20 self-harming high-school-aged adolescents (15 females and 5 males) to learn from them the following: what they considered major aggravating factors that contribute to why so many adolescents self harm today, key family and peer causal factors, what positive effects they had gained from self-harming, and how parents, therapists, and treatment programs could best manage this behavior. Although this was a very small sample size, these resourceful experts on self-harming behavior had a wealth of valuable wisdom to offer me, the professionals I train and consult with, and the parents I work with in my private practice (Selekman, 2005). Most of their experiences and recommendations about what worked for them in resolving their self-harming were consistent with other self-harming adolescents I treated who had not participated in this study.

For the majority of adolescents in the study and in my private practice, self-harming behavior serves as a coping strategy for managing emotional distress triggered by a combination of family, peer, and school stressors. Once they cut or burn themselves, their bodies rapidly secrete endorphins into their bloodstreams producing a numbing or euphoric sensation. One adolescent in the study said that self-harming became "a friend" for her in that she could "always count on it" for quick relief. This adolescent's parents were reportedly too involved with their careers and social lives to make themselves available to soothe her when she would experience emotional distress. In fact, several adolescents reported in the study that their parents were either not available to them to provide emotional support or invalidated their feelings by "not listening to" or "not respecting" them. In these situations, the adolescents reported that their self-harming behavior was employed to soothe them, stimulate them if they felt emotionally dead inside, or in extreme situations, it served as a form of self-punishment. The latter adolescents truly believed that they were "not worthy of being loved," and felt "worthless." Some of the adolescents in the study who were experiencing peer conflicts and rejection also self-harmed for these reasons.

Other adolescents reported that self-harming behavior was "like abusing a drug," in that it produced a numbing sensation or had a euphoric effect on them. In fact, close to 70% of the time, self-harming adolescents and adults report experiencing immediate relief after engaging in this behavior (Selekman, 2005; Favazza & Selekman, 2003). Based on this statistic, it is easy to see how this behavior can become addictive for adolescents. However, a few hours later the analgesic or pleasurable effects of the self-harming behavior wears off, and many adolescents report feeling "empty," "guilty," "bummed out," "anxious," or "angry at themselves" for not being able to control their impulses and disfiguring their bodies. To quickly alleviate these unpleasant thoughts and feelings and being at a loss for alternative coping strategies, they turn again to self-harm for quick relief from further emotional distress.

PREVENTION OF SELF-HARM

When parents can establish close and meaningful relationships with their children, instill healthy family values and attitudes in them, and provide a secure, predictable, and nurturing home base, children will be less likely to develop difficulties during adolescence (Catalano, 2005). The parenting guidelines below are based on important developmental and resiliency research studies (Wylie, 2004; Siegel & Hartzell, 2003; Siegel, 1999; Haggerty et al., 1994; Main, 1995; Bowlby, 1988), key findings from my research, and my 23 years of clinical practice experience working with adolescents and their families. Even if their adolescents are already self-harming, parents can use the guidelines as a checklist to critically examine their parenting styles and the type of family environments they have provided. The guidelines offer parents many valuable and practical ideas for how to change their interactions with their adolescents and strengthen their relationships with them.

- Adolescents need to know that their parents will be there for them when they seek emotional support from them.
- Parents uphold the importance of spending time together as a family. This time is considered sacred and protected by all family members.
- Adolescents should be involved in family decision-making regarding rules and consequences, chore selection, planning family activities and vacations.
- Parental rules and consequences are clear, fair, and consistently enforced. Setting limits is a loving act and helps adolescents develop impulse control and make better choices.

- Parents are flexible and respect their adolescents' needs for more autonomy.
- Parents consistently strive to create an inviting, positive, and nurturing home environment.
- Parents provide firm and consistent guidelines for their adolescents' use of the computer, TV, and other high tech equipment. It is important that parents tightly monitor and are aware of the websites their adolescents are visiting.
- Parents should know their adolescents' friends, their parents, and the activities their sons or daughters engage in outside the house with their peers. They should intervene early if their son or daughter becomes affiliated with a negative peer group that could set the stage for future trouble.
- Parents strive to consistently respond to their adolescent's disappointments, failures, and poor choice-making with emotional support, validation, and optimism.
- Parents expect that the adolescent contributes to the family by being responsible about chore completion, pitching in when family members need assistance, and in general serving as a valued member of the family team.
- Parents need to avoid at all costs over-scheduling their adolescents in too many extra-curricular and academically-oriented activities to make them more attractive candidates for earning college scholarships or for getting into top-notch universities. Some parents live vicariously through their adolescents, that is, treat them like extensions of themselves, not separate and unique individuals with their own wishes, aspirations, and goals. In these situations, the parents put a lot of pressure on adolescents to be the *best* student or *star* athlete. The unspoken or spoken parents' messages may be: "We want you to be everything that we failed to become" or "You need to get more 'A's so you can get a scholarship."
- Parents respect their adolescent's attempts to establish his or her individuality, such as musical preferences, dress, personal interests, leisure activities (as long as these are legal), and ideals and values (as long as they are not harmful to family members and others outside the home).
- Parents strive to take a strong interest in their adolescents' lives, are good listeners, and keep the lines of communication open.
- Parents regularly solicit from their adolescents feedback on how well they are doing in the parenting department and welcome

without defensiveness any recommended adjustments. Parents need to commit to making these changes.

- Parents need to become skilled solution detectives and pull out their imaginary magnifying glasses to capture and praise their adolescents' responsible and respectful behaviors. Furthermore, they should celebrate their adolescents' personal accomplishments daily.
- Parents should model for their adolescents healthy and constructive ways to manage work and life stressors, such as running, walking, biking, meditating, engaging in a pleasurable hobby, and talking about what is bothering them (unless this is private adult business).
- Parents should regularly talk to their adolescents about their thoughts, feelings, perceptions, memories as an adolescent, and share their attitudes, beliefs, and intentions. This helps adolescents to develop a deeper understanding of their parents as people, strengthen their connections with them, adopt an empathic view of others, and become compassionate people (Siegel & Hartzell, 2003).
- Parents refrain from overindulging their adolescent, which provides him or her with the opportunity to develop a healthy level of frustration tolerance and learn the value of working for things you really want.
- Parents model and teach their adolescents assertiveness, conflict-resolution, and problem-solving skills. They can share with their adolescents stories of themselves as teenagers and as adults where they successfully employed these skills to constructively resolve difficulties.

For several decades, developmental and resiliency researchers have stressed the importance of parents establishing strong bonds with their children, which provides them with critical emotional insulation to cope with life's stressors and disappointments (Siegel & Hartzell, 2003; Siegel, 1999; Main, 1995; Bowlby, 1988; Haggerty et al., 1994; Anthony & Cohler, 1987). Unfortunately, in today's consumerist and highly toxic cultural landscape, family attachments are eroding away and we are allowing our kids to live in a computerized world of isolation. Siegel & Hartzell (2003) and Main (1995) have found in their research that the more coherent and emotionally rich parents' narratives are about their own childhood experiences, the more likely they are to form healthy and secure relationships with their children. In fact, how clearly parents made sense of their past lives or did not was the most powerful predictor (85% accuracy) of whether their own children would be securely attached to them (Wylie, 2004; Main, 1995). This is why parents need to set aside time in their busy schedules to maintain a strong presence in their adolescents' lives. I like to encourage parents to share their most cherished and memorable stories from their childhoods with their adolescents, such as meaningful experiences with their own parents and peers, their struggles as teenagers, and how they overcame adversity in tough situations. Every child likes a good story, particularly one that is filled with wisdom and normalizes their own struggles as an adolescent. Besides taking a sincere interest in their adolescents' lives, parents also should invite their adolescents to select some fun or meaningful activity they would like to do with them.

When parents can provide a nurturing and positive climate at home, their adolescents will be more likely to want to engage in activities with them and keep the lines of communication open. They also will be more likely to talk to and treat parents in a respectful way, not lie, and not engage in sneaky behaviors. In my private practice, I always share with parents that respect is a two-way street. Fredrickson (2002) has found in her research that when individuals experience regular doses of positive emotion or are working in settings where the climate is positive and upbeat, they tend to perform at a much higher level with their creative problem-solving abilities than when they are in environments that trigger negative emotion. She also found that positive emotion helps strengthen our resiliency, protective factors, and immune systems and helps us be more confident and optimistic when faced with adverse situations. Because of all of the physical, psychological and social benefits of positive emotion, I strongly encourage parents to refrain from blaming, lecturing at, humiliating, and being too negative and critical with their adolescents and instead, strive to keep the atmosphere at home more inviting, positive, and upbeat.

Parents rarely check in with their adolescents about how well they are doing in their parenting jobs. This is because many parents believe that it is up to their adolescents to change and not them. Not only can this helpful feedback guide parents in better matching their responses to the unique needs of their adolescents in different situations, but it demonstrates that they are committed to doing whatever it takes to strengthening their relationships with them. Adolescents are often quite surprised and pleased that their parents are sincerely interested in getting feedback from them on their parenting style and abilities, particularly when they want to find out what they could do differently to further improve the quality of their relationships.

MANAGEMENT OF SELF-HARMING EPISODES

Many parents are at a loss for how best to respond to their adolescents' self-harming behavior. Because this behavior is so intimidating and appears to be life-threatening, parents tend to respond in extreme ways. Some parents become extremely overprotective, others may become paralyzed by guilt, some resort to lecturing about the dangers of this behavior, while others may view this behavior as "manipulative" or "attention-seeking" and manage it like any other form of misbehavior. However, the truth of the matter is that the self-harming behavior is a dramatic indication that something is not right in the adolescent's life. The guidelines below offer parents many practical ideas for how best to approach their adolescents after a self-harming episode to gain a good grasp of what the key stressors are in their lives that might be fueling this behavior, effective ways to comfort them, and steps to reduce the likelihood of future self-harming episodes from occurring.

- Parents should avoid getting angry with, becoming too emotionally reactive to, and allowing their anxiety to further overwhelm their adolescent following a slip.
- Parents need to soothe their adolescent and provide emotional support following a self-harming episode. Invite him or her to share his or her story about the slip. The parents need to make eye contact and be respectful listeners before offering their thoughts on the situation.
- Parents need to try and understand the precipitants for the slip and the meaning of this behavior for the adolescent. Some useful questions they can ask their adolescents are:

  - "Now that I know that you are cutting yourself, can you help me understand what it means to you?"
  - "How has it been helpful for you to do this?"
  - "Is there anything really stressing you out in your life right now that I might be able to help you out with?"

- "If you don't wish to talk about it right now, I understand. I just want you to know that I care and am here for you when you are ready to talk about it. Would you like me to check in with you or would you prefer to come to me when you are ready to talk?"

- Parents should tap into their adolescents' expertise and find out from them what they may be doing that is contributing to their self-harming behavior. They can ask their adolescents:

  - "In what ways have we contributed to your cutting yourself?
  - "What specifically do we do that bothers you the most?"
  - "Which one of these behaviors do you want us to change first?"
  - "How will that make a difference to you when we stop doing that?"
  - "In the future when something is really bothering you or you are feeling really stressed out, how would you like us to respond?"
  - "What should we avoid doing at all costs?"
  - "Is there anything missing in our relationship, that if it were present, would make a difference?"

  They should avoid lecturing, yelling, put downs, harsh and lengthy punishments, going through the adolescent's bedroom without him or her present, threats of sending the adolescent off to boarding school or residential treatment. All of these unproductive parenting responses can set in motion a prolonged relapse and other acting out behaviors.

- Following a slip, explore with the adolescent what he or she learned from the slip that he or she will put to use the next time they are faced with a similar situation. In addition, parents should encourage their adolescent to use the coping strategies and tools he or she learned in counseling, as well as employ his or her key strengths to better manage these type of stressful situations.

- One powerful trigger that might have contributed to the adolescent's slip was his or her visiting websites that glorify self-harming behavior. When it is clear that this is what happened, the parents should provide a time-limited consequence. Most of the adolescents in my research project reported that the graphic images of

self-inflicted violence shown on these websites was a very powerful trigger for them, and led to a self-harming episode.

- If it appears that the adolescent is self harming as a way to get
  even with, divide, or disempower the parents after losing his or
  her privileges or being grounded for getting into trouble, the parents need to be a united team and enforce their consequences
  without getting into a power struggle with their son or daughter.
  Later, once the adolescent has settled down, the parents can in a
  loving way review with their son or daughter what led to him or
  her receiving the consequence and he or she should be encouraged to talk about his or her difficulties rather than acting out.
- Parents need to be sensitive to the fact that slips go with the territory of change and should not think their son or daughter is
  back to square one. In a supportive and loving way, the parents
  should find out what steps their son or daughter needs to take to
  quickly get back on track. Also, the parents should find out from
  him or her what specifically they could do to help out in the best
  way possible.
- If the adolescent is experiencing difficulties at school due to conflicts with particular teachers or learning issues, these major stressors can trigger self-harming episodes. Parents need to serve as
  advocates for their adolescents and collaborate with these teachers to find out how best to resolve conflicts and meet their son or
  daughter's academic needs. Adolescents greatly appreciate when
  their parents are willing to champion their cause in this way
  because it shows that they care and are committed to them.
- Parents should celebrate their adolescent's short and long-term
  gains at staying on track and not self-harming. The celebration
  can take the form of taking the son or daughter out to one of his
  or her favorite restaurants, surprising him or her with a cake, or
  honoring his or her hard work with a special privilege. The parents should also find out from their son or daughter what specifically they have been doing that is contributing to his or her
  success. Once the adolescent identifies what specifically the parents are doing that is working, the parents should increase these
  solution-maintaining behaviors.

Most self-harming adolescents have grave difficulty with soothing themselves when experiencing emotional distress. This is why they resort to self-

harming, substance-abusing, and eating-distressed behaviors as attempts to rapidly comfort themselves. One former adolescent client found the sensation of "warm blood dripping down her arms" had "a calming effect" on her. For this adolescent, the use of the razor on her arms helped her to neutralize painful and anxious feelings triggered by her parents' intense arguments. She felt that she could not count on her parents to comfort her when she was in a bad place emotionally. Ideally, parents need to be like super sleuth detectives and intervene as early as possible when they observe their adolescents experiencing emotional distress or following a self-harming episode. They can soothe their adolescents by speaking to them with calm and comforting vocal tones, and by offering hugs and reassurance that together they will get through this tough situation. The more consistent parents become with timely soothing responses in these situations, the more their adolescents will begin to internalize their empathic and caring responses, and eventually develop mastery at soothing themselves rather than relying on self-harm and similar behaviors to provide this function for them. A consistent theme in my research project was the adolescents' desire to have positive and strong connections with their parents, not grow apart from them. They wanted to know that their parents loved them, embraced their uniqueness, and respected them as people. All of these adolescents valued the importance of family.

It is critical that parents provide firm guidelines around technology usage. Spending several hours a day, seven days a week in chat rooms, visiting psychologically harmful websites, e-mailing and instant messaging friends, and playing computer games creates selfless, moody, and emotionally disconnected kids. According to Gladwell (2002), allowing adolescents to have excessive and unmonitored time in isolation online with their peers can create "a world ruled by the logic of word of mouth," where ritualized, dramatic, and self-destructive behaviors are quite contagious and endorsed. Many of the self-harming clients in my research project and on my caseload spent several hours a day instant messaging their friends while they were cutting or burning themselves, exchanging digital photos of their fresh cuts, burn marks, or their scars, in chat rooms with other adolescents and adults who were self-harming, and visiting websites loaded with graphic images and live demonstrations of self-inflicted violence, such as *Blood Red*, *Razor Blade Kisses*, *Xanga*, and *The Cutting World*.

When asked about how parents should respond to their adolescents' self-harming episodes, the adolescents in my research project felt that parents should "not yell at," "lecture at," or "punish them," but "provide support" instead. They also felt that parents should "first hear them out" and "try and understand" what led to the slip. Furthermore, they felt that parents should "look at the big picture," that is, what is going *right* in their lives as well (Selekman, 2005).

In situations where it appears that the adolescent is using the threat of self-harm or has returned to self-harming behavior as a trump card or an attempt to disempower or divide the parents, the latter should provide an immediate consequence. However, rather than taking away privileges or grounding their adolescent, why not surprise them with something novel, a positive consequence? Positive consequences can take the form of having the adolescent volunteer at a soup kitchen serving the homeless, doing some other good deed in the community, or, having him or her make a card for an ill relative. Not only are adolescents often quite surprised by their parents' novel consequences, but they tend to be much more cooperative in accepting them without power struggles.

Despite parents' best efforts to change their parenting responses and resolve their adolescents' self-harming difficulties, they may find themselves getting frustrated or stuck, or the situation may be getting much worse with their adolescents. Prior to seeking professional help, parents can do some deep soul-searching and should ask themselves some critical questions which might help them better meet the needs of their adolescents. They can ask themselves:

- "When I was experiencing emotional distress as an adolescent, what specifically did my parents do to comfort me that worked?"
- "How was that helpful for me?"
- "Could this work with my daughter?"
- "What kinds of things did my parents do with me that made me feel invalidated or unloved by them?"
- "In what ways am I re-enacting those patterns with my son?"
- "What experiences from my past may be blocking me from having a closer relationship with my daughter?"
- "What steps can I take today to stand up to those past negative experiences and not allow them to get in the way of my having a stronger and more positive relationship with my daughter?"
- "What would my daughter appreciate the most that I could do today for her?"
- "As an adolescent, what adult outside the home did I have a highly positive and meaningful relationship with?"

- "What did he say and do with me that strengthened my connection with him?"
- "When I was experiencing rough times as an adolescent, what did he say or do that helped me the most?"

When I have had parents ask themselves these valuable and tough questions, often times they have gained important insight into what patterns from their past are blocking them from having stronger connections with their adolescents and how they can use what worked for them as adolescents in their relationships with parents and others outside the home to change their interactions with them. I also have found that these questions can empower parents to generate some high quality strategies for helping their adolescents resolve their self-harming difficulties.

WHAT PARENTS CAN DO TO GET THE MOST OUT OF PROFESSIONAL HELP

If the questions mentioned above fail to make a difference, parents should seek out a therapist, preferably a family therapist who specializes in adolescent self-harming problems. The ideal therapist should serve as a consultant to them in inviting them to determine their treatment goals, building on their strengths and past successes, helping them see how they get stuck, and collaborating with them to generate some novel experiments for changing their problem-maintaining patterns, improving their communications, and strengthening their relationships with their adolescents. It is important that the adolescent feels comfortable with and supported by the therapist. Parents must practice using their new parenting skills, in order to become proficient at using them when needed. If the parents are experiencing any difficulties implementing these parenting skills, they should seek assistance from the therapist to help remove the roadblocks or modify these strategies to make them more doable. Parents also should hold their adolescents accountable for using the various coping strategies that they are learning in counseling. By working together, parents and their adolescents are maximizing their chances for treatment success.

Individual therapy should be offered to the adolescent in the following situations: if he or she has grave difficulty opening up in the presence of the parents due to intense conflicts with them, if the parents' marital or post-divorce difficulties are so severe that they cannot tolerate being in the same room with one another, if the parents' individual difficulties demand so much attention that they overshadow the adolescent's issues, or to support the adolescent's developmental needs to separate and launch from the family. Once their adolescent begins individual therapy, the parents should avoid interrogating them about what they are talking about in sessions with the therapist. If the parents continue to engage in this behavior, it will further intensify the adolescent's conflicts with them and shut down the lines of communication.

The majority of adolescents in my research project indicated that the use of art therapy, visualization, and other multi-sensory interventions was most beneficial to them in both their individual and family therapy sessions. They found these interventions to be "calming" and "enjoyable to do." One adolescent said of her therapist's use of art therapy interventions with her, "They were really relaxing . . . sometimes it's just easier to draw out your feelings and thoughts, then to put words on them" (Selekman, 2005).

Group therapy should be pursued if the adolescent is experiencing peer difficulties, has poor social skills, can benefit from additional support outside the home, and in situations where the parents' work demands or childcare responsibilities make it difficult to schedule appointments for family therapy. This treatment modality can be a valuable adjunct to both individual and family therapy. Parents should locate a group that is skill-based and teaches adolescents effective tools for strengthening their mood management and cognitive, problem-solving, and relationship skills. The Stress-Busters' Leadership Group described in Chapter 8 provides adolescents with training in these critical areas.

During the course of treatment, if parents feel like their son or daughter is not improving and they are not being offered effective parenting strategies to change the situation at home, they should share their concerns with the therapist and see if necessary adjustments can be made to put them on the road to change. In some cases, what are contributing to the treatment impasse are goals that are vague, too big, or highly unrealistic. If re-negotiating the goals and other adjustments of the treatment plan are not making a difference, parents should not hesitate to pursue treatment for their adolescent elsewhere.

Therapists' weak therapeutic alliances and ruptures in their relationships with adolescent clients also may contribute to the lack of progress or their investment in the treatment process. Most of the adolescents in my research project were quite outspoken about what their previous therapists had done with them that put them on the defensive, ruptured their relationships with them, and led to their prematurely dropping out of treatment (Selekman, 2005). They identified the following negative therapist behaviors:

- "Being lectured at!"
- "After a relapse, don't overemphasize it. 'This is really awful . . . you have come back to the beginning.'"
- "Accept what I offer . . . even if I really don't know."
- "Too many questions . . . Interrogating me!"

A seasoned and highly competent therapist would pick up on their adolescent clients' or their parents' concerns early in the treatment process, would quickly abandon therapeutic strategies that were not working, and go to great lengths throughout the course of treatment to make sure his or her clients are satisfied with the service they are receiving.

Acknowledgments

There are several people I wish to acknowledge for greatly contributing to the ideas discussed in this book. First and foremost, I want to thank Michele Weiner-Davis for showing me a variety of shortcuts for empowering clients and rapidly navigating them to "possibility land." From "down under," I would like to thank Michael White and David Epston for introducing me to the creative therapeutic pathway of externalizing problems. A special thanks goes to Harry Goolishian and Harlene Anderson for teaching me the importance of giving therapy veteran clients plenty of room to share their problem-saturated stories and how to collaborate respectfully and effectively with all of the larger systems' professionals often involved in these families' lives. I would like to thank my friend and colleague Scott Miller for introducing me to the groundbreaking research and therapeutic ideas he and his colleagues are responsible for. A big thanks goes to Bill O'Hanlon for graciously agreeing to write the foreword and for being an important inspirational other in my professional development as a trainer and a consultant.

There are a few important people I would like to thank for paving the way to the creation of this book. A big thanks to Deborah Malmud at Norton, whose helpful editorial comments, support, and tremendous patience, helped me to put together a solid product. A very special thanks goes to Rhiannon for contributing two wonderful poems to my book: Your tremendous courage and ability to prevail over adversity teach therapists that self-harming kids are resourceful and possess the necessary strengths and talents to resolve their difficulties. Finally, I would like to thank my loving and supportive wife Åsa, and Hanna, my little angel and other love.

Working with
Self-Harming Adolescents

Introduction

The razor cuts into my skin, and this is how it
all begins! I blame myself for all of the fights
and cried a lot of lonely nights! The flowing
blood is on the floor, but I still cut me more
and more. I do the drugs to escape my pain
after all I have nothing to gain, drugs and
razors are my life. They take away my pain
and strife. When they're with me I am glad,
and the best thing is, I don't get mad.

— Rhiannon

RHIANNON'S POWERFUL WORDS graphically capture some of the reasons why adolescents have turned to self-harming behavior as a coping strategy. Her personal story is filled with many repeated experiences of being invalidated by key caregivers, feeling rejected and "not good enough," and discovering that cutting and heavy abuse of alcohol, marijuana, and methamphetamines were highly effective ways to anesthetize her pain. Rhiannon's experiences are no different than many other adolescents in this country who are struggling to cope with high levels of individual and family stress, toxic cultural environments, and a longing for connection with and validation from their parents and significant others in their lives.

Adolescent self-harming behavior appears to be on the rise today. Many of the mental health professionals and school social workers I provide consultation to on the local, national, and international levels are indicating that they have more self-harming adolescents on their caseloads than ever before. Unfortunately, research literature on the behavior is scant. And most of the research that has been conducted on this treatment population has been with adult samples or included only a small percentage of adolescents as subjects in the studies. Alderman

(1997) found in her research that somewhere between 1 and 2 million youth and adults have engaged in self-harming behavior across the country. Research indicates that the majority of self-harming individuals are women or adolescent girls and that cutting and burning are the leading forms of this behavior reported (Alderman, 1997; Conterio & Lader, 1998; Levenkron, 1998; D. Miller, 1994). However, as Alderman (1997) has pointed out, there are probably as many adult men as women who are engaging in self-harming behavior but do not present themselves for treatment due to traditional male socialization practices and the belief that going for therapy would be perceived as a "sign of weakness." Alderman's research shows high rates of self-harming behavior among the male prison population. According to Dusty Miller, women are not socialized to express violence externally. She believes that women act out by "acting in" (D. Miller, 1994), whereas men find it much more culturally acceptable to externalize their anger and act out. In line with Miller's observation about how women tend to "act in," Favazza (1998) has found that fifty percent of the adolescents and women he has treated for self-injury had eating disorders as well.

In this introduction, I first dispel some common myths about self-harming adolescents, discuss five major aggravating factors that contribute to the development and maintenance of this problem among youth, and present an integrative and flexible solution-oriented brief family therapy approach for treating this population. I discuss four ways I have expanded the basic solution-oriented brief family therapy model to build in more therapeutic flexibility and options. The introduction concludes with a brief overview of the rest of the book.

MYTHS ABOUT SELF-HARMING ADOLESCENTS

"Self-Harming Adolescents Are Borderlines"

The intimidating and repulsive nature of adolescents' deliberate brutalization of their bodies by burning or cutting themselves with sharp objects often leads therapists to gravitate toward an equally nightmarish diagnostic label for them: borderline personality disorder (Caplan, 1995; Lerman, 1996; Kutchins & Kirk, 1997). Therapists who frequently use this diagnosis with self-harming clients are probably clinically informed by the adult borderline personality disorder literature, which indicates that self-mutilation and other forms of impulsive behavior are considered major diagnostic features of borderline clients (Linehan, 1993; Kernberg,

1975; Masterson, 1981). However, as indicated by leading authorities in the area of self-injury and as can be seen by the case examples described in this book, adolescent self-harming clients do not engage in this behavior because of an underlying personality disorder (Conterio & Lader, 1998; Alderman, 1997). There are a multitude of reasons why adolescents engage in self-harming behavior. Brown (2000) contends that the borderline personality disorder diagnosis is often assigned to clients who "create discomfort for the powerful [therapists]" (p. 302). Not only is the borderline label one of the most stigmatizing labels an adolescent can be given, but it also is inaccurate: According to *DSM-IV*, a client must be at least 18 years old to receive this diagnosis!

"Most Self-Harming Adolescents Have Been Sexually or Physically Abused"

More often than not, therapists who are referred self-harming adolescents tend to formulate diagnostic impressions and entertain possible labels for their new clients based on the available intake information, such as drawing the immediate conclusion that there must be a history of sexual or physical abuse in the clients' backgrounds (Brown, 2000; Caplan, 1995; Dawes, 1994; Gergen & McNamee, 2000; Raskin & Lewandowski, 2000). After all, why else would these youth engage in such extreme self-destructive behaviors? However, much of the research on self-harming clients indicates there was no history of childhood sexual or physical abuse (Brodsky, Cliotre, & Dulit, 1995; Zweig-Frank, Paris, & Grizder, 1994).

I am not discounting the fact that there may be some self-harming adolescents who have experienced past sexual or physical traumatization and may or may not wish to address these issues. However, the clients ultimately must be invited to take the lead in determining what issues we focus our attention on and what their goals are. At all costs, therapists must avoid being privileged "experts" and editing their clients' stories. I have worked with far too many adolescents who, pushed by their previous therapists to "work through" their past traumatic experiences, ended up increasing their self-destructive behaviors or tried to kill themselves.

"Self-Harming Adolescents Are Suicidal"

Most self-harming adolescents engage in self-injurious behaviors as an efficient way to gain quick relief from emotional distress or other major stressors in their lives. They do not want to die. When self-harming adolescents die, it is usually due to accidentally severing veins during a cutting episode. According to Armando Favazza, an internationally renown expert on self-mutilation: "Self-mutilation is distinct from suicide. Major reviews have upheld this distinction. A basic understanding is that a person who truly attempts suicide seeks to end all feelings, whereas a person who self-mutilates seeks to feel better" (p. 262).

In school settings, once these adolescents are identified as engaging in self-injurious behaviors, they are often perceived as being suicidal and in need of immediate psychiatric intervention. This may lead to the adolescents' being admitted to a psychiatric hospital and placed on antidepressants.

"Adolescents Who Like to Pierce and Tattoo Their Bodies Have a Serious Problem With Self-Injury"

Body piercing and tattooing are a popular fad among youth today. For many adolescents, this type of self-decoration is a fashion statement. It also may serve as a membership card into the popular peer group the adolescent wishes to be a part of. Body piercing and tattooing are not a new phenomenon. Many ancient and modern cultures around the world have used tribal markings to communicate identity, status, and to convey a sense of belonging (Conterio & Lader, 1998; Favazza, 1998).

Self-harming adolescents, on the other hand, engage in this behavior not to make themselves more attractive but for quick relief from emotional distress or other stressors in their lives. This is the major distinction between true self-harming youth and those who are self-decorating (Alderman, 1997).

MAJOR AGGRAVATING FACTORS THAT FUEL ADOLESCENT SELF-HARMING BEHAVIOR

The Tipping Point

The medical research area of epidemiology provides some useful tools for analyzing and understanding why we are seeing an increase in adolescent self-harming behavior today. One of these tools is the concept of the *tipping point*. For medical epidemiologists, a tipping point is the moment in the development of an epidemic at which only a small change in the presence of the germ produces a big change in the rate of infection. The tool also can be employed to help explain the evolution of social epidemics. For example, geographer Jonathan Crane found that when the number of "affluent leadership class" families drops below 6% in an urban neighborhood, there is a rapid increase in adolescent social problems such as delinquency, dropping out of school, and out-of-wedlock pregnancies (Crane, 1991).

In his fascinating and thought-provoking book *The Tipping Point: How Little Things Can Make a Big Difference*, journalist Malcolm Gladwell employs the tipping point framework to help explain how social epidemics often happen suddenly and unexpectedly. Gladwell (2002) contends that if you carefully analyze any social epidemic, you will find three particular personality types or agents of change who are the "natural pollinators" of new ideas and trends. He calls these three agents of change: the *Law of a Few*, the *Stickiness Factor*, and the *Power of Context* (p. 19). Individuals who fit into Gladwell's Law of a Few personality type possess superb social skills, are energetic, and are quite knowledgeable or influential among their peers. One great historical figure that fit into this category was Paul Revere, who set in motion a word-of-mouth epidemic.

Revere was carrying a sensational and important piece of news: The British were coming. At the same time that Revere set out to warn people about the British invasion, a tanner by the name of William Dawes set out on the same urgent mission, with the same important information. So why did Revere make it into the history books instead of Dawes? According to Gladwell, the success of any kind of social epidemic is heavily dependent on the involvement of people with strong social skills. Revere's news "tipped" and Dawes's did not because the former had a much more dynamic personality and was highly respected in his community. The Reveres of this world are *connectors*. Connectors not only have a knack for creating an enormous social circle of friends and acquaintances, but they also manage to occupy many different worlds, subcultures, and niches.

Two other personality types or agents of change that fit into Gladwell's Law of a Few category are the *mavens* and the *salesmen*. A maven is an information broker who shares and trades information about people, places, and products. Salesmen are individuals who master the art of persuasion and play a critical role in the tipping of word-of-mouth epidemics. They are the catalysts for the Stickiness Factor, as their uncanny ability to present their ideas in a simple, irresistible, memorable way moves people into taking action. However, epidemics are sensitive to the conditions and circumstances of time and place, and unless the Law of a Few and Stickiness factors are in order, social change will not occur. This is known as the Power of Context (Gladwell, 2002).

Gladwell's tipping point framework can serve as a useful guide for understanding how self-harming behavior develops and spreads in peer groups and across entire schools. For example, I provided consultation to a junior high school that was plagued by student self-harming behavior. One could clearly identify the connectors, mavens, and saleswomen at this particular school: The main connector was a charismatic, outstanding student, a great actress, and one of the most popular and powerful teenagers in the school. However, despite her multitude of strengths, she had had several outpatient and inpatient treatment experiences for family problems, depression, and borderline personality disorder. For this teenager, cutting proved to be a much more effective medication than the Paxil and Depakote her psychiatrist had prescribed. Shortly after she discovered the powerful, endorphin-releasing effects of cutting, a word-of-mouth epidemic was set in motion at the school. Her popular saleswomen friends began to convince other students about how "cool" it was to "cut yourself." To further complicate matters, one of the connector's best friends, a true maven, turned her onto "witchcraft." Soon, the connector and their inner circle of friends began engaging in blood-sharing rituals and got into trouble for drawing symbols of Satan in their school workbooks. As the cutting and witchcraft fever spread across the school, increasingly more students wanted to join this powerful social club.

Self-harming behavior can be as contagious as a measles outbreak. Moos (1979) calls this contagion effect among peer groups *progressive conformity*, that is, human behavior comes to reflect what is stimulated, encouraged, rewarded, and successful in a particular social context.

Family Breakdown

Adolescents today are suffering from a lack of intimate time with their parents. Due to financial reasons, both parents in many families increasingly are being forced to work and, in some cases, split shifts. In some families, children are raised by adult caregivers who are not relatives. Furthermore, people are becoming increasingly more isolated from their extended families. The rise in single-parent and divorce rates also is contributing to family disconnection. Research indicates that time spent together as a family is not only an important characteristic found in strong families (DeFrain & Stinnett, 1992; Stinnett & O'Donnell, 1996), but also that developmentally it is critical for adolescents to be able to turn to their parents for emotional support and validation, which greatly contribute to their feelings of self-worth and self-confidence (Doherty, 2000; Garbarino, 1995; Gilbert, 1999; Grotevant & Cooper, 1983; Papini & Roggman, 1992; Pipher, 1994; Reimer, Overton, Steidl, Rosenstein, & Horowitz, 1996; Taffel & Blau, 1999, 2001).

As one former self-harming client said about her parents: "I feel invisible in their eyes." Alison was a Caucasian 14-year-old who had turned to cutting as a way to confirm her existence in the family. She further added: "I feel dead inside . . . cutting makes me feel like I'm alive!" Both of her parents were highly successful lawyers who regularly worked long hours. When the parents were around, they were quite irritable and preoccupied. They had failed to create firm boundaries between their work and home lives. In family therapy sessions, Alison would frequently complain about how her parents failed to listen or pay attention to her when she reached out for their support, which increasingly made her feel like her existence was meaningless to them. Alison's experiences of feeling invalidated, "invisible," and "emotionally dead inside" are frequently voiced by self-harming adolescents.

Renowned psychiatrist Robert Coles has this to say about the breakdown of today's American family: "The frenzied need of children to have possessions isn't only a function of the advertisements they see on TV. It's a function of their hunger for what they aren't getting—their parents' time" (Mattox, 1991, p. 10).

According to one study on adolescents, mothers tend to average 8 minutes per day of conversation time with their teens, and fathers only spend 3 minutes (Sparham, Roy, & Stratton, 1995). Cloud (1999) found in his research that parents are spending 40% less time with their kids now than 30 years ago. With statistics like these, it is no surprise that adolescents often report feeling disconnected from their parents.

Mary Pipher, author of *Reviving Ophelia: Saving the Selves of Adolescent Girls*, argues that therapists need to move away from family therapy models and instead begin "treating people's schedules" (Simon, 1997). In fact, in my clinical practice with self-harming adolescents and their families I have found that many of the presenting problems "are directly or indirectly related to time" (Simon, 1997, p. 31). Research supports this idea. Califano (1998) found that children and adolescents who regularly have dinner with their parents tend to have reduced rates of use or no use at all of marijuana. His study demonstrates how simply having dinner together as a family can serve as an important protective factor for our children and adolescents, who are growing up in toxic cultural environments. Family therapy in the new millennium must incorporate the importance of time and daily family rituals into the treatment process to help strengthen family ties and preserve the sanctity of family life.

Hurried Teens

In today's highly competitive, fast-paced cultural environment, adolescents are growing older younger. There is tremendous pressure put on teenagers to achieve academic excellence, to outperform their peers in classes and activities, and to devote their leisure time to intellectual pursuits—on top of all the stress involved in coping with much higher academic standards and heavy homework loads. Many parents pressure their teens to get involved in extracurricular activities or even take it upon themselves to over-schedule their children, all in the spirit of wanting them "to be the best they can possibly be!" These parents act as if life can be programmed or micromanaged, with the ultimate goal of their teenagers getting into the most prestigious colleges (Rosenfeld & Wise, 2000).

Another way adolescents are hurried today is through the process of *parentification* (Breggin, 2000; Elkind, 1994, 1988; S. Minuchin, 1974). The parentification process may be set in motion when a parent is underfunctioning due to health, mental health, substance abuse difficulties, or a relationship breakup. With some families, long work days have forced single or dual-career parents to recruit their most responsible child or teenager to take on important adult responsibilities, such as taking care of their younger siblings for extended periods of time, cooking, cleaning the house, and so forth. Some parents cannot afford childcare and consequently rely on one of their children to take on the adult responsibility of caring for siblings.

In some cases, the parentified child may become like a surrogate spouse, serve as a therapist for a single parent, or be triangulated (Bowen, 1978) into the parents' marital relationship as a go-between or confidant. The following case example illustrates the emotional and social consequences of being a parentified child.

Jane, a bright and highly popular Caucasian 13-year-old, was referred to me by her school social worker for cutting and possible suicidal ideation. Jane began cutting herself following her parents' divorce. The father had engaged in an extramarital affair and left his wife for the other woman. Jane was quite bitter about this. Her mother became extremely depressed after the breakup. She also was forced to get a job to support Jane and her other child, a 10-year-old girl named Lisa who had Down's syndrome. The mother put a lot of pressure on Jane to take care of Lisa during the week due to her long work hours. Jane begrudgingly agreed and thus sacrificed her formerly busy after-school social life. Whenever she attempted to share her frustrations about her diminishing social life or voiced her anger about the father's "wrecking the family," the mother would start to cry and share her feelings of guilt rather than respond to Jane's needs. In response to this regular invalidation process, Jane eventually found a powerful and effective way to avoid further burdening her mother and simultaneously keep a lid on her anger and frustration. One day, after a negative interaction with her mother, Jane took a razor blade into her bedroom and began cutting her arms. She found that not only did the cutting serve as "a friend," but also, as she put it, "would quickly get rid of my anger." In the context of this family, it is understandable why Jane gravitated toward cutting and was not eager to give up this behavior. Cutting helped her to cope with the family stressors and was a fast-acting solution that, like a good friend, she could always count on to be there for her when she needed relief.

The biggest tragedy of parentification is the sacrificing of young people's childhood. Today's parents often assume that their teenagers are more sophisticated and self-sufficient and can handle day-to-day stress better than they could have managed as teenagers. Unfortunately, the parentified child's needs for support, validation, and security are often left unmet (Breggin, 2000; Elkind, 1994, 1988).

The Second Family

In their relentless search for connection, and disenchanted with their parents' failure to adequately meet their needs, many adolescents have sought refuge in a "second family" (Taffel & Blau, 1999, 2001). The second family may take the form of a street gang, the rave/danceclub culture, or an unsavory peer group of teenagers who may engage in substance abuse or self-harming behaviors. The rave/danceclub culture is becoming one of the most popular second families. In this context teenagers feel empowered: There are no cultural or gender barriers;

everyone is accepted. For many youth, the rave/danceclub scene has become their identity, defining their friends and style of dress and providing them with a world they can call their own. For example, Julie, a 17-year-old lesbian, cut herself to cope with her parents' constant verbal abuse about what they perceived as her lifestyle choice and because she was underachieving in school. Her father was Middle Eastern and her mother was a staunch Catholic from Bolivia who frequently reminded Julie about how she was "sinning" and would "go to hell" for her lifestyle choice. For Julie, going to rave dances provided her with a context where she felt unconditionally accepted; as she put it, "I could leave my family problems at the door."

According to parenting expert Ronald Taffel, "Adolescents turn to the second family to fill the void created by parents too busy to spend time with them. Today's kids are angry because they feel invisible and ignored by parents who do not hear or see them. They are desperate to be seen and known, rather than scheduled or psychologized. They are craving one-on-one time. We are in a life-and-death struggle over who will connect with the core selves of our children—mothers or fathers, or the enveloping world of the second family" (Feldman, 2000, p. 16). While on their journey in search of a second family, many adolescents fall prey to the media and materialistic values. Teenagers find it difficult to resist or challenge the dominant cultural messages perpetuated and reinforced by the media and they end up buying an image—not a piece of clothing— that they believe will transform their lives, making them look better or more "cool" (Kilbourne, 1999). The world of advertisement promises teenagers products that can deliver what can only be generated in healthy interpersonal relationships.

In her scholarly critique of the advertisement business, Kilbourne (1999, pp. 90–93) applies the relational therapy theoretical framework of Jean Baker Miller (1976) to point out five ways advertisements artificially try to replace what we get naturally from meaningful relationships with others:

1. *Zest and vitality.* Ads promise that products will make us feel more alive and will help us to experience more intensely. Everywhere we look, we are offered false excitement, pseudo-intensity. Not only does this promise inevitably disappoint us, but it also contributes to the general feeling in our culture that every moment of our lives should be exciting and fun and anything less is boring.

2. *Empowerment to act.* Ads also promise us that products give us courage, will empower us to act. "Just do it," the slogan for Nike high-priced sneakers promises to help us to achieve our goals and perform with excellence. Ads define empowerment as power over other people.

3. *Knowledge and clarity of self and others.* Ads constantly tell us that products can help us find our identity, can make us unique, can help us understand ourselves better. Calvin Klein tells us, "Be good. Be Bad. Just Be," as if somehow his perfume had something to do with our core identity. Ads also promise that products will lead instantly to better communication.

4. *Sense of self-worth.* One of the central messages of advertising is that products will enhance our self-worth. "And I'm worth it," says actress Heather Locklear for *L'Oreal* hair products. Spend a little more money on hair coloring and this will improve your self-worth the slogan implies.

5. *Desire for more connection.* Ads are a key component of our consumerist culture, constantly exhorting us to be in a never-ending state of excitement, never to tolerate boredom or disappointment, to focus on ourselves, and never to delay gratification. These messages are a blueprint for how to destroy intimate relationships.

Our consumerist culture also wreaks havoc in the lives of adolescents by means of popular high-tech products and constant bombardment of violent images in the media. Thanks to *Game-Boys*, play stations, computer games, and chat rooms, leading a socially disconnected lifestyle has become much more appealing than participating in extracurricular activities at school or maintaining and building new friendships. For some teenagers, computers have become a second family. However, staring at a computer or television screen does not teach adolescents how to be empathic, how to be loving, or the importance of showing concern for others. Naisbitt, Naisbitt, and Philips (1999) contend that, "Screens are everywhere, in every setting, directing us, informing us, amusing us. And without conscious awareness, they are shaping us" (p. 12).

Brazelton and Greenspan (2000) report that children and adolescents spend 5.5 hours per day in front of a computer screen or television set. Today, many teenagers have TVs, VCRs, and DVD players in their bedrooms, which greatly increase the opportunity for them to be exposed to violent images in the media. Over time, this constant exposure to violent images has a desensitizing effect on teenagers' tolerance levels for violence, including self-harm. They become numb to it (Huston et al., 1992). Their heroes on TV shows, in the movies, and in rap or other types of music videos convince them that they are invincible. Singers such as Marilyn Manson, who cuts himself on stage with broken bottles, do a masterful job of glorifying self-mutilative behavior. Interestingly, when discussing his teenage years, Manson described himself as being disconnected from his parents and peers and often bullied. He says of teenagers today, "Teenagers are not considered human beings in some ways. Until you turn 18, you really don't have any rights, so in a sense you really don't have any soul. You're not really a real person" (Carlson, 2000, p. 77). This view of teenagers and Manson's description of disconnection is very similar to the stories self-harming adolescents have shared with me.

Disconnected, frustrated youth who gravitate toward unsavory peer groups often end up being mentored by equally troubled, disconnected, and frustrated teenagers who head such groups. To further complicate matters, the other members of the group may share similar psychological and family background profiles, and are also seeking new families to connect with. These teenagers soon learn that there are benefits to being loyal followers. They get a lot of attention, they feel powerful, they have control, they are connected to a group that seems to care about them, and they may receive immediate rewards like money or material items. The peer-group second family meets many of their basic human needs. Once an individual is totally immersed in this peer group subculture, there is no turning back.

Some adolescents' peer groups today are much more powerful than their nuclear families. If there is any hope for parents to reclaim their sons and daughters from a negative peer group, they must figure out a way to neutralize the powerful influence this group has on their teens. In my clinical work, I often invite adolescents to bring their closest friends into our family therapy and individual sessions (Selekman, 1991, 1993, 1995b). I also strongly encourage them to bring in the leader of their peer group. Once I have been able to establish some leverage and mutual respect with the peer group leaders and their high-ranking followers, I have been able to steer my adolescent clients in a different direction socially, as well as help the parents and their teenagers to establish more nurturing and meaningful relationships. Another added bonus to collaborating with an adolescent's peer group leader and other high-ranking peers is that they may decide to become clients themselves!

It is important to point out that not all self-harming adolescents gravitate toward a negative peer group. Some of these adolescents are quite resourceful and resilient and have carefully selected a supportive peer group in an effort to help themselves to better cope and self-heal.

Societal "Quick-Relief" Solutions

We live in a feel-good, quick-relief society. Legal mood-altering drugs such as Prozac and Ritalin have become magic bullets in our cultural landscape. Major pharmaceutical companies own our politicians and our healthcare industry. No other presidential administration has endorsed with such great fervor and financial support the use of mood-altering medications for the mental health problems of children and adolescents than the Clinton administration had (Breggin, 2000).

Following the Columbine High School tragedy, President Clinton called for a White House conference on mental health, where Steven Hyman and Harold Koplewicz, both expert biologically based psychiatrists, totally dismissed the role of "childhood traumas," "inadequate parenting," or "absent fathers," that possibly lie at the root of why children and adolescents become violent. Instead, they successfully sold the Clintons and the Gores on their scientific views that violent kids have biochemically disordered brains, which can best be treated by mood-altering medications. They neglected to mention the fact that one of the Columbine shooters, Eric Harris, was already on Luvox, a drug that is rarely prescribed today because of its awful side effects. They also did not mention that in the United States there are close to 6 million children already taking antidepressants, Ritalin, Dexedrine, and Adderall (Breggin, 2000).

Congress subsequently funded a federal initiative aimed at providing nationwide training programs to help school systems and communities to identify "troubled" children and youth and provide them with better school mental health services. Sadly, this federal initiative ended up spreading an even larger "psychiatric net" over our nation's schools with the aim of drugging increased numbers of students (Breggin, 2000). Some federally funded school districts manage "troubled" students, including self-harming youth, by referring them to a psychiatrist for a comprehensive evaluation. More often than not, these students are placed on medication in an attempt to biochemically stabilize their mood and behavioral difficulties. Such a school protocol for "troubled" students may alleviate the administrators' and other personnel's headaches and worries about the safety of students, but what about the identified students' personal needs? Surprisingly, biologically based psychiatrists and school officials seem to be oblivious to the fact that the outcome research on the effectiveness of medications for child and adolescent behavioral problems is sparse, and studies have not indicated that in the long term the use of medications has led to improvements in social functioning or academic achievement (Greenberg, 1999). Many of these psychiatrists also assume that medication treatment regimes for children and adolescents should be no different than those for adults (Breggin, 2000; Greenberg, 1999).

Ritalin, the number one medication prescribed for attention deficit disorder, has now become a popular street drug of abuse. Young entrepreneurs are now selling their prescriptions as a form of speed to teenagers and adults alike. Low cost and accessibility make it an enticing purchase for youth seeking a "quick rush" or wishing to get out of a melancholic state of mind. Some of my clients have reported that peers at school are even dealing Prozac and Zoloft.

INTEGRATIVE SOLUTION-ORIENTED
FAMILY THERAPY PRACTICE

Over the past decade, a number of solution-focused brief therapy practitioners both in this country and abroad have recognized the limitations of being too formulaic or rigidly adhered to one particular model (Beyebach & Morejon, 1999; Chang & Phillips, 1993; Geyerhofer, personal communication, 2000; Lamarre & Gregoire, 1999; S. D. Miller, Hubble, & Duncan, 1995; Nylund & Corsiglia, 1994; Selekman, 1993, 1997, 1999). Some of the major pitfalls of practicing within the box of a particular model are: (1) It greatly limits what therapists can see and hear; (2) therapists are limited to a set of therapy model assumptions, strategies, and techniques; and (3) therapists rob themselves of the opportunity to allow their creativity to run wild in crafting questions and therapeutic experiments.

For me, solution-oriented clinical practice gives me the freedom to be improvisational, integrative, and to tap my imagination powers and test out whatever I think might work in any given moment in any given session. This is not to say that what we do in the therapeutic process should not be purposeful or in line with the client's treatment goals, but rather that there are unlimited ways to empower clients to succeed in achieving their goals. Being therapeutically flexible, adopting a kaleidoscopic view of clients' unique problem stories and interactions, and giving ourselves the freedom to traverse therapy model boundaries will help us to stay fresh and grow professionally. It also will help to liberate our clients from their oppressive problem stories more efficiently and effectively. Therapeutic flexibility is a must. Often these families are grappling with multiple issues and require therapeutic intervention on the individual adolescent, family, peer-group, school, and other larger systems levels. Each family member also may be at a different stage of readiness to change (Prochaska, 1999), to do something about their problem situations, or to address what the referring agent and other helpers want them to work on. I have added four important guidelines to the basic solution-oriented brief family therapy model (Selekman, 1993, 1997) to help to build in more therapeutic flexibility and to better meet the unique needs of self-harming adolescents and their families.

Bring Forth Client Expertise: Integrate What Works in Psychotherapy

After conducting a scholarly review of 40 years of treatment outcome studies, Miller and his colleagues have identified four important variables that clients identified as the key to their success in treatment (Duncan & Miller, 2000; Hubble, Duncan, & Miller, 1999; S. D. Miller et al., 1995). Clinicians should concentrate their therapeutic efforts in maximizing these four common factors in their clinical work with families.

- *Clients' extratherapeutic factors.* These factors include the clients' strengths and resources, theories of change, protective factors contributing to their resiliency, spiritual involvement, supportive elements in their environments, chance events, and client-generated pretreatment changes. Forty percent of what accounts for outcome variance has to do with what the clients bring to therapy and the therapist's expertise in capitalizing on the client's expertise.

- *Therapeutic relationship factors.* These factors include therapists' caring, warmth, empathy, acceptance, validation, humor, and encouragement of positive risk-taking. *Structuring skills* (Alexander & Parsons, 1982; Henggeler & Alexander, 1999) include the therapist's ability to convey confidence and competence and to take charge in family sessions when things get out of hand. This skill in particular has been identified by clients as being an important contributing factor of successful family treatment outcome for antisocial, violent, and substance-abusing adolescents. Thirty percent of what accounts for outcome variance has to do with these therapist-client relationship factors.

- *Placebo, hope, and expectancy.* This category of factors consists of the client's faith that the therapist's abilities and treatment procedures will be of benefit. Frank and Frank (1991) found that in successful therapies both the therapists and the clients believed in the healing powers of the treatment procedures provided. Several researchers in the field of psychiatry have demonstrated that antidepressants are no more effective than an active placebo, particularly if the placebo mimics the side effects of the real drug being tested (Greenberg, 1999; Greenberg, Bornstein, Zborowski, Fisher, & Greenberg, 1994; Kirsch & Sapirstein, 1998). In other words, if clients truly believe that a particular medication will help them because the prescribing psychiatrist has instilled optimism about the effectiveness of the medication, the placebo being administered will produce favorable results. Placebo, hope, and expectancy account for fifteen percent of outcome variance (Lambert, 1992).

- *Model/technique factors.* The last contributing factor to the client's success in treatment is the therapist's technical skills. All therapeutic models strive to create a safe climate for clients to take action. Technically skilled therapists are often quite accurate in matching therapeutically whatever they do with the clients' problem views, theories of change, goals, and stages of readiness to change (Duncan & Miller, 2000; Hubble, Duncan, & Miller, 1999; Prochaska, 1999; Prochaska, DiClemente, & Norcross, 1994; Reimers, Walker, Cooper, & DeRaad, 1992). According to Lambert (1992), model/technique factors account for 15% of outcome variance.

By inviting self-harming adolescents and their families to share their expertise, unique needs, expectations, and goals, as well as to take the lead in guiding therapeutic activity, therapists can improve their chances of succeeding in treatment. To maximize treatment success, therapists should check in with their clients at the end of every session to find out what they found most useful, not helpful, or wish for them to address or change about their approach in future sessions.

Make Room for Client Storytelling

One of the major criticisms of the solution-focused brief therapy approach (de Shazer, 1985, 1988, 1991) is that clients are not given enough room to share their problems stories and address affect-laden or unresolved conflict material that may surface during the course of therapy. This can occur because the solution-focused therapist avoids "problem talk" and actively tries to coauthor solution-determined stories (de Shazer, 1991; Nylund & Corsiglia, 1994; Selekman, 1997). Spence (1987) refers to this therapeutic strategy as the "singular solution." He argues that therapists who operate from a singular-solution framework ignore or downplay client statements that don't fit with their therapeutic framework. Spence contends that making use of all clients' raw data (problem-saturated or not) opens the door for a multiplicity of therapeutic possibilities. P. Minuchin, Colapinto, and Minuchin (1998) argue that the solution-focused approach deliberately avoids the open exploration of family conflicts and that "families will often founder over their inability to face and deal with disagreements" (pp. 208–209) unless the therapist helps them to find more adaptive ways of resolving their differences.

The late and brilliant family therapy pioneer Harry Goolishian had the following to say about the limitations of the solution-focused brief therapy approach:

> The ideas are not wrong but perhaps too sharply focused in one direction with reference to the development of new meaning. If we were to point to one danger in solution-focused approaches it would be the risk of trying so hard to produce a brief change-oriented experience that one can lose sight of, or contact with, the story of the client. This is particularly so with families which have been recycled through the mental health system. They have a long story to tell. (Goolishian, personal communication, March 7, 1988)

These important words of wisdom have stuck with me for years and have greatly contributed to my becoming a much more flexible solution-oriented practitioner. I now find myself spending more time in the beginning of initial family sessions carefully listening to families' problem-saturated stories and validating their experiences. Throughout the course of therapy, whenever a family member begins to have a strong affective nonverbal or verbal response to important material being discussed, or when he or she discloses affective-laden material, I avoid being a narrative editor and give him or her plenty of room to share the meaningful story.

Because many self-harming adolescents often feel invalidated and emotionally disconnected from their families (Conterio & Lader, 1998; D. Miller, 1994; Strong, 1998) it is crucial that therapists avoid inadvertently contributing further to this feeling by failing to support or bring out their "voices" in family sessions. Three powerful forces contribute to the development and maintenance of invalidating family interactions and the silencing of self-harming women—the mismanagement of anger, strong patriarchal cultural proscriptions for how women should think and act, and family secrets. The mismanagement of anger is one of the most common family characteristics of families with self-harming women (Conterio & Lader, 1998; D. Miller, 1994; Walsh & Rosen, 1988). Often the fathers in these families wield all of the power and have made it very clear to their wives and daughters that it is not okay to challenge or question their authority in any way. In some cultures, such as with Middle Eastern families, this unspoken rule is enforced by the oldest son in the family, who is next in command when the father is away (Abudabbeh, 1996). Self-harming women have learned that it is much safer to keep a lid on their anger by cutting or burning themselves than to risk being verbally ridiculed or harshly disciplined. In a similar fashion to bulimia, cutting in particular can serve as a way to purge one's anger and frustration and to rapidly release tension. In some cases, the traditional fathers in these families may not resort to verbal or physical aggression but instead are conflict avoidant and use extended periods of silence, an equally powerful weapon. Problems and conflicts are never resolved when family members' anger and frustration has to be swept under the carpet. Therefore, family members are forced to come up with other ways to manage their anger and frustration with fathers who will not tolerate or listen to their concerns or frustrations with him. The use of parental silence can be quite effective at squelching the "voice" of an adolescent woman who is seeking validation, support, and more autonomy. When an individual is feeling a strong sense of hopelessness, a lack of power, and relatively little control in his or her family, cutting or burning, like substance abuse and eating disorders, can give the person a false sense of being in control.

In family therapy sessions, the therapist has to be very active in disrupting the invalidating family interactions occurring in the room by using reframing, externalization of the problem (White & Epston, 1990), and curiosity. One effective way that I disrupt invalidating patterns of interactions in families with self-harming women is to change how the self-harming behavior is viewed. For example, I was working with Debbie, a Caucasian 13-year-old who was cutting herself, experimenting with speed, and had a highly conflictual relationship with her father. Her father, who was a very tall, burly businessman, apparently had no problem giving commands to family members and putting them in their place if they dared to challenge him or question his decision-making abilities. For the first time in one of our family sessions, Debbie took a big risk and began to confront her father about how he "never would listen" to her when she spoke to him. When the father began to reprimand her in the session, I turned to him and said, "That was absolutely beautiful the way your daughter stood up for herself! Do you think Debbie inherited your gene for assertiveness?!" Although initially he was puzzled by my comment, he soon began to smile and appeared proud that he could have given his daughter a "genetically important life trait." The father's style of communicating with Debbie began to change after he reframed her behavior as a positive "trait" that she had inherited from him. In future sessions, the father totally abandoned his blaming style of interacting with his daughter, began to make better eye contact with her, and would listen to her in our sessions. Once Debbie found it increasingly safe to assert herself with her father and effectively elicit more support from him in and out of our family therapy sessions, her cutting and substance abuse behaviors stopped.

As can be seen in Debbie's case, two of the most important therapeutic tasks to accomplish in family therapy with self-harming adolescents are: (1) to actively challenge and disrupt the invalidating family interactions that are often connected to traditional patriarchal socialization practices and (2) to create a safe therapeutic climate that gives the self-harming adolescent permission to externalize her anger or any other unpleasant thoughts or feelings she may be experiencing in particular family relationships or in any other social contexts. Replacing impulsive action with "words" is one of the main keys to successful treatment with self-harming adolescents.

In some cultures, young women have very little say when it comes to asserting their personal wishes (such as their desire to date), participating in other social activities outside the family, and deciding how to dress. Some of the adolescents I have worked with are in intense conflict with their parents over these issues, especially as they become increasingly immersed in the American teenage cultural world. The parents, on the other hand, cling to the traditional beliefs, customs, and expectations for their children that clash with the teenage world they often view as sinful. The self-harming behavior often exhibited by these young women is an attempt to cope simultaneously with the stress of acculturating and the strong family pull to conform to the traditional patriarchal proscriptions for women's behavior. In very religious families the guilt for "sinning" can be so intense that the self-harming behavior becomes an act of repentance and self-punishment (Conterio & Lader, 1998; D. Miller, 1994).

The challenge for therapists in these clinical situations is to support the parents but at the same time build a solid alliance with the adolescent. The first step is to validate both parties' positions. Secondly, the therapist should normalize for the family how most immigrant families struggle with similar issues and how this transition period of adjusting to the American culture creates a lot of family stress and conflict. Finally, the therapist needs to serve as an intergenerational negotiator (Selekman, 1993) and help the parents and their adolescents learn problem-solving and negotiation skills, as well as how to compromise. With some families, I have been able to unite the parents and adolescents against the "negative effects of the transition period" which is wreaking havoc on their family relationships.

Besides externalizing the negative effects of this transition period for immigrant families, I sometimes externalize societal and intergenerational *rigid gender socialization practices* as the real enemy that is getting the best of family members (Philpot, Brooks, Lusterman, & Nutt, 1997; White, 1989). The therapist has to help family members see that these rigid gender socialization practices brainwash them to think that there is a "right way" to view and relate to the other gender. Therefore, it is not the other gender that is the enemy, but it is "the inflexibility of gender messages that do not allow for growth" (Philpot et al., 1997, p. 163) that has to be challenged and addressed in family therapy.

Another family dynamic that sometimes exists in families of self-harming adolescents is the presence of family secrets (Conterio & Lader, 1998; D. Miller, 1994). Family secrets may involve parental substance abuse or mental health difficulties, parental extramarital affairs, family violence, sex abuse, patterns of family cutoffs, being in a cross-generational coalition with a parent or grandparent, a family history riddled with suicides and unresolved losses, or undisclosed adoptions. The parents and older siblings of the self-harming adolescent may collude to prevent these unspeakable and anxiety-provoking family secrets from leaking out. In some cases, the self-harming adolescent may be harboring such secrets as having been physically or sexually abused by a family member, a relative, or an adult outside the home, or possibly discovering a family member engaging in illegal or other troublesome behaviors of which other family members are not aware. Often the adolescent is either threatened not to disclose the secret or, out of loyalty to her family, decides to keep a lid on what is happening to her or what she knows about that is occurring secretively behind the scenes. Over time, the secret-keeping process can take its toll psychologically and physically on the self-harming adolescent, for instance, by intensifying depressed feelings and anxiety, which in turn increase the likelihood of self-harming behaviors. Self-harming behavior can also be a metaphor for family secrets, such as family cutoffs or feeling cut in two due to being caught in the family web of divided loyalties.

In clinical situations where family secrets appear to be surfacing, I use curiosity and ask the family open-ended, conversational questions (Andersen, 1991, 1995, 1998; Anderson & Goolishian, 1988; Selekman, 1993, 1997) to explore with them if there are any significant untold family stories that may be contributing to what is keeping the treatment situation stuck. I ask the family the following types of questions:

- "It is clear to me that all of you have been working hard to improve your situation. However, it feels like we have run into a brick wall at this point in our work together. Is there anything we have not talked about that you think might be keeping us stuck?"
- "Are there any issues or concerns that you are surprised that I have not asked you about?"
- "Before we started working together, was there one thing that any of you told yourselves that you would not talk about with me or in the company of your family in our sessions?"

These types of questions can help pave the way for the disclosure of family secrets that may have been contributing to the development and maintenance of the self-harming behavior of the adolescent.

Integrate Cognitive-Behavioral Therapy Ideas and Self-Soothing Strategies

With some self-harming adolescent case situations, disrupting invalidating family interactions and altering constraining family beliefs fails to have an impact on the adolescent's self-harming behavior. This may be because the self-harming adolescent still is being pushed around by automatic self-defeating thoughts (Beck, Rush, & Emery, 1979), such as irrational "I" statements or catastrophizing (Ellis, 1974; Seligman, 1995). She also may be experiencing grave difficulties coping with overwhelming emotions and high levels of stress in her family and in other social contexts. Her capacity to identify and verbalize her different feelings, as well as soothe herself when overwhelmed by these emotions, may be deficit areas that require therapeutic attention.

Prior to teaching the adolescent effective tools for challenging her irrational self-defeating thoughts and useful self-soothing strategies to employ when plagued by emotional distress and other stressful situations, I first explore with her in great detail any past or present successes she has had in which she effectively coped with oppressive emotional states and negative thoughts that had been pushing her around. For example, Eloise, a Jewish 17-year-old who cut up and down her legs "50 times" with a razor blade following her boyfriend's breaking up with her, used "journaling" as an effective coping strategy to get back on track with her life. After learning about Eloise's use of journaling as a helpful coping strategy, I decided to capitalize on this important client extratherapeutic factor (Hubble et al., 1999) by having Eloise bring in her three-volume set of journals so we could incorporate them into our therapeutic work together. What was most fascinating about Eloise's style of journaling was her deliberate use of different color print to capture her shifting emotional states from the relationship breakup to "feeling happier" and "more self-confident." Immediately after the relationship breakup, Eloise began using black print and gradually moved into blue, green, red, and brown print in the first two volumes of her journals as she started to cope better with the loss. She began painting and exercising again and stopped isolating herself from the family. Her third volume of the journal began in orange print and finished in yellow print, which Eloise claimed represented "the sun and feeling happier." By making maximum use of Eloise's unique coping strategy in individual and family therapy, I was able to help further empower her to get back on track with her life.

Although Eloise found her journaling to be of great help to her, she still reported being plagued by self-defeating thoughts. Knowing that she was an avid fan of detective stories and murder mysteries, I had her pretend to be a super sleuth detective over a 2-week period and search for evidence to support her thoughts. By the end of her 2-week investigation, she came up empty handed and was successfully able to erase her self-defeating thoughts.

Besides teaching adolescents how to challenge and disrupt their self-defeating irrational thought processes, it is critical to increase their repertoire of self-soothing strategies and techniques. This includes teaching them how to visualize, meditate, use relaxation training, and journal, as well as helping them to access their inner resources and unique talents when experiencing emotional distress.

Facilitate Connection-Building

One of the major gaps in the solution-focused brief therapy model (de Shazer, 1985, 1988, 1991) is the lack of importance placed on the therapist's use of self as the catalyst for helping to build meaningful connections among the adolescent and more distant family members, as well as in strained and conflictual peer relationship situations and in relationships with concerned and involved helping professionals from larger systems, particularly when clients identify these areas as playing a role in their problem situations. The leading proponents of the solution-focused brief therapy model would argue that a therapist engaging in such activity would be creating too much complexity for herself/himself and the clients and that if you do the model "right," such therapist activity is totally unnecessary (Berg, 1994; de Shazer, 1988, 1991), because change will occur across the various social contexts the client interfaces in the form of a "ripple effect"(de Shazer, 1985). However, in my clinical practice, particularly with more complex and chronic case situations, I have found the standard solution-focused therapeutic strategies and techniques to fall short in helping create possibilities. For one, some of the solution-focused questions may block the self-harming client from telling her story by keeping the interview too sharply focused on the "positives" both in the present and in the past. In some cases, a "ripple effect" does not occur when the self-harming adolescent reduces or stops her problematic behavior, and the parents remain emotionally disconnected from her. Sometimes the reverse happens: The parents abandon their past unhelpful patterns of interaction with the adolescent but the child remains symptomatic and emotionally disconnected from her parents. Finally, I have also experienced case situations where the self-harming adolescent has made some important changes but those changes have failed to have an impact on her strained peer relationships or on her relationships with more pessimistic professionals from larger systems.

Many self-harming adolescents grapple with the establishment and maintenance of meaningful connections with one or both parents, other family members, peers, teachers, and other adults in their communities. In some cases, one or both parents have not been emotionally available to connect with and soothe them when they are overwhelmed by stress or painful thoughts and feelings. Similar to substance abuse, cutting or burning becomes a substitute comforter or a "friend" to help adolescents to cope. The self-harming adolescent may interpret the parent's disengagement from her as a sign of rejection. All children and adolescents need to feel a *sense of place* or belonging in their families. This concept can be extended to every social context that the adolescent interfaces with outside the family as well. In Native American culture, children are considered "sacred beings." The Maori Indian culture views their children as "gifts of the gods." In both of these cultural groups there is much love, care, and attention given to children in their immediate and extended families and by the entire community (Brokenleg, 1998).

According to Bronfenbrenner (1979):

> The capacity of a dyad to serve as an effective context for human development is crucially dependent on the presence and participation of third parties, such as spouses, relatives, friends, teachers, clergy, and neighbors. If such third parties are absent, or if they play a disruptive rather than supportive role, the developmental process breaks down. (p. 5)

Bronfenbrenner also contends that an adolescent's ability to establish and maintain meaningful connections across multiple social contexts can greatly enhance his or her psychological and physical levels of functioning.

Some self-harming adolescents report feeling alienated and lack meaningful connections with their teachers. This is in line with a recent Search Institute survey of 100,000 students from 6th through 12th grades, which found that only one in four students reported that they went to a school where adults and other students cared about them (Applebome, 1999). I honestly believe that if every child or adolescent had a meaningful connection with at least one teacher in their school for emotional support and guidance, there would be far fewer extreme behavioral difficulties such as youth violence and self-harming behaviors occurring in our schools. Some good empirical evidence supports this belief. In his longitudinal research, Anthony (1984, 1987) found that the primary protective factor that at-risk inner-city children identified as helping them to overcome adversity while growing up was their *inspirational others*. The inspirational others were older siblings, extended family members, teachers, coaches, clergy, adult friends of the family, and community leaders. I have found it useful in clinical work with adolescents in general to involve their inspirational others in the family treatment process. These people can not only provide added support for the adolescent in other social contexts in which she is struggling outside the family, but they also may have some valuable words of wisdom and offer creative problem-solving ideas.

Self-harming adolescent case situations are notorious for attracting an army of concerned helping professionals well before an initial family therapy session. Often the school principal, dean, social worker, or teachers are worried that the adolescent is "suicidal" and may need to be psychiatrically hospitalized. The family physician may be the first helper to observe the adolescent's cuts or burn marks and will more than likely refer the client to a psychiatrist colleague for an evaluation. This visit may result in the adolescent's being diagnosed as clinically depressed, having a borderline personality disorder or obsessive-compulsive disorder, and being placed on medication and admitted into a psychiatric hospital. The self-harming adolescent's voice is often lost in these dialogues about what the concerned professionals think is "wrong" with her and how to treat her. This is why it is best to mobilize as many of the involved helping professionals constituting the *problem system* as possible to share their concerns, expectations, ideal outcome pictures, and treatment plan ideas with the family and treating therapist as early as possible in the treatment process, if not in the very first family session (Anderson & Goolishian, 1988). This allows everyone to know where everyone else is coming from, both the adolescent and the family to have an active voice in their own treatment, and the involved helping professionals to have ample opportunity to notice changes occurring with the adolescent and her family, which can lead to shifts in their original ways of viewing the client's problem situation.

OVERVIEW OF THE BOOK

Chapter 1 presents a multisystemic family assessment framework that takes into consideration the complex interplay between individual, family, peer-group, larger-system, gender, cultural, and community factors in the development and maintenance of adolescent self-harming behavior. This multisystemic assessment process informs therapists of which systems levels they should target interventions to.

Chapter 2 describes guidelines for crafting and selecting therapeutic questions that grow out of the interviewing process to help foster therapist-family member cooperative relationships, to elicit their expertise, to challenge constraining family beliefs, and to help empower families to achieve their goals. The therapist's use of spontaneous reflections, curiosity, and imagination is also discussed in this chapter.

Chapters 3 and 4 will present a wide range of therapeutic techniques and strategies for the self-harming adolescent and her family to experiment with both in and out of therapy sessions. Case examples are provided throughout both chapters.

In Chapter 5, I discuss a variety of ways to help disentangle larger- system-knot situations that often occur with self-harming cases. Guidelines for how to foster cooperative and successful collaborative relationships with involved helping professionals from larger systems and the concerned members of families' social networks will be covered.

The one-person family therapy approach is described in Chapter 6. I discuss how this is a viable therapeutic option with older adolescents wishing to address their family or individual issues alone, in case situations where conjoint family therapy proves to be counterproductive or the parents are reluctant to participate in family therapy, and when one or both parents' undisclosed individual or marital issues greatly contribute to the maintenance of the adolescent's self-harming behavior.

Chapter 7 presents a variety of individual and family solution-enhancement strategies to minimize the likelihood of client slips. Several goal-maintenance techniques are discussed.

The eight-session stress-busters leadership group, specifically designed for self-harming adolescents, is presented in Chapter 8. This skill-building group combines solution-focused, narrative, and cognitive-behavioral therapy ideas with experiential, art-therapy, and meditation techniques.

Chapter 9 summarizes the major themes of the book and offers some implications for future clinical work and research with self-harming adolescents and their families.

CHAPTER 1

The Multisystemic Family Assessment Framework: A Kaleidoscopic Method of Inquiry

There's nothing wrong with you that what's right with you couldn't fix.

—Baruch Shalem

I PRESENT HERE A MULTISYSTEMIC family assessment framework that takes into consideration the complex interplay between the adolescent, family, peer-group, larger-system, cultural, gender, community, and societal factors in the development and maintenance of self-harming behavior. This assessment framework informs therapists of which systems levels they should target interventions to and indicates where they need to adjust their methods of interacting and intervening to better accommodate the unique needs and expectations of the adolescent, the family, and concerned others. In keeping with constructivist and postmodern therapy traditions, the therapists/assessors need to include themselves as part of whatever they observe "out there" in so-called reality. As Hoffman (1988) contends, there is no such thing as a "God's eye" view from which to look at our clients. If throughout the assessment and treatment process we critically self-reflect and challenge the various ways we get wedded to certain ideas or explanations about our clients' problem stories, we will be better able to entertain a multiplicity of views, gain a clearer understanding of the families' theories of change, and have many more avenues for possible interventions available to us.

Whenever possible, in my initial telephone contact with the parents I secure permission from them and the adolescent to invite the referring person and any other involved helping professionals from larger systems to the family assessment session. This way we can gain a clear understanding of the events that lead up to the referral, how each of the helping professionals originally got involved, and what their concerns, expectations, and goals are for the adolescent, her family, and myself as the treating therapist.

Thus, I view the assessment process as intervention, and not as a separate stage before the treatment process begins. After providing the family with ample space to share their problem stories, their theories of change, information about their unique strengths, and important family background information, I invite the family to take the lead in determining their treatment goals and in coauthoring a treatment plan with me. By the conclusion of the assessment session, the family should leave my office feeling understood, validated, empowered, and optimistic about resolving their difficulties. If the referring person and any other helping professionals were able to attend our initial family meeting, my hope would be that they, too, would leave my office feeling that a meaningful, collaborative relationship has been established.

MULTISYSTEMIC FAMILY ASSESSMENT SESSION FORMAT

Joining

I begin the family assessment session by inviting family members to share what their individual and family strengths are. For example, I may ask the adolescent the following question: "If your best friend asked you what are two things you really like about your mother, what would you say?" I ask the parents a similar question: "If someone stopped you on the street and asked you what are three of your daughter's strengths, what would you say?" I also like to ask the whole family group: "What are your family's strengths?" These types of questions help create a positive climate and offer the therapist valuable information about the adolescent's and the family's strengths. If the referring person and any other involved helping professionals are present in the meeting, they, too, can learn more about the competency areas of the adolescent and her family, and this information can help challenge any client deficit views they may hold.

The Referral Process and Problem Clarification

The next stage of the session involves securing a clear understanding of the referral process and the specific trigger that made the family seek treatment. In the context of this discussion, the therapist can also explore with the family what they found helpful and not helpful with past treatment providers and programs. The therapist needs to make sure that each family member has plenty of room to share their problem stories and avoid being a narrative editor. Once problem areas and concerns have been shared, the therapist's job is to invite the family to identify which problem they wish to tackle first and to negotiate it with them into solvable terms—that is, into bite-sized pieces. One question that assists the family in identifying the "right" problem to work on changing first is: "If there were one question you were dying to ask me about this problem situation, what would that question be?" Not only does the answer to this question provide guidance for the therapist in determining where the family wishes to begin in treatment, but it also can help to point him or her in the direction of potential change strategies.

After clarifying with the adolescent and her parents what they view as the "right" problem area to address first, treatment goals can be established. It is not unusual for the parents and the adolescent to want to address separate problem areas and not agree on a mutual treatment goal. In fact, many adolescents and parents do not see eye-to-eye on their problem views and their treatment goals. In some cases, the adolescent may want to initially focus her attention more on pressing individual and peer issues, rather than address the parents' concerns with her or other family difficulties. However, it has been my clinical experience that meaningful changes can still occur through the establishment of separate treatment goals and intervening top-down through the parents and bottom-up through the adolescent. Each party can be engaged in separate work projects.

Working with Subsystems

During this assessment session, I find it quite useful to divide the family and meet separately with the parents first and then alone with the adolescent. However, if the adolescent has had an extensive treatment history and controls the family mood with her extreme acting out behaviors, tactically it may make better sense to meet with her first in order to gain some therapeutic leverage. When meeting alone with the parents, the therapist can accomplish the following: explore in great detail their theories about why the self-harming behavior is occurring, identify their expectations of the therapist, ask about their attempts to resolve this problematic behavior, renegotiate their treatment goal into more solvable terms, and, perhaps, offer them a therapeutic strategy to experiment with in relationship to their self-harming adolescent.

The individual session time alone with the adolescent can be used to explore the following: her expectations of the therapist, how she thinks the therapist can be most helpful to her, what she believes the self-harming behavior does for her, and what specifically she would like to see changed with her parents (that is, the parents' most troublesome behavior and the privileges they are withholding). The therapist can attempt to negotiate the parents' goal or establish a separate treatment goal with her. If the adolescent is in the action stage of readiness to change (Prochaska, 1999), I may propose a manageable therapeutic experiment in line with her treatment goal for her to test out in relationship to her parents over the next week.

The Editorial Reflection

Approximately 15 minutes before the conclusion of our hour-long session, I take an intersession break to reflect on the family's strengths, their problem views, areas of the family story I am still puzzled about, and their treatment goals, and I come up with compliments for each family member and a menu of therapeutic experiment options for the family to choose from. When we reconvene, I share my editorial reflection with the family and present the therapeutic experiment options, which are in line with their unique cooperative response patterns (de Shazer, 1988, 1991) and stages of readiness for change (Prochaska, 1999). In concluding the session, I invite the family to share with me what the meeting was like for them. I inquire about what they found to be most helpful and ask if they learned anything new about themselves or their situation and if they would like me to make any adjustments in our future sessions together. If this is a regular indemnity insurance case situation, and for reimbursement purposes, I also collaborate with the family on picking a *DSM-IV* label that they feel most accurately captures the adolescent's problem situation. With managed care case situations, the family and I coauthor the assessment form information, including their family background information, treatment goals, and the treatment plan, which is sent back to the referring care manager in charge of managing their health plan benefits.

MULTILEVEL ASSESSMENT CONSIDERATIONS

There are various categories of inquiry for each level of the multisystemic family assessment framework. By thoroughly covering all of the contextual dimensions of the self-harming behavior, the therapist will have access to multiple pathways in which to intervene and will empower the adolescent and her family to resolve their difficulties in the most effective and efficient way.

Adolescent Level

The therapist needs to conduct a balanced interview with the adolescent—that is, inquire about both her strengths and the problematic areas of functioning that the adolescent, her parents, and the referring person reported as concerns. It is also crucial to assess the meaning and the purpose of the self-harming behavior for the adolescent. There are eight key assessment questions that I typically ask the adolescent while meeting alone with her to help secure this important information:

1. "Where did you learn how to cut/burn yourself?"
2. "Has anyone ever hurt you in the past?"
3. "What does cutting/burning do for you?"
4. "What effect does your cutting/burning have on family members and your relationships with your friends?"
5. "Do your friends cut/burn themselves?"
6. "Are there any particular things that happen to you or thoughts or feelings that you experience when you are more likely to cut/burn yourself?"
7. "If you could put a voice to your cutting/burning, what would it say about you or your situation?"
8. "When you avoid the temptation to cut/burn yourself, what do you tell yourself or do that works?"

As readers can clearly see, answers to questions like these offer the therapist a wealth of information about the various ways the behavior serves as a coping strategy for the adolescent. The adolescent's responses to these questions can help inform the therapist about specific target areas for intervention.

One therapeutic option that can grow out of the adolescent's responses to the seventh question is the narrative therapy in-session experiment of *interviewing the problem* (Epston, 1998, 2000). With this therapeutic experiment, the adolescent plays the part of cutting or burning, or whatever she calls her presenting problem. From this unique inside-looking-out perspective, she is interviewed about the problem's place in the life of the client, her family, and in her relationships with significant others. Family members are also free to pose questions to the cutting/burning problem as well. The therapist plays the role of an investigative reporter trying to cover a story on the cutting/burning problem, asking the problem about when it feels thwarted by or loses its grip on the adolescent, her parents, and significant others. After thoroughly covering all angles of the story, the therapist can explore with the adolescent and her family what they learned.

The next important step when implementing the interviewing the problem experiment is to have the adolescent play the role of her most potent solution strategy that successfully prevents cutting or burning from pushing her around. Again, the therapist plays the part of an investigative reporter covering a follow-up story on the adolescent's potent solution strategy. Questions can be asked of the solution strategy: How can it be implemented more frequently? What has it taught the adolescent? How will it benefit the adolescent and her relationships with family members and significant others in the long run? What other ways will the adolescent's life be different in the future when the cutting/burning problem has been defeated?

Finally, I like to devote ample time to learning more about the client's strengths, talents, and adaptive coping strategies. It is helpful to ask the adolescent about pretreatment changes (Hubble et al., 1999; Weiner-Davis, de Shazer, & Gingerich, 1987), such as useful self-talk or problem-solving strategies that she already employs to avoid cutting or burning herself. She also can be asked about how her parents, friends, and significant others help her to stand up to the self-harming behavior and not fall prey to it. Two other competency areas I like to inquire about are: *multiple intelligence areas* (Gardner, 1993, 1999) and *resiliency protective factors* (Anthony, 1984, 1987; Anthony & Cohler, 1987; Haggerty, Sherrod, Garmezy, & Rutter, 1994; Selekman, 1997; Wolin & Wolin, 1993).

MULTIPLE INTELLIGENCE AREAS

Howard Gardner, a Harvard University professor and psychologist, developed the multiple intelligences model as a revolutionary way to assess human intelligence. According to Gardner (1999), children and adolescents should be assessed in terms of 10 distinct intelligence areas rather than be judged solely by their verbal and academic performance scores on the IQ test. The 10 intelligence areas are: linguistic, logical-mathematical, musical, bodily-kinesthetic, visual-spatial, interpersonal, intrapersonal, naturalist, spiritual, and existential. As Gardner (1993, 1999) has pointed out, all humans possess these intelligence areas, however, each person has a unique style of learning and he or she can learn best when teaching methods are matched with his or her natural gifts and talents in particular intelligence areas. Unfortunately, our traditional educational system has placed great emphasis on linguistic and logical-mathematical intelligence, whereas the child or adolescent's other intelligence areas are often ignored.

The implications of Gardner's ideas for family therapy are far-reaching. For example, once the learning style of the adolescent or parent has been accurately assessed, this important information can help inform the types of question categories the therapist should select from and craft in the interviewing process. Therefore, if an adolescent tends to be strong in the visual-spatial intelligence area, she may respond well to the use of imagination type questions, such as the miracle question (de Shazer, 1988) or the imaginary crystal ball (Selekman, 1993). She also may respond well to the use of family art therapy techniques like the *imaginary feelings x-ray machine* (Selekman, 1997), which can be employed as an in-session task, particularly if she is artistically talented and complains about having difficulty identifying and verbalizing her feelings. The imaginary feelings x-ray machine helps to empower adolescents to use their own natural artistic abilities to visually express their inner emotional world through drawing pictures of what they think their feelings look like and telling stories about each picture. Not only can this exercise help to provide her with some valuable insight into what's behind the self-harming behavior, but it also may prove to be a newsworthy experience for her family.

Gardner's multiple intelligences model can also be useful to family therapists in the following treatment areas: with offering families alternative constructions or explanations for their problem situations, with the presentation of rationales for testing particular out-of-session therapeutic experiments, and with therapeutic experiment selection and construction. Once therapists have identified each family member's key intelligence areas, they can carefully match their language and metaphors with their unique learning styles. Family members thus will be more likely to accept the therapist's ideas and be receptive to proposed out-of-session therapeutic experiments, particularly when their natural talents and skills in certain intelligence areas are being tapped and channeled into the presenting problem areas.

RESILIENCY PROTECTIVE FACTORS

Over the past 30 years, there have been a number of studies conducted with at-risk children and adolescents growing up in high-stress, abusive, and chaotic home and community environments who have "beat the odds" and prevailed over adversity (Anthony, 1984, 1987; Anthony & Cohler, 1987; Garmezy, 1994; Haggerty et al., 1994; Masten, Best, & Garmezy, 1990; Werner & Smith, 1992; Wolin & Wolin, 1993). In some cases, these "super kids" (Kauffman, Grunebaum, Cohler, & Gamer, 1979) had to cope throughout their childhoods with a parent who grappled with a chronic mental illness or a serious alcohol or substance abuse problem. Researchers have identified a core set of *protective factors* that appear to contribute to the resiliency of these children and adolescents. They are: effective and creative problem-solving abilities, strong social skills, the presence of at least one responsible and supportive caretaker, and successful experiences in school.

During the family assessment session I explore with the adolescent her unique coping strategies for managing emotional distress and other stressors in her life. Often, self-harming adolescents report possessing one or more of these protective factors, which they have used to resist the temptation to cut or burn themselves or to resort to other maladaptive attempted solutions like bingeing and purging or substance abuse. It is crucial that the therapist secures all of the details on whatever past successes at coping the adolescent reports and explore how these strategies can be increased and employed on a more regular basis. The following case example illustrates nicely the resourcefulness and creative problem-solving abilities of a self-harming adolescent.

Gina, a 17-year-old Latina, had a long history of cutting herself. Her boyfriend of 3 years had just broken up with her and she was devastated by this loss. However, instead of carving up her arms as a form of "self-punishment," which was her usual justification for cutting herself, Gina used her red lipstick to draw multiple lines on the various locations where she typically cut her arms. In our next therapy session, Gina reported her tremendous accomplishment with great joy. I gave her a big high-five and explored with her how she had come up with such a highly creative problem-solving strategy. Gina told me that she had used self-talk prior to using the lipstick on her arms. She had told herself: "Why am I going to

punish myself? I should be mad at him, not at myself." This was a different way of thinking for Gina. Typically she blamed herself for everything
that went wrong in her life. Although she was still a little hard on herself
about having to mimic the cutting, Gina could see herself continuing to
use the lipstick as an alternative to cutting until she could totally abandon anything that resembled this behavior. After amplifying and consolidating all of Gina's important gains, I asked her if I could recommend
that other self-harming women experiment with her creative lipstick coping strategy and she kindly granted me permission to do this. I am happy
to say that thanks to Gina's creativity, many other self-harming clients I
have worked with have benefited from this strategy.

When assessing an adolescent's social skills, evaluating her ability to
create a support system for herself, and trying to determine if there are
any responsible and caring adults outside the family, I ask the following
questions:

- "When you are really stressed out or in a bad place, which one of
  your friends do you turn to first?"
- "What advice does he/she offer you that you have found to be
  most helpful?"
- "Are there any adults other than your parents that you typically
  turn to for advice or support when the going gets rough?"
- "In what ways is this (teacher, coach, aunt, clergy, neighbor,
  friend of the family, etc.) most helpful to you?"
- "Are there any particular words of wisdom that he/she has offered
  you in the past that have stood out in your mind and helped you
  in tough situations?"

The answers to these questions can furnish the therapist with valuable
information about protective factors. In addition, it may be advantageous
to involve these important resource people in future family therapy sessions for brainstorming new ideas and added support outside of the therapy office.

One therapeutic task I use that capitalizes on the adolescent's protective factors and strengths is the *victory box* (Selekman, 1997). I have the
adolescent cut a slit in the top of an old shoebox. Then, on a daily basis,
she keeps track of her personal victories by writing down on a piece of
paper the accomplishment, the useful self-talk, and the problem-solving

or coping strategies she employed, and then she deposits the victories in the box. These victories can take the form of avoiding the temptation to cut or burn herself, scoring high on a class test, giving a great performance in a school band concert or theater production, performing with excellence in a sports event, doing a good deed, and so forth. Ultimately, it is up to the adolescent to decide what is a personal victory. I ask the adolescent to review all of her daily victories before she goes to bed each night and bring her valuable victory box into our sessions to see what blueprints for success we can put into action more often or channel into problem areas that are still a source of stress.

COGNITIVE FUNCTIONING

There is no question that a combination of distorted thought processes and an inability to consistently manage and cope with high levels of emotional distress often drives self-harming behavior (Alderman, 1997; Conterio & Lader, 1998; D. Miller, 1994). One helpful way to assess cognitive distortions is to have the client describe a recent stressful event that resulted in her cutting or burning herself. The next step is to have her identify her negative self-defeating thoughts and what feelings were triggered as a result of thinking this way about the stressful situation. The more proficient the adolescent gets at identifying these negative self-defeating thoughts and learning how to successfully dispute them, the more likely we are to be able to eliminate the distorted thinking that supports the behavior.

Some self-harming adolescents have grave difficulties with self-observation and misread social cues, creating serious problems for themselves in their social world. In these situations, I have the adolescents imagine themselves high up in a bubble looking down at themselves in various social situations. By having this aerial view, clients can see themselves more clearly in social situations. The parts of themselves that are in the bubbles are trustworthy and are looking out for their best interests and carefully researching the different ways they may be getting themselves into trouble in their interactions with others. Most adolescents who have tried this experiment have found it to be helpful to them in challenging their irrational beliefs and in improving both their perceptual and social skills.

MOOD MANAGEMENT

Many self-harming adolescents also have difficulty coping with their emotional distress. Perhaps the adolescent has grown up in a family envi-

ronment where it is not okay for her to voice her angry or depressed feelings. In such a family, it may be safer to check one's anger by self-harming than to get hit or receive a verbal tongue-lashing. The more
self-soothing strategies and techniques the adolescent has available to her,
the better able she will be to manage her moods. If the adolescent's self-
soothing options are highly limited, the therapist needs to help expand
her repertoire by teaching or proposing tools such as: visualization, relaxation training, meditation, journaling, yoga, martial arts, or some other
form of aerobic exercise. In addition to proposing the coping strategies
mentioned above, the therapist should also explore with the adolescent
any past successes she has had at adequately managing her moods and
comforting herself in stressful situations.

Family Level

At this systems level, I want to gather information from the family about
their strengths and assess certain family characteristics or dynamics that
may serve as the life-support system for the self-harming behavior. From
the very beginning of the multisystemic family assessment session, I carefully observe where family members sit, who talks for whom, who domi-
nates the floor, who protects whom, and whether the parents are a united
or divided team, and I listen carefully for central family themes,
metaphors, beliefs, key words used by family members, and clues for
identifying each family members' stage of readiness to change (Prochaska
et al., 1994). I begin by discussing with each family member their
strengths and past successes as a family group.

FAMILY STRENGTHS

Stinnett and O'Donnell (1996) and DeFrain and Stinnett (1992) have
done extensive research with large samples of families to determine the
characteristics of strong families. They have identified the following six
characteristics: open lines of communication, spending time together,
unconditional commitment to one another, family members consistently
showing appreciation for one another, dealing with crises in a positive
way, and spiritual wellness.

When asking a family about what they view as their strengths as a
group, I listen carefully for elements of any of these six characteristics.
Once one or more of these characteristics have been identified, I like to
share with the family that the strengths they have identified have been

found in several research studies to be the characteristics of strong families. By sharing this with the family, I can instill hope and encouragement that they have the strengths and resources to change. I also like to explore with the family how its strengths benefit them both individually and in their relationships. Finally, I like to ask if they would like to do any therapeutic work in the family characteristic areas that they are either weak in or lacking.

I also ask the parents about their past and present successes with managing family difficulties. There may be some parenting strategy they used a year ago to resolve their daughter's marijuana abuse problem that can be employed with the present self-harming problem. I also ask both the parents and the adolescent if anything they have done lately is having a positive impact on the self-harming behavior or any other reported difficulties they are grappling with. Perhaps the parents are nagging or yelling less or trying to spend more time with their daughter. Any of these past and present successes can serve as building blocks for future successes.

EXCEPTIONAL FAMILY BELIEFS AND PATTERNS OF INTERACTION

I also ask the parents if they are aware of any existing useful beliefs and patterns of interaction from their families of origin that we may want to harness and channel into the presenting problem areas. Often when therapists elicit this information from clients they inquire about negative and dysfunctional intergenerational belief systems and patterns of interaction rather than about exceptional beliefs, ideas, values, and positive family interaction patterns. I ask parents the following questions to elicit this important information:

- "Can you think of any specific beliefs or words of wisdom that your parents shared with you while you were growing up that helped you to take responsibility and constructively manage difficulties you faced as a teenager?"
- "In what ways are you putting these beliefs or ideas into practice as a parent?"
- "Can you think of specific ways that your parents interacted with you as a teenager that made you feel loved by them and brought out the best in you?"
- "Can you think of any times lately when you interacted with your daughter in a similar fashion?"

- "Can you think of any beliefs, values, or ideals that your mother lived by, that you found empowering as a young woman, and that you wish to make known to your daughter?"

These types of questions can open the door to a vast reservoir of family-of-origin wisdom and solution strategies that can be put to immediate use in the presenting problem areas.

Some parents already may be having success using these ideas and solution strategies with their children. If this is the case, the next step in therapy may be to explore with the parents how they can increase these solution-maintaining patterns. If there have been substantial pretreatment changes due to major adjustments on the parents' behalf, it may be helpful to ask them if their views of themselves as parents have changed as well. Parents can be asked questions like: "Have you gotten any new ideas about yourself as a parent now that you're yelling/nagging less?" or "How do you view yourself differently as a parent now as opposed to how you used to view yourself when things were out of hand?"

REFERRAL CONTEXT AND PAST TREATMENT HISTORY

It is critical that the therapist gather from the family detailed information about the referral process, particularly the specific trigger that led them to pursue treatment. I ask the following questions about the referral process:

- "Whose idea was it that you should seek help at this time?"
- "What specifically was the referring person seeing you do or was concerned about that he/she wants to see you work on changing?"
- "Do you have any idea about how the referring person will know you are done here so you won't have to go for counseling anymore?"
- "What are your thoughts about the referring person's concerns?"
- (To the parents) "Have you seen any of this behavior with your daughter at home?"

The answers to these questions can help provide a clear focus for the treatment, particularly in situations where the family members are in agreement with what the referring person has identified as a problem area warranting clinical attention.

Some families either fail to be troubled by or totally disagree with the referring person's claims that there is a "problem" needing immediate attention. In these situations, I adopt a therapeutic stance of curiosity and employ the tactics of the popular TV detective Columbo (Selekman, 1993, 1995a, 1997) to invite the family to help me understand. I ask the family the following questions:

- (*Scratching my head and looking puzzled*) "Help me out . . . I'm confused. You said the referring person claims you were burning yourself. How did he/she get that idea?"
  "So one of your teachers told the referring person about the burn marks on your arms. What do you think was going on in your teacher's mind that made her decide to contact the referring person to check up on you?"
- (*To the parents*) "Did you know that your daughter was burning herself?"
  "Oh, so you didn't know about this. Tell me, do you have any thoughts about why your daughter would be doing such a thing?"
- "Lisa, how did you first get the idea to burn yourself?"
  "Oh, so your friend turned you on to this idea?"

As the reader can clearly see, by employing curiosity and Columbo tactics, the therapist can successfully move the family from a position of "not having a problem" to the identification of a serious problem to address. Because many self-harming adolescents conceal their burn and cut marks from their parents and other adults by wearing long sleeves and pants and tend to function quite well in most areas of their lives, parents may not think there is a "problem" with their daughters until the previously mentioned interviewing methods are employed and the self-harming secret is fleshed out.

Many adolescents I have worked with have had past treatment experiences. When this is the case, it is important for the therapist to ask family members what they found most and least helpful with past providers, including treatment programs. I ask families the following questions to secure this information:

- "You have seen a lot of therapists before me, what did they miss or overlook with your situation that is important for me to know?"
- "What sort of things did past therapists do that you disliked the most?"

- "If you were to work with the most perfect therapist, what would he/she do that you would find to be the most helpful?"
- "Has there been anything that any of your past therapists tried with you that you found to be most helpful?"
- "On your way over here, did you think about all of the various ways I could screw up your case situation?"

By placing the family in the expert role, the therapist can learn how best to cooperate with them, can avoid replicating past therapists' unsuccessful attempted solutions, and can help the family in the most meaningful way possible.

UNSUCCESSFUL PARENTAL SOLUTION PATTERNS

When meeting alone with the parents I conduct a detailed investigation of all of their past and present attempts to resolve their daughter's self-harming behavior or other behavioral difficulties. In trying to gain a clear picture about how the parents are attempting to manage the identified problem, I ask the parents to give me a detailed description of how they typically respond to their daughter when she engages in the problematic behavior and how she in turn responds to them. I have parents draw their circular problem-maintaining patterns with their adolescents out on a flip chart in my office. This way the parents can see how in their best efforts to be helpful or do the "right" or "best" thing they inadvertently perpetuate or exacerbate the very problematic behavior they want resolved. After having the parents map out the problem-maintaining family dance, I ask them the following hypothetical questions:

- "If your daughter were sitting here, what advice would she give you about how best to manage her?"
- "If you did it her way, what difference do you think it would make in helping change her behavior and with getting along better with one another?"
- "If we asked your daughter what the number one thing that you guys do that ticks her off the most is, what would she say?"
- "If we asked her to rate your (nagging/lecturing/yelling/ distancing) behavior on a scale from 1 to 10, with 10 being the best and 1 being the worst, what do you think your daughter would rate you today?"

- "So your daughter would give you a 1 with the nagging. What steps would she need to see you take to get you up to a 2?"

If the parents find this type of inquiry helpful and are committed to begin working on changing themselves in relationship to their self-harming daughter, a therapeutic experiment can be offered.

CONSTRAINING FAMILY BELIEFS AND STRUCTURAL ISSUES

Positive relabelling and spontaneously reflecting alternative constructions or explanations about the problem situation are two ways to test how constrained family members' beliefs are. If the therapist is met with nods of acknowledgement or any comments like: "I never thought of it that way" or "That's an interesting idea," he or she can begin to widen this crack in the outmoded family belief system and set in motion the coauthoring of a new family story.

In some cases, constrained family beliefs are kept intact due to unresolved family conflicts. By helping family members identify what their key conflict issues are, the therapist can begin to assist them in finding more productive ways of resolving their disagreements. Once family members learn effective conflict-resolution skills, their views of the presenting problems and interactions with the self-harming adolescent will change.

Often, families with self-harming adolescents become entrenched in unhelpful patterns of interacting, rigid role behaviors, and family structures that keep them stuck. In some cases, the self-harming adolescent becomes parentified (Breggin, 2000; S. Minuchin, 1974; S. Minuchin & Fishman, 1981). I have witnessed some self-harming adolescents use their behavior as a way to regulate distance between the parents when their conflicts surface or they are arguing more.

One common structural pattern observed with families of self-harming adolescents is disengagement (S. Minuchin, 1974). Many of these adolescents report feeling disconnected from one or both parents. This could be due to the parents being emotionally spent by their oppressive jobs, their own individual issues, unresolved parent-child conflicts, or possibly the parents' chronic marital difficulties. In some families, the generational boundaries are so diffuse that the only way the self-harming adolescent can maintain some sense of self and control is to create her own physical boundaries by cutting herself. Conterio and Lader (1998) have observed this attempted solution with self-harming clients who have been sexually abused.

STAGES OF READINESS FOR CHANGE

For the past 20 years, James Prochaska, John Norcross, and Carlos DiClemente have been studying how people change. Prochaska and his colleagues have found that individuals that have had no past treatment history or never attended a self-help group change in a similar fashion to individuals who have had serious health and psychological problems (Prochaska, 1999; Prochaska et al., 1994). They have identified six distinct stages that self-changers go through before conquering their problems: *precontemplation, contemplation, preparation, action, maintenance,* and *termination.*

1. *Precontemplation.* Precontemplators do not think they have a problem, but the referral sources and their family members often think they do. There may be some very good reasons why they are not ready to change their behaviors or situations. Some precontemplators may be feeling demoralized by their intractable and chronic difficulties. They may have already experienced multiple treatment failures or repeatedly failed to conquer their problems on their own. Finally, perhaps they had no parents, siblings, or significant others who modeled the benefits of changing.

2. *Contemplation.* Contemplators have no problem clearly identifying the difficulties they are struggling to cope with, but they are feeling ambivalent about what to do about their problem situations. Often it is their ambivalence that acts as a roadblock for either taking action or abandoning their unsuccessful attempted solutions. Some contemplators believe if they continue to persist with employing a particular solution strategy that eventually they will resolve their problem situations. However, they are oblivious to the fact that in their best efforts to try and resolve their difficulties they are further compounding and exacerbating them.

3. *Preparation.* Individuals in the preparation stage are very concerned about the problem, are less ambivalent, and are voicing a strong desire to want to take action. However, they are at a loss as to how to take the first step. They need help with devising an effective action plan.

4. *Action.* Individuals in this stage have successfully set goals and are ready to launch their action plans. They tend to be excited and more self-confident about taking the first step.

5. *Maintenance*. Individuals in the maintenance stage are pleased with the changes they have made in their lives but are worried about relapsing. Once they develop a plan for constructively managing slips and setbacks, they regain their self-confidence and are better prepared for achieving long-term success.

6. *Termination*. Once individuals reach this stage, they confidently report having no concerns about relapsing or ever returning to their original problematic behaviors. In their minds, they have changed for good.

In applying these ideas to family therapy practice it is important to remember that each family member can be at a different stage of readiness for change. Therefore, the therapist needs to match his or her questions and proposed therapeutic experiments carefully with whatever stage family members are in and capable of responding to or managing. This rapidly fosters therapist-family member cooperation. Most adolescents begin treatment as precontemplators (Prochaska, 1999). This is often because their parents, school dean, or another authority figure has made them go for counseling. The first step in these situations is to try to build a relationship with the adolescent and offer her compliments for "taking responsibility," "cooperating," and "opening up" about her plight of being forced to go for counseling. Because they are nowhere near the action stage, it would be senseless to give these adolescents tasks to experiment with.

It may be helpful to present parents in the contemplative stage with the decisional balancing scale (Prochaska et al., 1994) so that they can take a look at both sides of their ambivalence, particularly the advantages and disadvantages of continuing to engage in attempted solutions that are not working for them. The decisional balancing scale can either be drawn on a flipchart or on a sheet of paper. I draw two columns on the page. One of the columns is labeled *advantages* and the other *disadvantages*. For example, a parent who is "super-responsible" may discover that there are many more disadvantages to continuing this behavior than advantages once she realizes that her daughter has become increasingly "super-irresponsible" with taking care of her chores, schoolwork, and so forth.

Another important dimension of Prochaska and his colleagues' empirically based model is its preparation of family members for the inevitability of slips and setbacks. Not only is it important to normalize slips and explain that they go with the territory of change, but it also is advantageous to provide them with helpful tools and an action plan for how they can constructively manage slips or setbacks when they occur. This will enable the family to achieve long-term success (Prochaska, 1999; Prochaska et al., 1994).

Peer Level

In the introductory chapter, I discussed how important and powerful the "second family" peer group is in the lives of self-harming adolescents. Therefore, it is critical that the therapist ask the adolescent about the nature of her peer group culture. The following types of questions can be used:

- "Do your friends also cut or burn themselves?"
- "If not, what do they think about your doing this?"
- "How do your friends typically manage their problems?"
- "If I were to ask you to invite in two of your friends that have always been there for you and really care about you as a person, who would you bring to our session?"
- "How will they be helpful to me in better understanding you and your situation?"

The answers to these questions can give the therapist a good sense of whether or not the adolescent's peer group has a positive or negative influence on her self-harming and other behavioral difficulties. Clearly, if it appears that one or more of the adolescent's friends are described as caring and good problem-solvers, I may want to recruit them as guest consultants for future individual and family therapy sessions.

SOCIAL SKILLS

As discussed earlier, one key protective factor for children and adolescents that can help them to cope effectively with high levels of stress and life's challenges is having strong social skills (Anthony, 1984, 1987; Garmezy, 1994; Wolin & Wolin, 1993). Resilient children and adolescents are masters at making new friends and creating support systems for themselves. It is helpful to know from the adolescent how skilled she is at making new friends, if she has at least one or more close friends or if she is somewhat limited in this area, if she has difficulty with self-observation in social situations, and how well she can reach out to other kids or adults when she needs support. If there are difficulties in any of these areas, the therapist should explore with the adolescent if she would like to address these issues in future sessions. The observing-oneself-from-a-bubble experiment mentioned earlier can be a very effective social-skill-building tool for adolescents struggling in this area.

One important developmental task that the adolescent needs to master is to become affiliated with a peer group. Without adequate social skills this can be an arduous task for the young adolescent seeking to make meaningful connections outside of her family. As Pipher (1994) has accurately pointed out, adolescent girls can be quite vicious in spreading nasty rumors around the school and in rejecting those seeking affiliation with their "cool" in-groups. The consequences of being blacklisted or having one's reputation tarnished by these cold-hearted adolescents can prove to be devastating for the adolescent who is seeking a peer group to connect with. As a last resort, this adolescent may end up gravitating toward a peer group of other troubled adolescents who also feel disconnected. It is here that the adolescent may for the first time get exposed to self-harming, substance abuse, or eating disorders. However, not all rejected or alienated adolescents end up on this dead-end street. In fact, the adolescent's one and only friend may be the one who serves as a faithful supportive other to help her through the stormy periods of adolescence.

In situations where the self-harming adolescent reports not having any friends or her whole peer group plays a major role in maintaining her self-harming behavior, I ask her about the possibility of bringing in some former clients as a peer group support system for her in one of our future sessions (Selekman, 1995b). This makes the adolescent less isolated, connects her to a positive peer group, and gives her the opportunity to learn the creative ways these peers conquered their self-harming problems.

Finally, if the adolescent reports being involved in a serious intimate relationship but is experiencing relationship difficulties, I may propose that she bring in her partner for future couples counseling. Clearly, if the adolescent feels that her relationship difficulties are contributing to the maintenance of her self-harming behavior, this should be a future target area for intervention.

Cultural and Gender Issues

When conducting my assessment at the adolescent, family, and peer group levels, I am always listening carefully and thinking about the role cultural and gender issues play in the maintenance of the self-harming behavior problem. While intently listening to my clients' problem stories and observing their patterns of relating to one another and to me, I am mindful of how my own traditional background as a white Jewish male and the essentialist views of cultural groups different from my own that I was exposed to growing up can get in the way of my trying to understand their unique cultural values, rituals, customs, and gender role expectations. According to Laird (2000), "Learning about culture can teach us how to ask good questions in a way that not only helps to surface clients' cultural meanings for our inspection, but makes it possible for clients to hear their own cultural stories in a newly reflective way" (p. 343). The therapist's use of curiosity can invite the clients to take him or her on a grand tour of their cultural worlds.

In some cases, the adolescent's cutting behavior may be a metaphor for her newly immigrated family's feeling isolated and cut off from extended family and friends in their homeland. One transition area that sparks intense intergenerational conflict and high levels of stress in immigrant families is the Americanization process, which often poses a major threat to the preservation of traditional cultural values and role behaviors. This may take the form of the adolescent wanting more autonomy, to wear different clothes, to go to parties or go clubbing, or to engage in premarital sex. For example, I once worked with a Middle Eastern adolescent who was cutting and burning herself and abusing cocaine and heroin. After her parents found out that she was pregnant, they threatened to move back to their homeland without her and not tell her where they were going unless she immediately got an abortion. She did, but because of this painful loss, combined with all of the threats of physical abuse for "sinning" and tremendous guilt placed on her, she became quite depressed. In these types of cultural conflict situations, the therapist needs to work both sides of the intergenerational fence (Selekman, 1993) and help family members see the destructive and unproductive ways they try to solve their problems.

It is also helpful to ask the family the role spirituality plays in their lives. The therapist can ask: "Tell me, in what ways spirituality has been important to you?" or "What gives your life purpose or meaning?" With families in which spirituality or religion plays a central role in daily life, I actively involve their spiritual leaders in the treatment process.

GENDER POWER IMBALANCES IN THE FAMILY

While listening to family members share their varying views about the presenting problem and observing them interact with one another, I red-flag in my mind certain language, themes, and beliefs that are rooted in traditional patriarchal ideology are supporting gender power imbalances in the family. In some families of self-harming adolescents, the father wields all of the power in their families when it comes to decisions being made and having the last word. In some cases, the fathers in these families may use aggression or various forms of intimidation to silence the female voices in their families. As mentioned earlier, the use of reframing and the externalization of rigid patriarchal patterns of relating across the genders (Philpot et al., 1997; White, 1989) can be pursued as therapeutic options in these clinical situations.

Therapists should also listen carefully for and support the voices of self-harming adolescent women that are resisting patriarchal and cultural proscriptions for how they are "supposed to" think and act. Brown (1998) found in her qualitative research with young adolescent women from poor and middle class families that the resilient "resisters" in her study had the "capacity to name sources of ill treatment, injustice, and bad feelings that freed them to deal with anger constructively and reasonably; this anger motivated their resistance and strong voices" (p. viii). According to Brown, the young women in her study asked "through their resistance both implicitly and explicitly, whose construction of reality is to be given legitimacy and authority" (p. x). Once the therapist identifies the adolescent's natural resisting abilities in the assessment process, he or she should harness those abilities in order to help the adolescent to avoid falling prey to conventional patriarchal beliefs and practices. She can also be helped to channel this personal strength into problem areas in her life and possibly serve as a teen leader doing prevention work at her school and in her community.

Larger Systems Level

Because adolescents who self-harm tend to attract many helping professionals from larger systems, it is critical that the therapist assess with them and their families which helpers who are part of the problem system he or she needs to collaborate with (Anderson & Goolishian, 1988). Two larger system areas often play a role in the development and the maintenance of the adolescent's self-harming and other behavioral difficulties: the school context and family-helping-system knot situations.

THE SCHOOL CONTEXT

We know from resiliency research findings that being successful at school can serve as an important protective factor for at-risk children or adolescents (Haggerty et al., 1994; Werner & Smith, 1992). Therefore it is important that the therapist take the time to assess with the adolescent, her parents, concerned teachers, and other involved school personnel how well the student functions academically and socially. I ask the adolescent which particular classes is she struggling the most and how much of her difficulty is related to conflicts with particular teachers versus not grasping the material due to its being too hard or because of her learning difficulties. Once I have secured signed consent forms from the family to collaborate with the involved helpers at school, I set up meetings with the relevant teachers and inquire about all of their concerns, attempted solutions, and frustrations with my client. In some cases, the same unproductive interactions that occur between the adolescent and her parents at home get played out with particular teachers. After I have listened respectfully to the teachers' stories, I offer to collaborate with them to brainstorm some new strategies for disrupting negative interactions in their relationships with the adolescent, as well as find out from them what they think I should work on and address with the client in my family therapy sessions.

I also explore with the adolescent if she has established any meaningful, close relationships with particular teachers to whom she typically goes for support and advice. These inspirational others (Anthony, 1984, 1987) can serve as valuable resources for the therapist to have present in both the adolescent's individual and family therapy sessions.

If the adolescent or her parents are very concerned about specific learning difficulties, but the school is not responding to their concerns by providing testing or special remedial services, the therapist may need to act as their advocate. Once a case study evaluation has been conducted, it is important that the adolescent and the parents have an opportunity to review the testing results and be coauthors in the construction of the Individual Educational Plan (I.E.P.), particularly when it comes to goal-setting and selecting what special school services they think could be helpful to them. More often than not, adolescents have very little input—if any—in the I.E.P. goal-setting process. In fact, many of my adolescent clients who previously have had case study evaluations conducted on them were not only not asked if they would like to review what was written about them but also had never even seen their evaluations!

FAMILY-HELPING-SYSTEM KNOT SITUATIONS

Sometimes antagonistic, conflictual relationships develop among the adolescent, her parents, members of her social network, and the involved

larger systems professionals. These may play a major role in the maintenance of the client's self-harming behavior. In these situations, the therapist has to walk a tightrope between advocating for and supporting his or
her clients and simultaneously respectfully listening to and conveying his
or her interest in the helpers' concerns. The therapist may also need to
be like a labor relations arbitrator and help both parties learn more productive ways to resolve their difficulties. In addition, the therapist must be
willing to critically examine how his or her views and actions in collaborative meetings may be fueling conflicts or keeping things stuck. I like to
refer to family-helping-system entanglements or impasses as *knot* situations. A common example of this is when the involved helpers, including
the therapist, fall into the trap of enacting the family's problem-maintaining interaction patterns and role behaviors in their relationships with
one another.

Community Level

It is also important to determine how community factors may be contributing to the maintenance of the self-harming adolescent's behavior
and to other family difficulties. As Laird (2000) contends,

> Therapists need to move beyond therapeutic conversations to a position
> between the family and the community. Interpersonal family practices
> reflect injustices in the larger surrounds, just as family troubles often
> reflect oppression and the lack of opportunities. (p. 352)

It is critical that therapists advocate for marginalized clients who are
experiencing institutional racism and social injustice.

It is also important to assess with the family if they have a strong or
weak social-support system. The more isolated families are, the more vulnerable they are to developing a wide range of stress-related difficulties.
The adolescent's cutting behavior may be a metaphor for how "cut off"
she and her family feel in their community. One way the therapist can
advocate for and help strengthen an isolated family's ability to function
and cope more effectively is to offer to connect them to family support
groups, the local church or synagogue congregations if they are unaffili-
ated, and community organizations that may share similar cultural or religious backgrounds. As mentioned earlier, spiritual involvement has been
identified as being one important characteristic found in strong families
(DeFrain & Stinnett, 1992; Stinnett & O'Donnell, 1996).

CLIENT-DIRECTED FACTORS INFORMING
THE THERAPIST'S USE OF SELF

While conducting the multisystemic family assessment interview, I listen carefully and observe family members' verbal and nonverbal responses for clues to how best to tailor my therapeutic actions to match their unique needs, expectations, beliefs, and styles of cooperating. I strive to create a therapeutic climate that will maximize the presence of the four common factors cited by clients and researchers as contributing to successful treatment outcomes: *extratherapeutic factors*; *relationship factors*; *hope and expectancy*; and *model/technique factors* (Duncan & Miller, 2000; Hubble et al., 1999).

Extratherapeutic Factors

As therapists, we maximize the likelihood of our clients' being able to achieve their ideal treatment outcomes rapidly by inquiring about and capitalizing on their strengths and resources, key resiliency protective factors, unique coping strategies, client-generated pretreatment changes, and chance events (Duncan & Miller, 2000; Hubble et al., 1999) the family brings to treatment. During the assessment, it is important to make mental notes or write down key extratherapeutic factors that the family members indicate have been instrumental in helping them to cope or begin to resolve the original presenting problem. These may include any of the following: journaling, practicing useful ideas from a particular self-help book, gaining personal strength from attending church or a synagogue more regularly, or taking up yoga or a new hobby that relieves stress. The therapist's sincere interest in family members' expertise and resourcefulness and strong desire to accentuate the positive can help to create a therapeutic climate ripe for change.

Relationship Factors

If the therapist fails to give family members ample space to share their problem-saturated stories, they may feel slighted or disrespected. This is especially true with self-harming adolescent clients who may have experienced a long history of being invalidated by their parents and misunderstood or mishandled by former therapists. Families who have experienced a number of treatment failures and are grappling with longstanding difficulties will have long stories that should not be edited by the therapist.

In order to be effective helpers, therapists need to have solid relationship and structuring skills (Alexander & Parsons, 1982; Henggeler & Alexander, 1999). The therapist's empathy, warmth, validation, concern, and humor are an important set of ingredients that need to be present in the therapeutic relationship with the family. If a particular family seems to respond well to my use of humor in the therapeutic process, this is an important indicator that I should continue to interact with the family in a playful and humorous way to help to create possibilities. Structuring skills, such as disrupting destructive family interactions in the room or deciding when to work alone with individuals or with subsystems of the family, are employed by therapists to take charge in sessions if things get out of hand (Alexander & Parsons, 1982; Henggeler & Alexander, 1999).

Beyebach and Carranza (1997), Beyebach and Morejon (1999), and Beyebach, Morejon, Palenzuela, and Rodriguez-Arias (1996) have found that relationship factors play a major role in clients' prematurely dropping out of treatment and with treatment outcome satisfaction. These researchers found that "one-across messages"—that is, the moments in the therapeutic process in which the therapist does not attempt to dominate the interview with too many questions or comments, makes no attempt to introduce change, and refrains from using any technique—are important relationship factors that help strengthen therapeutic alliances and promote client satisfaction with the treatment.

Prior to ending each session with the family, it is important for the therapist to check in with them to see how well they are working together as a team. The family's feedback will help guide the therapist in making whatever adjustments are necessary to help improve the quality of their therapeutic relationship.

Hope and Expectancy

Research indicates that both the therapist's ability to instill hope and the client's own level of hope brought to the therapeutic arena can also contribute to the success of treatment (Duncan & Miller, 2000; McDermott & Snyder, 1999; Snyder, Michael, & Cheavens, 1999). When joining with families in our very first interviews, I like to convey confidently to them that change *will* happen with their situations and it is only a matter of *when*. The therapist's use of presuppositional language (O'Hanlon & Weiner-Davis, 1989; Selekman, 1997) and spending ample time amplifying and consolidating family members' pretreatment changes and eliciting their expertise can empower them to believe in their ability to resolve their presenting problems.

McDermott and Snyder (1999) encourage therapists to listen carefully for elements in clients' problem story reports and clients' descriptions of their treatment goals regarding whether they are high- or low-hope individuals. According to these researchers, high-hope individuals display little pessimism, have no difficulty identifying their goals, are often excited about them, and confidently believe in their ability to achieve them. High-hope clients possess high levels of both wayfulness and willpower (Snyder et al., 1999). Wayfulness consists of the client's perceived capability of finding pathways to achieving his or her goals. Willpower is the driving force or the energy that propels clients towards achieving their goals. High- hope clients also use what McDermott and Snyder (1999) refer to as high-hope markers, that is, descriptors of self and self-talk like the following: "I am proud of what I have accomplished," "I feel confident," "I am a good person," and so forth.

Throughout the family assessment session, I listen carefully for indications of where each family member is in terms of their ability to establish goals for themselves, their levels of wayfulness and willpower, and the high- or low-hope markers they may be using in the interviewing process. Sometimes I ask family members the following scaling question to measure their levels of hope about resolving the presenting problem: "On a scale from 1 to 10, with 10 being totally hopeful that we can resolve this difficulty, and 1 indicating that your situation is completely hopeless, where would each of you have rated things 4 weeks ago? How about last week? How about today?"

Model/Technique Factors

As therapists, we need to take good care of the quality of our relationships with our clients. We must regularly assess with our clients if the questions we ask and the therapeutic experiments we propose are in line with their problem views, theories of change, and treatment goals. During the assessment session and in future therapy sessions, therapists must ask themselves what techniques or strategies family members respond to and what they should abandon because it is not helpful. This is why it is important for therapists to build in some end-of-session time to explore with the family what they found helpful or not helpful in the session. The research on treatment acceptability indicates that clients will cooperate with therapists and implement their techniques or experiments when they perceived them as being sensible, practical, and having the potential for success (Reimers et al., 1992).

This research also indicates that the rationales that therapists present to clients for pursuing particular courses of action or implementing prescribed experiments need to be in line with the clients' views of their problem situations (Conoley, Ivey, Conoley, Schmeal, & Bishop, 1992). Therefore, it is important that therapists incorporate into their rationales the clients' language and problem views in order to gain their cooperation with the implementation of the proposed therapeutic experiments. I have found it extremely useful to offer families a menu of therapeutic experiments to choose from at the end of our sessions. By doing this, therapeutic cooperation can be further enhanced and family members have ample room to choose which task fits best for them.

COLLABORATIVE TREATMENT PLANNING AND GOAL-SETTING

The Goal-Setting Format

To help launch the goal-setting process with the family, I begin with the miracle question (de Shazer, 1988) or other presuppositional questions (O'Hanlon & Weiner-Davis, 1989; Selekman, 1993) to elicit family members' ideal treatment outcome pictures. With both of these type of questions, it is most advantageous to expand the possibilities with each family member—that is, have them spell out in great detail the changes they envision in their family and extrafamilial relationships and in every social context with which they interface, such as with peers and at school. Absent family members can be brought into the miracle question inquiry as well. For example, I may ask the self-harming adolescent: "If your father were sitting here, what would he be the most surprised with that changed in your relationship with you and your mother after the miracle happened?"

MIRACLE QUESTION

When asking the miracle question, it is important that the therapist give family members plenty of time to think and respond. The therapist should not take the lead in guiding family members in any one particular direction. If family members appear to have difficulty responding to this question, I may ask them to pretend or play around with this fun idea that all of their problems have magically disappeared. Often, this helps stuck family members allow their imagination to flow.

Once each family member has had the opportunity to share his or her miracle pictures, I explore with them if any pieces of their miracles have been happening already. This question helps elicit important client-generated pretreatment information that the therapist can amplify and consolidate and use in the solution-construction process with the family. I respond to family members' reports of pretreatment pieces of the miracle happening with the following questions:

- "Are you aware of how you did that?"
- "What did you tell yourself to pull that off?"
- "What will you have to continue to do to get that to happen more often?"
- "How has that made a difference in your relationship?"
- "What else is better?"

These consolidation questions (Selekman, 1993) empower families by inviting them to compliment themselves on their creativity and resourcefulness.

My work with Suzanne, a Caucasian 17-year-old self-injurer who was doing poorly academically in school, illustrates how the miracle question cannot only elicit family members' ideal treatment outcome pictures, but also can create possibilities in the very first family interview. Earlier in the session, Suzanne had talked about how she cut herself to cope with how "everyone was always bitching" at her. She was referring to her parents and some of her teachers that were on her back for not completing her homework assignments. When describing cutting herself with a razor Suzanne said, "the warm blood dripping down my arms relaxed me." What was most surprising to me about the mother was her total lack of concern about Suzanne's cutting behavior. She appeared to be much more concerned about Suzanne's "academic performance problems" than anything else. Unfortunately, the father could not attend this family assessment session due to a mandatory evening work meeting.

Barbara: I don't understand what is going on with you. I mean, you used to be a straight-A student in junior high. Your father and I are very disappointed in you. Why can't you be like your sister Jill who is on the honor roll?

Suzanne: You guys are always comparing me to Jill. I am sick of it! Fuck you!

Barbara: You watch your mouth, young lady! See what I mean, Matthew? She has an attitude problem. Her teachers have complained to me about her attitude problem as well.

Matthew: I would like to ask the two of you a fun question. Suppose you were to go home tonight and while you were sound asleep a miracle happened, and all of these problems were solved. When you wake up the next day how will both of you be able to tell?

Suzanne: Well, my parents would stop nagging me about doing my homework. They would stop comparing me to my genius sister Jill.

Matthew: When your parents make those changes, what effect will that have on your relationship with them? How will you treat them differently?

Suzanne: I guess I wouldn't have the "attitude" problem—you know, not cuss at them when they make me mad.

Matthew: Barbara, what will that be like for you when the attitude problem is gone?

Barbara: I'm sure we would all get along better. I probably would not get any more calls from your teachers about your mouth or missing assignments.

Matthew: Suzanne, if your father were sitting in this empty chair right next to me, what would he be the most surprised with in the miracle picture?

Suzanne: I guess I would be getting better grades in school. I don't know.

Matthew: How will that help the two of you get along better?

Suzanne: He wouldn't be bitching at me as much about school. I'd probably stop cutting myself. . . . Things would be how they used to be with my dad.

Matthew: How did it used to be with you and your dad?

Suzanne: We used to talk about other things like music. I could talk to him about anything. . . . He actually listened to me back then.

Matthew: Back when?

Suzanne: When I was 15. Before he became a partner in his law firm.

Barbara: She's right, life has changed for all of us since Harold became a partner. There are some nights where I never even see him before I go to bed. He is always so stressed out by his job when he is around that he does not hear me when I talk to him.

Matthew: It sounds like both of you are on the same page with this family issue. I'm curious, if I were a fly watching your family after the miracle happened, what will I see the three of you doing together as a family that you used to do for fun?

Suzanne: On Sundays, we used go on long bike rides as a family.

Barbara: I also miss those fun bike rides in the forest preserve.

Matthew: Besides reinstating the fun Sunday bike rides, what other fun things will I see the three of you doing together after the miracle happens?

Suzanne: My dad used to take me to Cubs games. He'd get great box seats through his job.

Matthew: I'm curious, are there any pieces of the miracle happening a little bit already now?

Barbara: Lately, I have seen Suzanne doing her homework and not on the phone as much with her friends.

Matthew: Wow! Is that different for her to be doing her homework on a more regular basis?

Barbara: Up to this past week, I used to have to check up on her.

Matthew: How did you get her to do that?

Suzanne: It was my idea. If my mom promised to stop nagging and comparing me to my sister, I promised her that I would show her my completed homework.

Matthew: Suzanne, how did you come up with such a creative contract?

Suzanne: I don't know. . . . I just came up with it.

Barbara: See how bright she is? Honey, if you buckled down more at school, you could probably graduate in the upper percentile of your class.

Matthew: Suzanne, if I ever needed to tap your creative mind to help me come up with another great contract for another mother and daughter I am working with who have similar difficulties, can I consult with you?

Suzanne: Sure! (*Both Suzanne and Barbara are smiling now.*)

Not only did the use of the miracle question successfully elicit Barbara and Suzanne's ideal treatment outcome pictures, but it also helped create possibilities in two major ways. First, Barbara identified the important client-generated pretreatment change of Suzanne's doing her homework on a more regular basis without reminders. Suzanne had come up with the brilliant idea of a quid pro quo contract with her mother around homework completion, which set in motion this important pretreatment change. Second, in the process of expanding the possibilities of the family members' ideal miracle pictures, the mother's initial problem-saturated worldview of Suzanne as the main family problem dramatically shifted to the father's not spending enough quality time with his family. For the first time in the session both Barbara and Suzanne were in agreement about how the "lack of quality time spent with Dad" was a family stressor they both wished to see changed.

PRESUPPOSITIONAL QUESTIONS

Presuppositional questions (O'Hanlon & Weiner-Davis, 1989; Selekman, 1993, 1997) help to instill hope and convey the inevitability of change. They can be used for goal-setting purposes and for amplifying and consolidating client-generated pretreatment changes. These empowering questions can effectively elicit the who, what, when, and how of goal-attainment for family members. Clients bring their own unique presuppositional language to the therapeutic arena. Therefore, once the key presuppositional words used during the interview have been identified, the therapist can match his presuppositional language with the client's. For example, if a family member gazes into my imaginary crystal ball (Selekman, 1993) and describes how she "fixed" a problem, I will ask her what specifically she *did* to "fix it." This helps to strengthen my cooperative relationship with the client and elicits her problem-solving expertise. Some examples of presuppositional questions are as follows:

- "How will you know when you have really succeeded in counseling?"
- "Let's say all of you leave here tonight and while driving home you tell yourselves, 'Gee, that meeting with Matthew was really helpful.' What will have changed with your situation?"
- "If you were to gaze into my crystal ball in 2 weeks when you have stopped cutting yourself, what will you see yourself doing differently?"

- "How surprised will you be when you have completely changed in 2 weeks' time?"
- "What will be a small sign of progress over the next week that will tell you that you are making good headway?"
- "Let's say we ran into one another three months after we successfully completed counseling together, and in reflecting back you told me the steps you took to get out of counseling. What will you tell me you did?"

Following the miracle question inquiry with Barbara and Suzanne, I utilized presuppositional questions to elicit a solvable problem from them and to begin the goal-setting process.

Matthew: How will you know that you really succeeded in counseling?

Barbara: Suzanne would continue to do her homework on a regular basis without any reminders. She will have picked up her grades up to As and Bs. No more Ds, no more calls from her teachers.

Matthew: Since Suzanne is already succeeding in the homework- doing area, what will be the next big step she will take with school that will tell you she is continuing to succeed there?

Barbara: I guess no more calls from the teachers would be the next indication of success on Suzanne's behalf.

Matthew: Suzanne, let's say I handed you my imaginary crystal ball and we all took turns gazing into it seeing you being successful in Mrs. Brown's and Ms. Smith's classes over the next week. What will your mother and I see you doing that is making those teachers feel like fainting in amazement because they don't recognize you as a student?

Suzanne: Well, first of all, I will make it to both of their classes on time. You will probably see me sitting up in front in both classes so I can take better notes. I won't be talking to my friends in class. I won't cop an attitude with them—you know, be sarcastic. I will make sure I take home the right books from my locker. I will also be turning in my homework assignments.

Barbara: That sounds very impressive! You think you can pull all those things off in one week?

Suzanne: I definitely think I could do most of those things.

Matthew: On a scale from 1 to 10, with 10 being you're totally confident that you can accomplish all of those things in one week's time and 1 being absolutely no chance at all, where would you rate yourself today?

Suzanne: An 8!

Matthew: Wow! You sound very confident, Suzanne! How about you, Barbara, where would you rate your daughter on the confidence scale?

Barbara: I think I would give her a 6.

Matthew: How will you know she made it up to a lucky 7?

Barbara: I will not get one call from Mrs. Brown or Ms. Smith.

Matthew: How will the two of you celebrate Suzanne's getting up to that lucky 7 next week?

Suzanne: Could we talk to Dad about going on a family bike ride next Sunday?

Barbara: Sure, that sounds like a great idea.

Through the use of presuppositional questions we were able to negotiate a solvable problem and establish a treatment goal with the help of the imaginary crystal ball (Selekman, 1993). Suzanne was able to spell out each step she would have to take to prevent her two teachers from being tempted to call her mother. Although she had stated confidently that she could see herself having no problem pulling off all of these steps in one week's time, I further underscored her high level of confidence through the use of a confidence scale. Surprisingly, Barbara had rated Suzanne higher on the confidence scale than I expected by giving her a 6. By this point in the interview, she appeared to be much more hopeful about things continuing to improve with Suzanne than she was at the beginning of our session. We concluded the goal-setting process by discussing how they would celebrate Suzanne's goal attainment. By doing this, I instilled hope and raised their levels of expectancy that Suzanne will continue to improve in the school problem area. Both Barbara and Suzanne were quite excited about the prospect of reinstating the Sunday family bike ride and of being together as a family, an important value that mother and daughter shared.

SCALING QUESTIONS

Scaling questions (Berg & de Shazer, 1993; de Shazer, 1991, 1988) are particularly useful for securing from family members quantitative measurements of where they would rate the presenting problem prior to treatment, presently, and where they would like to be in a week's time. As a therapeutic tool, scaling questions can help therapists negotiate realistic and well-formed behavioral treatment goals with their clients. If they have a clear focus for treatment, both the therapist and the clients will know when they have arrived at their targeted destination. Scaling questions also can be used to assess family members' levels of self-confidence or hope that the presenting problem can be solved. Finally, scaling questions can effectively flesh out client-generated pretreatment change material that had not been discussed earlier in the family assessment session. Some examples of scaling questions are as follows (subzero scales, which appear in the following transcript, are used for pessimistic clients):

- "On a scale from 1 to 10, with 10 being you are not arguing at all and 1 being you are arguing all of the time, where would you have rated your situation 4 weeks ago? How about today?"
- "So you used to be at a 1 and now you rate the arguing situation at a 5. What steps have the two of you taken to get up to a 5?"
- "On a scale from −10 to 0, with −10 being that there is absolutely no chance ever that this cutting problem can be resolved, and 0 being you are hopeful that things can improve a little bit with your situation, where would you rate your situation today?"
- "You think you are at a −4 now? Let's say we get together in a week's time and you have taken some important steps up to a −3. What will you tell me you did?"

Samantha, a Caucasian 16-year-old, had been referred to me by her school social worker for being depressed, cutting herself, and doing poorly in school. Apparently, the last psychologist she had seen diagnosed her with borderline personality disorder. Before this yearlong treatment experience, she had seen a psychiatrist and two other psychologists that had diagnosed her with bipolar disorder. She had taken Depakote for her mood disorder problems. The parents appeared to be very frustrated and burned out with mental health professionals in general, particularly with their inability to help their daughter. I might add that with all of the past treatment experiences, the parents were peripherally involved in the treatment process.

Samantha found that the cutting helped her to control her emotional reactions to frustrating and overwhelming stressors going on in her life. She contended that she was "addicted" to her cutting behavior, that "now it was controlling [her]." Samantha cited her parents' chronic "arguing problem," as well as peer rejection issues, as being a big source of stress for her.

The session transcript begins with my use of negative scaling questions to establish an initial treatment goal.

Matthew: I realize all of you are quite overwhelmed by the difficulties you're struggling with. However, we have to start somewhere in trying to resolve these difficulties. Which one of these problems would you like to work on changing first?

William: My fear is that sooner or later she may kill herself with this cutting she is doing. None of the other therapists addressed that issue.

Samantha: Dr. Kerr did. But she really didn't help me to stop the cutting.

Wilma: I'm also afraid that one of these times she might sever a vein.

Matthew: Samantha, would you like us to begin with trying to resolve the cutting problem first?

Samantha: Yeah, but nothing has ever worked before and I can't stop doing it.

Matthew: I hear you—the cutting problem has been pushing you, your parents, and other therapists around for a long time. It's going to require hard work and a family team effort! Let me ask all of you some questions to get a rating on where things have been with the cutting situation in the past and up to this present day. On a scale from −10 to 0, with −10 being that there is absolutely no chance ever that the cutting problem can be resolved and 0 being you are hopeful that things can improve a little bit with this situation, where would you have rated your situation a month ago?

Samantha: A month ago I would say . . . at a −10.

Matthew: How about you, Mom and Dad, where would you have rated the cutting situation a month ago?

William: (*looking at Wilma and agreeing on a number*) We would probably agree with Samantha the situation was at rock bottom then. . . . It was about at a −10.

Matthew: It's nice to see that all of you are on the same page with your ratings. Often parents and teens don't see eye to eye on problem situations. To help me have a sense of how all of you rate the cutting situation now, what would you rate it today?

Samantha: I would say that I am probably up at a −5 or −4.

Matthew: Which rating suits you best now in terms of having a little more hope?

Samantha: Let's go with the −4.

Matthew: Are you aware of what you did or told yourself to help get you from a −10 "rock bottom" situation up to a −4?

Samantha: Well, I've tried calling my friend a few times instead of cutting. I've looked at the scars on my arms a lot lately and told myself, "No wonder why I have a hard time making new friends or boys aren't interested in me. They probably think I am a psycho!!!"

Matthew: How did you come to that realization?

Samantha: I don't know. . . . Maybe I'm off, but I have been thinking a lot lately that maybe I set myself up to be rejected by other kids.

Matthew: How else has this piece of valuable insight helped you gain a little more control over the cutting?

Samantha: I talk to myself a lot about how nice it would be to make some new friends and hang on to friendships. I have lost two friends over my cutting.

Matthew: What other things have you been doing lately to stand up to cutting and not allowing it to push you around?

Samantha: When I have been frustrated or mad sometimes I have told one of my parents about it, rather than going up to my room and using the razor.

Matthew: Is that different for you to do that with your parents?

Samantha: Yeah.

William: We told her that we are very pleased with the way she has been coming to us lately. In fact, one night Wilma and I were arguing and she confronted us.

Matthew: Is that different for her to confront the two of you or does she typically do that?

William: Yes, my wife and I were very surprised by Samantha's doing this. She had told us that she is very troubled by our arguing. We have been working on not arguing as much.

Matthew: So it sounds like in some ways Samantha has been a big help to the two of you. Do you think she would make a good marital therapist?

Wilma: (*Everyone in the room laughs.*) Samantha seems to be doing much better. We also need to work on our arguing problem. In no way do we want to be the source of her cutting problem.

Matthew: Where would you rate things with Samantha today?

William: (*talking with Wilma*) We think she has gotten up to a −2.

Matthew: Other than the changes that have already been mentioned, what else have you seen Samantha do that got her up to that −2?

William: She is not hanging out in her bedroom as much. We are talking more with her about school and she is being more open with us about her life.

Matthew: Are all of those things different for her?

Wilma: Yes, she used to isolate herself in her room and not tell us about anything going on in her life.

Matthew: To help your parents out, is there anything they are doing differently now that is helping you open up with them more?

Samantha: They are arguing less and not asking me a million questions about school and my friends.

Matthew: Because we are running short on time, let's say we get together in one week's time and you guys come in here and tell me that we have made it up to −3 and −1, respectively, or higher. What will you tell me you did?

Samantha: I will keep talking to myself about the need to change. I will talk to my parents and friends more when I'm upset. I don't know, maybe I will come up with some new things.

William: (*talking with Wilma*) Samantha will keep talking with us, and my wife and I will try not to argue as much.

It is critical to give families like Samantha's that have experienced multiple treatment failures and are highly pessimistic about the likelihood of change plenty of room to share their long problem-saturated stories, as well as provide validation, empathy, and support in an effort to build relationships with them first. Clinically, I have found it quite useful to use a negative scale and externalize (White & Epston, 1990) the self-harming problem with these highly pessimistic families as a way to better cooperate with them and create possibilities with their entrenched problem-saturated situations.

The added bonus with Samantha's family was her parents' willingness to take responsibility for how their chronic arguing problem was contributing to the maintenance of their daughter's cutting problem. I had also relabeled Samantha's cutting behavior as being helpful to the parents and inquired about whether if she would be a "good marital therapist." By the end of the interview, the parents had voiced a desire to spend some future session time working on their arguing and other marital difficulties alone with me. Samantha left our first family session empowered and much more self-confident.

CHAPTER 2

Improvisational Systemic Interviewing: Crafting and Selecting Meaningful Questions

Music is your own experience, your thoughts, your wisdom. If you don't live it, it won't come out of your horn.

—Charlie Parker

IMPROVISATIONAL SYSTEMIC INTERVIEWING is in many ways analogous to the playing styles and the creative expressiveness of jazz artists. We give ourselves permission to take risks and expand on clients' concerns by responding with curiosity, introducing new storylines, and giving them invitations to liberate themselves from the shackles of their familiar problem-saturated family tunes.

Gary Klein, a cognitive psychologist and author of *Sources of Power: How People Make Decisions,* has provided empirical support for the use of improvisation, intuition, imagination, metaphor, and storytelling in the problem-solving process. Using naturalistic field research methods, Klein and his colleagues studied the decision-making processes of firefighters, pilots, emergency room nurses, military leaders, nuclear power plant operators, and chess masters. The research team identified seven cognitive skills that these highly talented professionals possessed that helped them to make life-and-death decisions and to solve problems with little margin for error under extreme pressure. They are: *pattern recognition, situation awareness, identifying anomalies, identifying leverage points and improvising, identifying events that already happened (the past) or are most likely to happen (the future), identifying differences that are too small for novices to notice,* and *critically examining one's own limitations* (Klein, 1998). Klein and his colleagues observed that these skilled professionals could see the big picture and patterns when they were involved in performing tasks. The professionals used their intuition to detect typicality of patterns and to determine if an anomaly they observed or heard about warranted prompt intervention or not. The professionals were observed masterfully identifying leverage points or opportunities to improvise, and they creatively were able to tackle the tasks at hand. They used mental simulation or visualization to transport themselves into the future to assess the potential pitfalls or problems with an intervention they wished to test out or a project that was on the verge of being implemented. Klein (1998) calls this thinking process a *premortem*. Finally, these highly skilled professionals had superb observation and listening skills and could detect subtle or small changes occurring and noticed anomalies or things that did not happen with work situations they were attempting to manage (Klein, 1998).

In this chapter, I will present an improvisational style of systemic interviewing. I will discuss a variety of ways therapists can tap their natural creative abilities in the interviewing process and present several categories of therapeutic questions.

THERAPEUTIC IMPROVISATIONAL MOVES IN THE INTERVIEWING PROCESS

Therapists can make three improvisational moves in the interviewing process to help to cocreate possibilities with clients: *spontaneous reflection, curiosity,* and *the use of imagination.* After discussing each one of these therapeutic moves, I will present five major categories of therapeutic questions that the therapist can use to help to coauthor solution-determined stories with more pessimistic clients.

Spontaneous Reflection

As therapists we can spontaneously reflect the ideas, metaphors, and stories that enter our minds during our therapeutic conversations with clients. Schon (1983) refers to this activity as *reflection-in-action*. According to Schon, reflection-in-action is the ability to stay alive and improvise in the midst of action without having to stop and think. The nature and contents of the therapist's spontaneous reflections are endless; therapists should allow their creativity to run wild. For example, therapists could offer tentative alternative constructions of the family's problem story, share an off-the-wall idea that just popped into their head, tell a story or joke that parallels or exaggerates the clients' problem views or situation, share a famous quote that fits nicely with the family's problem situation or offers them important wisdom, or wonder aloud how a famous historical figure, popular book character like Harry Potter, or popular television or movie family might approach and attempt to solve similar difficulties. In some cases, this type of improvisational use of self can dramatically alter family members' constrained or outmoded beliefs about the self-harming adolescent and their problem situations. Any shift in their habitual way of viewing their difficulties can help to disrupt the family's unproductive interaction patterns and have a positive impact on the self-harming adolescent's behavior as well.

The following case example with Rhiannon, a Caucasian 17-year-old girl, illustrates the profound impact and long-lasting effects a well-timed, spontaneous reflection can have in helping a self-harming client to rewrite her oppressive problem story. Rhiannon's parents were divorced and for several years she lived with her father, stepmother, and their children. At the time of our family consultation session, Rhiannon had moved back in with her mother Judy, who was granted custodial guardianship. Rhiannon had a long history of abusing alcohol, marijuana, methamphetamine, and cutting herself to manage her anger and emotional pain. She was doing poorly in school, was running around with a negative peer group, and was often violating her mother's rules. Rhiannon and her mother were receiving treatment and case-management services at a child and family clinic in their community.

Matthew: Is the cutting because you are angry or you are trying to comfort yourself?

Rhiannon: Yeah, it's better than crying. If I get sad, I can turn it into anger real quickly . . . and after I cut I feel better.

Matthew: Has anybody hurt you in the past in some way or another? It could be something physical or verbal, but something that had a major impact.

Rhiannon: Yeah, my . . .

Judy: . . . the stepmom—a lot of verbal abuse. Putting her down for things . . . anything. If she came back from somewhere, she would say, "The little princess is back!" Very demeaning to her.

Rhiannon: I could never do anything right for her. I would get good grades and went to a divorce group. There was nothing I could do. I was just this little princess, a Miss Know-it-all and everything with her. Well, fine! I just became myself—a piece of crap! I was just nothing!

Judy: For her to tell Rhiannon that she was the one who was causing all of the problems between her [the stepmother] and her dad!

Matthew: Wow! There were guilt trips and a lot of blaming!

Rhiannon: She would want me to clean like a little Cinderella, so I would and that would annoy her because I was around her too much and she didn't want to look at me. And I would go up to my room. Then we would fight about my being in my room too much and I would hear that I am lazy and didn't help around the house. It wasn't something she kept to herself, but something the whole family knew about!

Matthew: How come your dad didn't jump in there and protect you?

Rhiannon: I told him once and then they got into an argument and he left the house instead of hitting her. And as soon as he closed the door and left, she would say, "And now you are going to cause our marriage to break up and the kids and everything!" It was so stupid!

Judy: She also used a kind of reverse psychology on her. She would go and tell her, "I suppose you are going to tell your dad!" Well, Rhiannon would try and prove her wrong and would not go tell her dad.

Matthew: (*As I listened carefully to Rhiannon's difficult and painful story, I began to reflect-in-action.*) You know, I wonder if stopping the cutting thing would be in some ways a way to close the door on the past and the horrible things you have been through and allow you to move in a different direction with your life?

Rhiannon: Uh . . . I never thought of that. (*pause*)

Matthew: Because it sounds like cutting is attached to awful things that continue to haunt you.

Rhiannon: Yeah, it's kind of attached to me . . . like, when I lived over there she would put me down or whatever and I would just go and cut myself. Now whenever I get mad, like instinct I just go and cut myself. (*long pause, responding again to my spontaneous reflection*) I never even thought of that.

At this point, it became quite clear that Rhiannon's cutting behavior was symbolic of or a painful reminder of her horrific past. It kept her a prisoner of her past. Her painful story was full of double-bind situations, blaming, lack of connection with and support from key parental figures, and being forced to squelch the expression of her feelings, particularly her anger. The cutting worked for her because it gave her the control she lacked in this out-of-control remarried family situation. The spontaneous reflection I shared with Rhiannon was not only acceptable to her belief system, but also appeared for her to be a newsworthy way of looking at her problem story.

Curiosity

Using curiosity allows therapists to entertain a myriad of possible explanations for a family's presenting problem situation and to look for a pattern of how family members' and involved helping professionals' problem views fit together. The therapist also must be curious about how gender, cultural, and societal factors play a role in the development and the maintenance of the problem situation. By adopting a therapeutic stance of curiosity, we can critically examine our own premises and decision making. Operating like a curious super sleuth in the interviewing process, I try not to allow myself to become wedded to any one important clue, explanation, or grand solution strategy that should happen to enter my mind while in conversation with the family.

Patricia, a Caucasian 14-year-old, and her family had been referred to me by Jan, Patricia's school social worker, for her cutting behavior, signs of being depressed, and problem with bulimia. Patricia was also associating with a peer group of "troubled teenagers." Jan was a seasoned clinician and felt there was "much more to Patricia's story then we knew about at this point." I was curious about what Jan meant by her statement and asked her to elaborate. She replied that she had suspected there was something going on with Patricia and her family that was not being discussed in their individual sessions together. For example, whenever they discussed her relationship with her father, Patricia would "change the topic." Again, I adopted a stance of curiosity with Jan and explored with her what her thoughts were about this. She said she wondered if the father had possibly been abusive to Patricia in some way in the past. I asked her if she had picked up on any innuendos or signs of this. According to Jan, Patricia had mentioned to her on numerous occasions that her parents fought a lot in front of her and her 8-year-old sister Amanda. I also asked her if she knew whether the parents' fighting ever escalated into episodes of violence. Apparently, Patricia had not indicated that violence had ever occurred when the parents argued.

One of the main triggers for Jan's decision to refer Patricia to me was that teachers had twice caught Patricia taking laxatives and throwing up in the bathroom. In individual sessions with Jan, Patricia had reported a "regular pattern of bingeing and purging," as well as "cutting herself on her arms and abdomen."

Sid (the father), Elizabeth (the mother), and Patricia were present at the first family interview. Jan could not attend because of her work schedule. After joining with each family member around their strengths and resources, I explored with the family what their thoughts were about why the school social worker believed it was important that they pursue family therapy with me at this time. The following transcript begins with our conversation about the referral process and Jan's idea that they should seek family therapy.

Matthew: What do you think gave Jan the idea that all of you should come in for family counseling?

Elizabeth: Well, I know that Jan and a few of Patricia's teachers were worried about her cutting, throwing up, and using laxatives. . . . I was also concerned when Jan told me what was going on. Is it normal for teenage girls to do these sort of things?

Matthew: Is this the first time you heard about these "sort of things" with Patricia or does this ever happen at home?

Elizabeth: Not that I know about. . . . Honey, do you do this at home?

Patricia: Sometimes. . . . I do it when no one's around.

Sid: But why do you do it, period?

Patricia: Laurie and Candace [her friends] do it. It's weird—I actually feel better after I throw up.

Matthew: I'm curious, Patricia, is there anything going on in your family or in your life right now that you find real hard to stomach?

Patricia: Yeah. The last big fight my parents had. . . . I got real scared. My father picked up a chair and slammed it into a wall. I don't know . . . I mean, I said to myself, what if he really loses it on us?! Some nights I just sit up in my room and start to cut on my abdomen and arms so I can take my mind off of this.

Matthew: What do you guys think about what Patricia just said?

Sid: (angrily) That happened about a year ago! I really lost it. I had been demoted that day at work and I was really pissed off. And then to top it off, Elizabeth over here started pushing my buttons!

Elizabeth: (*interrupting*) You are cutting your abdomen and arms?! When did you start doing that? Aren't you concerned about this Sid?!

Sid: I was talking. Don't interrupt me!

Matthew: (*Rather than allowing the exchange to get out of hand, I decided to disrupt this negative interaction.*) It sounds like that day was difficult for all of you to swallow! (*turning to Patricia*) Patricia, things are starting to heat up with your parents right now, so I think this is a good place for you to hand off the baton to me and let me give it my best shot—you have already run your leg of the race against fear. Go catch your breath in the waiting room.

With some families, the adolescent's symptoms or problems may be metaphors for anxiety-provoking family events, relationships in the family, or a parent's problem. In this initial family interview with Patricia, I was particularly curious about what main stressors in her life she found most difficult to "stomach." This linked her bulimia and the self-harming behavior to the father's aggressive behavior and the threat of violence, his work-related problems, and the parents' marital difficulties. During our one-on-one time in the family meeting, Patricia had shared with me that her catastrophic fear was that one day her father would "really lose it" and "harm one of us in the family." This important piece of information was part of Patricia's untold story that the school social worker was picking up on. As I observed the family interactions, I noticed that the parents were not only disconnected from one another but from Patricia as well. Patricia had found that bingeing, purging, and cutting were effective coping strategies for dealing with her fears and the parents' marital problems.

When the parents began to show me their destructive interactive dance, I saw this as a great therapeutic opening for crossing the bridge to the parents' marital relationship. I also used this as an opportunity to relieve Patricia of carrying the burden of trying to save her family from destruction. I used the metaphor of a relay race and her handing "the baton" off to me to take over the mission of trying to help her parents and prevent future family disaster. After I had dismissed Patricia and began to address the parents' relationship concerns, I was able to establish a contract with them to work on their marital issues. I also set up a "no violence" contract with them. Before concluding our session, each family member had come up with three constructive things they each could do if violence were to erupt or if they felt unsafe.

Use of Imagination

One powerful way to help self-harming adolescents and their families break free from their problem-saturated realities is to use imagination questions (Epston, 2000; Selekman, 1997). Many of my incoming clients feel overwhelmed by their difficulties, have lost their spontaneity and playfulness, and are at a loss for solutions. Imagination questions propel them into a new reality where anything and everything is possible. I believe that every family likes a surprise! This is quite evident in the way that family members smile, laugh, and are intrigued by my use of questions that titillate their imagination powers. Once immersed in the imagining process, family members begin to generate creative problem-solving ideas and important information about their past successes.

When joining with family members in initial sessions, I take the time to learn about their unique interests and hobbies, the sports they like to play, the types of books they like to read and why, and who their favorite celebrities and characters are in current affairs, in television and film, in professional sports, in history, and in the books they like to read. After securing this important information, I can intersperse my imagination questions with the names of these key celebrities and characters and their unique storylines to capture a family's interest and cocreate possibilities with them.

Imagination questions also have a liberating effect on the therapist in that there are no formulas or rules for crafting them. The therapist is free to tap his or her own creative capacities. Some examples of imagination questions are as follows:

- "If you were Harry Potter for a day, how would you use your magical powers with your family to improve things at home?"
- "If all of us ended up stranded together on a deserted island in the Pacific Ocean, what strengths and talents would I come to know about your daughter and you as a family that would help us to survive the ordeal?"
- "Let's say you were to turn your parents on to two of your most favorite Korn tunes and they really liked them. What were the tunes? What effect would their liking your music have on your relationship with them?"
- "If you were a new character on the TV show *Friends*, which character's sister would you play? How would you act? What per-

sonal qualities would the original cast like most about you? How about TV viewers—what aspects of your character would they come to like best?"

The following case example demonstrates how imagination questions can help to create possibilities in a stuck situation. I had seen 17-year-old Caroline two times with her family for her cutting, marijuana abuse, and poor grades in school. I was the seventh therapist they had been to regarding these same problems over a 3-year period. The parents were quite pessimistic about Caroline's ability to "take responsibility" and "change." During our one-on-one session time in the family session, Caroline had shared that her parents put a "lot of pressure" on her to "get good grades." For Caroline, the marijuana and the cutting helped her to "tune out" the parents' voices in her head about "doing homework" and being "a- good-for-nothing." She was constantly being compared to her older sister Meredith, who was "a success story" in college. My attempts in the first two sessions to get the parents to put less pressure on Caroline and to stop blaming her went absolutely nowhere. Traditional solution-focused brief therapy methods were not working.

The transcript below was taken from our third session and begins with my asking the family imagination questions. Present in the session were Caroline, her father Paul, her mother Janet, the referring school social worker Sam, and Marci, Caroline's art teacher and inspirational other (Anthony, 1987) with whom she had a meaningful connection.

Matthew: Let's say we all got stranded on a deserted island in the South Pacific, not a soul in sight. What strengths and talents would I come to know about Caroline and your family that will help us survive this ordeal?

Sam: (*looking at Caroline*) Well, Caroline's got a great sense of humor. She would provide the good cheer.

Janet: You're right, despite all of her problems, Caroline can be very funny and give me a good laugh once in a while.

Marci: Caroline is very creative and is great with her hands. Maybe she would design a new kind of raft or floatable contraption with her father.

Paul: I remember last year we went on a camping trip as a family and a terrible storm rolled in which wiped out our campsite. It was

Caroline, not my older son Peter, who offered to help fix the tent and clean up.

Caroline: (*looking at her father and smiling*) I remember that camping trip! What a mess! It was so muddy. Our things got blown all over the place. Peter didn't help out a bit.

Janet: What an ordeal that camping trip was! I think it rained three of the five days we were there. Caroline was a real trooper! She didn't complain once. It was Peter who was constantly demanding to leave and giving us a hard time.

Matthew: It sounds like Caroline can really step up to the plate and take responsibility when the going gets rough for the family. Mom and Dad, can you think of some of the ways Caroline will be most helpful to you on the deserted island?

Paul: She will probably help me find food on the island . . . and like Marci said, try and help build a raft so we can head out to sea.

Matthew: Let's say that Caroline continues to evolve into a strong family leader and is instrumental in helping all of you survive this ordeal and make it home safely. As parents, how will your viewing of and relationships with Caroline have changed?

Paul: I will see her as being a responsible young adult. I won't be yelling at her anymore. We will probably go on long bike rides together like we used to in the past.

Janet: Homework will get done with no reminders. We will enjoy each other's company again.

Matthew: Caroline, what difference will it make for you when you return home from the deserted island adventure and your parents have stopped yelling and reminding you to do your homework?

Caroline: We won't be arguing as much. I will be happier. I will get my work done when I'm not stressed out by them.

Matthew: Let me ask your parents something. How will you know that Caroline really changed after the deserted island experience?

Paul: When we ask her to do something, like help out around the house, she will pitch in without battles and reminders. She will get her homework done without us saying a word.

Matthew: If you were to pick one of these two things you want to see Caroline change first, the one that is the highest priority for you, which one would it be?

Janet: Caroline's taking charge of the homework situation.

Paul: I agree.

Through the use of imagination questions, I was successful in moving the treatment system into a more workable reality. We were finally able to establish a realistic treatment goal. I could negotiate with the parents and Caroline a quid pro quo contract around the homework issue. Caroline discovered that by complying with the parents' wishes she could earn privileges she wanted, such as coming home an hour later on weekend nights.

THERAPEUTIC QUESTIONS TO USE
WITH PESSIMISTIC CLIENTS

Coping Questions

With some families, one or both parents and possibly the self-harming adolescent do not respond well to the use of the miracle question in the interviewing process. Even after valiant efforts on the therapist's behalf to invite family members to play around with this idea and entertain how the miracles will be making differences in their lives, he or she still is met with pessimism or "Yes, but" and "I don't believe in miracles" responses. In order to cooperate with these more pessimistic family members, the therapist needs to be prepared, even in the midst of the miracle question inquiry, to shift gears and ask them the following coping questions (Berg & Gallagher, 1991; Selekman, 1993, 1997):

- "Your situation sounds pretty tough right now. I'm curious, Mom and Dad, what steps have the two of you taken to prevent this situation with your daughter from really escalating and getting out of hand?"
- "How has that been helpful? Do you think your daughter would agree?"
- "What are you doing that seems to help you keep going and not give up?"
- "What would be one indicator that would tell you that your situation is getting a little bit better?"

The following case example with Tasha, a 16-year-old from the former Soviet Union, illustrates how coping questions (Berg & Gallagher, 1991; Berg & Miller, 1992; Selekman, 1993, 1997) not only can help to create possibilities when family members are feeling stuck and pessimistic, but also can elicit from the family past and present coping and problem-solving strategies that can be harnessed to empower them.

Tasha and her family had immigrated to the United States from the former Soviet Union when she was 6 years old. Her 12-year-old sister Tatiyana was a straight-A student. According to the parents, Tasha's behavior had changed dramatically when she turned 15. Her "school grades had dropped," she was "abusing marijuana," she was "sneaking out of her bedroom window to go out clubbing," and the mother had "caught her in her bedroom cutting and burning herself." Beth, the school social worker, had referred Tasha and her family to me after she had "made several cigarette burn marks on her right arm." Apparently the school dean was also involved in the referral process and had spoken to Maria, Tasha's mother, after the cigarette burn incident. Beth described the family as being "highly resistant" and known to "drop out of treatment when Tasha decides to stop going for counseling." It was Beth's contention that Tasha had all of the power in the family. She also mentioned that Tasha and her family had been in treatment three times before. According to Beth, Tasha had "blown off" their weekly scheduled counseling sessions a number of times in the past month.

Having worked with a number of Russian families in the past, I have found that what is often considered by helping professionals to be "resistant behavior" has a lot more to do with the cultural meaning of being sent for "therapy" in the former Soviet Union. Not only is there a tremendous stigma attached to going for therapy—that is, you must be "crazy" or "bad"—but there also is a great deal of fear about being locked up in an institution, especially when a governmental authority is sending you to treatment because something is wrong with you or your family. Although Tasha's social worker was not representing the government, the parents were quite up-tight about her referring them to me. My clinical experience working with Russian families has taught me that it is critical to take the time to address their fears, concerns, and the stigma issues they may have about being referred for therapy in a respectful and culturally sensitive way before launching into a discussion about what they would like to address or accomplish in therapy.

Boris (the father), Maria, and Tasha were present at the first family interview. Beth also attended our family meeting. The session transcript begins with the tail end of my miracle inquiry with the family.

Boris: I don't believe she's going to change. Therapy has not worked. She doesn't care. All she wants to do is be with her friends going clubbing. So what if she doesn't go to the university.

Maria: Yeah, I don't believe the miracles are going to happen. We've tried and nothing has worked. We spent all of that money on that last psychologist. . . . What was her name, Tasha?

Tasha: Dr. Swenson. I don't know why you kept on paying her. I never went anyways!

Maria: Yes, this is the problem. She doesn't go to her appointments. She doesn't want help! I don't know what to do with her.

Tasha: Why don't you guys get off my back! You know I hate going for counseling. It's a waste of time!

Matthew: I hear all of you loud and clear—how frustrated all of you feel with your situation and how counseling hasn't worked. Tell me, what have all of you done to prevent your situation from getting much worse?

Boris: Well, I have offered to help Tasha with her math homework. I think this is one class she is failing. But she is never around so how can I help her?

Matthew: Is that different for you to make time to try and help her out with her schoolwork?

Boris: Yes, I suppose. I have felt like giving up on her.

Tasha: I have appreciated the times when you have helped me out. I've been trying to come home earlier lately.

Maria: This is true. Lately you have been coming home on time.

Matthew: Wow! Are you aware, Tasha, of how you have been able to pull that off?

Tasha: I'm tired of my parents yelling at me. I hate to see my mother cry.

Matthew: (*looking at the parents*) It seems like your daughter has a real sensitive and caring side. Who did she inherit those genes from?

Maria: (*Everyone smiles.*) Probably from me. I'm the crier in this family.

Matthew: Maria and Boris, can the two of you think of other things you are doing lately to help Tasha take more responsibility?

Boris: I think we are yelling less. In fact, just the other day I saw Tasha doing her schoolwork on her own. We didn't have to tell her to do it.

Matthew: Wow! You mean to say she is taking more responsibility with doing her homework lately?! How are you pulling that off, Tasha?

Tasha: This is the thing . . . if they don't yell at me and aren't pushing school on me so much, I'll do better.

By better cooperating with family members' pessimism through the use of coping questions (Berg & Gallagher, 1991; Berg & Miller, 1992; Selekman, 1993, 1997), I was successful in gaining more therapeutic leverage and eliciting some important client-generated pretreatment changes. There was a major shift in the parents' initial view of Tasha as being irresponsible and not wanting to change toward having more hope and observing her recent efforts to take more responsibility. Tasha also pointed out what the parents were doing differently to enable her to take more responsibility: not "yelling" at her all of the time and "pushing school on" her.

In my one-on-one time with Tasha, I discovered that she cut and burned herself and abused marijuana as a form of stress management. She felt that her parents "put a lot of pressure" on her to be "a good student" like her younger sister. Tasha felt that she could do better in school if her parents would "back off more with the pressure." I offered to work on changing the parents' behavior if she was willing to continue to take charge of her homework without reminders. We were able to set up a quid pro quo contract between her and her parents around the homework issue. I encouraged the parents to continue to avoid the temptation to yell at and remind Tasha to do her homework.

Pessimistic Questions

In clinical situations where family members cannot identify any useful coping or problem-solving strategies and are highly pessimistic, I use pessimistic questions (Berg & Gallagher, 1991; Berg & Miller, 1992; Selekman, 1993) in an attempt to cooperate better with them. Often these family members are demoralized by their oppressive problems and have experienced multiple treatment failures. They have very little hope that the current therapy experience is going to be any different. In the context of cooperating with the parents' pessimism, it can be worthwhile to find out what they have done in the past to resolve other difficulties with their adolescent. This blueprint for parenting success can be channeled into the presenting problem area and can serve as a way to instill hope with highly pessimistic parents. The following are examples of pessimistic questions:

- "What keeps you going? Some parents in your situation would have sent their kid off to boarding school a long time ago!"
- "You have been in counseling seven times before. Why haven't you thrown in the towel already?"
- "Why are you willing to give counseling another try?"
- "What would be the tiniest thing that your daughter could do over the next week that could give you an inkling of hope that things could get slightly better?"
- "When she pulls that off, how will that make a slight difference for you?"

Latisha, a 16-year-old African American, was referred to me by her school social worker for cutting, conflicts with her teachers, and poor grades. Latisha had an extensive treatment history, which included two psychiatric admissions for her suicidal behavior. Deborah, the school social worker, mentioned that she suspected that the hospitalizations were related to her cutting behavior and that she was not really suicidal. These admissions had occurred her freshman year in high school. Latisha lived with her mother and maternal grandmother. She had been born out of wedlock and had not seen her father since she was a toddler. One of the major stressors Latisha struggled with was being one of a handful of African Americans attending her school. She found it very difficult to make friends due to all of the tight-knit cliques, and she had voiced to Deborah that her peers had "racist attitudes." Latisha also felt "all alone at school."

Latisha had shared with Deborah that she cut herself "to not hurt other people." Apparently she had been suspended several times in past years for "fighting with peers." Deborah also reported to me that Latisha's mother, Sabrina, was "burned out" with all of her daughter's problems at school and was "not too thrilled" about being referred to counseling again.

Deborah, Sabrina, and Latisha were present in the first family inter-view. Neither Sabrina nor Latisha could envision any miracles happen-ing with their situation. The mother could not identify any useful coping or problem-solving strategies that worked either in the present or in the past with Latisha. Latisha could not identify any adaptive coping strate-gies she used to avoid cutting herself.

Matthew: You have seen six therapists before me, why are you willing to give counseling another try?

Sabrina: To be honest with you, I really don't think this is going to work. Nothing has in the past. I'm really here because Deborah thought it would be a good idea. I myself think this is a waste of time.

Matthew: Before we move on to hearing Deborah's story about what led to your referral here, I was wondering, in having seen all those other therapists before me, was there anything important that you think they missed or overlooked with your situation that I should know about?

Sabrina: Well, most of the counselors only saw Latisha. I was rarely included in the meetings. I didn't learn anything about how to deal with her behavior. Come to think of it, I don't think the counselors ever went up to the school and met with anyone when she was having trouble there.

Latisha: I didn't like any of them. Some of them asked me if I was being abused at home and stuff like that. They tried to tell me what to do. I hate going for counseling!

Matthew: I'm curious, Latisha, what did the counselors not hear that you were trying to tell them that would be helpful for me to know about your situation?

Latisha: How hard it is to go to an all-white school. There are times I feel like popping somebody, but I don't want to get suspended. A lot of the girls are rich and spoiled and think they are better than you. Sometimes I feel dissed [put down] by them.

Matthew: What do the girls say or do that makes you feel dissed by them?

Latisha: Sometimes they look at me funny, ignore me when I am trying to talk to them, or walk away from me.

Matthew: I imagine that it must be quite difficult being African American and going to a mostly white school. Do you have any African-American friends at school?

Latisha: Just one, Loretta.

Matthew: Does Loretta feel the same way as you?

Latisha: Yeah, we have talked about it before.

Sabrina: I know this is a problem. We had to move out here from the city. It is closer to my job. Latisha has to understand that we have to make it work out here.

Deborah: I just would like to share with you that I worked with some other African-American students who felt the same way as you do, Latisha. A lot of these suburban white kids can be very snotty and be part of closed cliques. Many have never lived in integrated communities.

Matthew: Latisha, how can Deborah and I be most helpful to you dealing with this difficult situation?

Latisha: I don't know. I mean, you guys can't give me friends. You guys can't teach these girls to be less racist.

Deborah: I would like you to let me know when you think students are treating you in a racist way. I will not tolerate that.

Sabrina: I deal with racist people all of the time. I don't like it either. But I don't go around threatening people or carving myself up.

Matthew: Sabrina, what kinds of things do you do to cope with or to combat racism?

Sabrina: I have in the past called white people on it. You know, pointed it out to them when it happens. It does no good to go after people or make threats.

Matthew: What has stopped you from taking it out on yourself?

Sabrina: My mama taught me "to be strong and be proud, not be weak." (*looking at Latisha*) I don't think I have ever shared that with you before.

Matthew: Those are some powerful words of wisdom! How do you like those words Latisha?

Latisha: (*smiling and looking intrigued*) I like them.

When we began our session, both Latisha and her mother had been uninterested in pursuing another counseling experience. Simply giving Latisha plenty of room to share her story about what was being overlooked with her past therapists opened the door for her to disclose how her former therapists were all so narrowly focused on the "causes of her behavior" that they did not hear her concerns about racism occurring at her school and how alienated she felt there. Apparently all of Latisha's former therapists were white. I explored with Latisha and her mother if they felt okay working with another white therapist again. Neither the mother nor Latisha voiced any concerns about this.

Another turning point in the session was my placing Sabrina in the expert role regarding how to cope with or manage racist people. Not only did she make some great suggestions, but she shared with Latisha for the first time some valuable words of wisdom that her own mother had given her to cope with racism. This was a sparkling moment in the session. I recommended to Latisha that she experiment with telling herself "be strong and be proud, not weak" every time she experienced racist comments or felt like cutting herself. Both Latisha and the mother thought this was a great idea. They both agreed that wanting to fight with someone or cut oneself would be "signs of weakness." Deborah and I also had shared with Latisha that we would serve as advocates for her in addressing the racism problem in the school.

Reversal Questions

In my clinical work with adolescents, I frequently use reversal questions (Selekman, 1997) to tap adolescents' wisdom about what their parents can do differently to gain their cooperation with following their rules, completing chores, and doing well in school, as well as what the parents could change about themselves to function better both individually and as a couple. Another advantage of using reversal questions is that they help to challenge the parents' unhelpful beliefs about their adolescents' skill deficiencies and lack of ability to take responsibility. Finally, placing the adolescent in the expert consultant role (Selekman, 1993) can help foster a cooperative relationship and strengthen the therapist's alliance with her. Some examples of reversal questions:

- "Do you have any advice for your parents about how they can get you to take more responsibility?"
- "What do you think your parents could do to argue less?"
- "Do you have any advice for your parents about how to be less stressed out?"

- "What is the first thing your parents could do differently that would help all of you to get along better?"
- "Is there one thing that your parents do that really ticks you off the most that you would like me to work on changing?"

Flora, a precocious 15-year-old Latina, was referred to me in crisis by Paula, her school social worker, after a teacher had observed deep cuts train-track style up and down both of Flora's arms. According to Paula, when Flora first was sent down to her office she was "crying a lot" but could not identify what was causing her tears. She called Flora's parents to pick her up immediately and take her to my office for an emergency evaluation. Although Flora had been running around with "a troubled group of kids," this was the first time Paula had ever seen her "butcher her arms" this way. In the past, Flora had visited Paula's office for "cutting herself in the girl's bathroom once," cutting classes, and truancy. Paula also suspected that Flora was experimenting with drugs.

Present in the initial family session were Flora, her father Juan, and Christina, her mother. Paula could not make our meeting. The atmosphere in my office was like that of a funeral. Everyone looked very worried and depressed.

Matthew: The heaviness in the room makes me feel like we are attending a funeral together. What's not being talked about that you think I should know about?

Flora: Well, last night my parents had a big argument and . . . (*looking at her father*) my dad was planning to move out today.

Matthew: Is that new for your father to want to move out?

Flora: Yeah. This was one of the worst fights they have ever had. My younger brother was real scared. I had to comfort him.

Juan: Flora, if I would have known that you were so worried about my moving out, I wouldn't do it.

Christina: Things are not good between your father and I. I asked him to leave. It's just not working out. I've told you that before.

Matthew: Flora, you did a great job of keeping your parents together. They are right here by your side. Do you have any advice for your parents about how they can argue less and try and make it work?

Flora: They always fight about money. Maybe they should go and see someone to help them better manage their money.

Juan: She's right, we do fight a lot about money. Christina likes to use our credit cards.

Matthew: Flora, do you have any other helpful advice for your parents?

Flora: They need to learn how to argue less. They once saw a counselor a few times but that didn't help. It's not good for us kids to hear you guys threaten divorce all of the time.

Christina: (*starting to cry*) You're right.

Flora: (*crying*) Dad, why don't you hug Mom and take care of her?

Matthew: Christina and Juan, would you be willing to meet with me alone?

Flora's cutting crisis at school was a desperate attempt to keep the family together. By placing her in the expert consultant role, she came up with some good advice for her parents on how they could improve their marital relationship. During most of my one-on-one time with Flora, she had shared with me that cutting comforted her when she was stressed by her parents' intense arguing and personal problems. She said that the warm blood running down her arms had a "calming effect" on her. Apparently her mother frequently went to her for support. Christina had very few friends and her family lived in Venezuela. Similarly, Juan had very few friends and his family lived in Bolivia. The parents' lack of a strong support system put a tremendous strain on their marital relationship. I was very pleased that the parents agreed to work with me to try and save their marriage. When we shared this news with Flora, she looked relieved. Flora also agreed to work with me on coming up with more adaptive ways of managing stressors in her life. Finally, to help address the parents' sense of isolation, I hooked them up with a Latino community association that provided social functions and support to adults, youth, and families.

Conversational Questions

Sometimes in the interviewing process family members display a strong need to share important elements of their problem stories. It is critical that therapists "stay close" to family members in the therapeutic conversation and give them plenty of room to share their concerns. This is why it is important to ask open-ended conversational questions (Andersen, 1991; Anderson & Goolishian, 1988; Selekman, 1993, 1997) to elicit the missing pieces of the family puzzle. By asking questions from a position of "not knowing" as opposed to "preknowing," we place ourselves in the position of learning and avoid being narrative editors (Anderson, 1993). Some examples of conversational questions that may grow out of the interviewing process are as follows:

- "On your way down here today, was there anything you told your-self that you wouldn't talk about with me in our meeting?
- "If that untold story were shared, who would be the most trou-bled by it?"
- "What have we not focused our attention on and might make a difference if it was included in our conversations?"
- "If there was one question you were hoping I would ask you while we are working together, what would that question be?"

Externalizing Questions

Members of families that have been oppressed by their problems for a long time may describe their problems as disempowering and demoraliz-ing to them and having a life of their own. One therapeutic option ther-apists can pursue with these types of family situations is *externalization of the problem* (White, 1995; White & Epston, 1990). The externalizion of the presenting problem must be based on family members' descriptions of the problem—that is, their language or their beliefs about why the problem exists. Once the therapist presents the new coconstructed and objectified description of the problem to the family, he or she needs to carefully listen for and observe verbal and nonverbal acknowledgement from family members that this alternative construction of their problem situation is acceptable or comes close to fitting their views.

After mapping out with the family the problem's influence (White, 1988; White & Epston, 1990) or the various ways the identified client, parents, siblings, peers, and significant others accept invitations from the problem to interact in unproductive ways with one another, the therapist can begin to explore with all members of the problem system what they have done in the past and do in the present to stand up to the problem. The useful self-talk and problem-solving strategies they employ during these times are called *unique outcomes* (White, 1988). A type of external-izing question, the unique-outcome question can elicit from family mem-bers their storylines of competency, which can help to thicken the new, preferred problem-free story they wish to author about themselves. For example, Diane, a former client of mine, decided one day to take a positive risk with her mother: Instead of rushing up to her bedroom after school and taking a razor to her arms, she talked with her mother about how depressed she felt after being rejected by a group of popular peers at school. This client-generated unique outcome is what White (1995) would call a "sparkling moment" for the client. In the past, not only would Diane typically go up to her bedroom and carve up her arms when overwhelmed by her emotions, but her mother also would not make herself available to her daughter to listen to her concerns. Diane would often share this complaint about her mother in both our individual and family sessions. However, with this unique outcome, Diane reported in our family session that the mother was "very loving and supportive" and appeared to "really listen" to her. The mother indicated in our family session that she was quite pleased that she could be a "big help to Diane" and how together they had successfully thwarted "cutting's" efforts to push the two of them around in this "sparkling moment" (White, 1995) situation. I responded to the family's great accomplishment with cheerleading and amplified and consolidated their gains.

Some examples of unique-outcome questions (White, 1995, 1988; White & Epston, 1990) are:

- "What words does cutting whisper into your ears that makes you cave into harming yourself?"
- "Have there been any times lately when cutting was lurking about and your parents did something that worked to prevent you from becoming vulnerable prey to it?"
- "What did they do to keep it from getting the best of you?"
- "What do you tell yourself to stand up to cutting and not allow it to push you around?"
- "As you continue to frustrate cutting and not cave into its clever ways, how are you viewing yourself differently as opposed to how you used to view yourself when you were a victim to it?"

Jill, a Caucasian 17-year-old high school senior, was referred to me by her school social worker, Bob. Bob and Jill had been working together since Jill's sophmore year. According to Bob, Jill had "lost total control" of her "self-mutilating behavior" and again was occasionally bingeing and purging, a problem that Bob, along with a psychologist in private practice and a psychiatrist Jill was seeing for medication management, had helped to stabilize during Jill's junior year. Although Jill was no longer on Paxil or seeing the psychiatrist and psychologist, Bob had been seeing her once or twice weekly since the beginning of the school year. He was quite concerned that Jill might end up "killing herself accidentally" while cutting on her wrists and forearms. Apparently, Jill was an honor's student who was "very hard on herself" when she achieved anything less than an A. Bob pointed out to me on the telephone how "perfectionistic" her parents had become during his past interactions with them. Jill's father was a highly successful businessman. Her mother was a freelance writer. Bob suspected that Jill's self-mutilating behavior was related to "all of the pressure" the parents put on their daughter to be a straight-A student.

Jill, her father, Gerald, her mother, Cassie, her 12-year-old sister, Marjorie, and Bob attended the initial family meeting. Marjorie was an A student as well. After taking the time to connect with each family member, I began the interview by inviting Bob to share his story of involvement with Jill and to clarify the specific trigger that led to his referring her to me for family therapy. While Bob shared his concerns about Jill's "brutalizing her body with razors" and his fear that she would eventually kill herself, the parents reacted with different levels of concern. The father showed absolutely no emotional reaction and seemed more troubled by his having to miss an important meeting with a new business client. Cassie, on the other hand, was quite troubled by Bob's report and hearing Jill chime in that she had "no control" of her self-harming behavior. Jill described her cutting behavior as if it were a monster haunting her and wreaking havoc in her life. Rather than shifting gears and asking the miracle question (de Shazer, 1988) in an attempt to establish goals with the family, I decided to avoid being a narrative editor and give Jill and her mother plenty of room to dialogue about the seriousness of the cutting and elicit their emotionality about taking a stand against it together. The family appeared ripe for trying to externalize (White & Epston, 1990) the cutting problem. Knowing that Gerald was a former star linebacker on his college football team, I decided to use football metaphors and language as a way to engage him and enlist his services in supporting his daughter's efforts to free herself from the clutches of cutting.

Matthew: It sounds like cutting is like a puppeteer and you are the marionette puppet, Jill.

Jill: That's how I feel sometimes. When I'm really stressed out there is something that takes me over—I go up to my room, pull out the razor and start to cut. I have no control at that point. I can cut for an hour or longer. I'm like in another world. . . . I feel numb.

Matthew: This might sound off the wall to all of you, but problems like cutting are like hypnotists: They put you in a trance and have you do things that you are not aware you are doing to try and solve a problem. How would you like to work with your family, Bob, and me in coming up with a plan to counter cutting's powerful trance inductions so that you are in charge of it versus it being in charge of your mind?

Jill: Yeah, whatever you guys can do to help I would appreciate it.

Cassie: Honey, why are you carving yourself up?

Jill: I think it is all of the pressure. I am always thinking that I am not doing good enough in school for you guys. I mean I always hear from Dad that I have to bring in those As.

Gerald: Your A grades will get you into Harvard and Stanford.

Jill: See what I mean? All you care about is my academic achievement, you couldn't care less that I am so stressed that I am cutting myself daily!

Cassie: Of course your dad cares about your well-being, dear.

Matthew: Here is a great example of how cutting is wreaking havoc in this family. Other families I have worked with where cutting was getting the best of them also fell into the traps of blaming each other, taking sides, and perfectionism, which this particular type of problem thrives on.

Cassie: What can we do to help Jill now?

Matthew: Jill, what can your parents do differently to help you to stand up to cutting and not allow it to push you around?

Jill: Well, I think if we could talk about things other than just school grades, I would not be as stressed out.

Matthew: Bingo! I think you hit it right on the head. I can't tell you how many young women and their families I have worked with that were being victimized by cutting, bulimia, and drugs where this was an issue. As I mentioned to you before, cutting and its other close cousins love to prey on stressed-out family members.

Cassie: Jill, can you think of other things Daddy and I could do so you are less stressed out?

Jill: I don't know . . . um . . . can we also give the college choice discussion a little rest, too?

Gerald: I hear that you are stressed out and I want to help you with the cutting thing, but you will have to get your acceptance letter back to the college you select very soon.

Matthew: This is a beautiful example, Gerald, of how you accepted an invitation from cutting to bring up something school-related, which in turn will lead to Jill's getting stressed out or having a negative interaction with you. There is no question that in order for us to be successful at defeating cutting, it will have to be a team effort. Gerald, you mentioned earlier that you used to be a star linebacker on your college team. As a linebacker, what techniques did you use in games that helped you make a lot of tackles?

Gerald: Well, I used a lot of forearm shivers, sometimes I would spin off of blockers, and I would keep my feet moving toward the ball carrier and drive my body right through him.

Matthew: Good thing I never had to face you when I played high school ball! I liked playing split end so I could be as far away from guys like you as possible! Gerald, are you willing to suit up again to help Jill to flatten out cutting in the game so it will be out for the season?

Gerald: Absolutely! What do you want me to do?

Matthew: When cutting is lurking about and trying to roadblock you off your feet by inviting you to bring up school-related conversation with Jill, I want you to give it a forearm shiver and change the topic. Think of Jill as your cornerback and teammate. It is cutting that we must tackle so hard that it is injured and sidelined and fearful of returning back to the game against your family.

What proved to be most effective in helping engage Gerald in the change effort was the use of football language and metaphors. By utilizing his expertise as a former star linebacker, his key football language, and his love for the game, I was able to get Gerald fired up to lead his family to the eventual defeat of Jill's cutting problem. Once the family interactions improved and Jill stopped cutting, the bulimia problem stabilized as well.

As the various case examples in this chapter illustrate, improvisational systemic interviewing helps to loosen fixed family beliefs, disrupts unproductive family interactions, and can effectively elicit family members' expertise and accentuate their self-healing capacities. Well-timed questions can also generate new meanings and help treatment systems in impasse situations to get unstuck. Finally, when interviewing families in this manner, therapists are free to transcend any particular therapy model's rules, go with their gut instincts on question category selection, and tap their own creativity to craft unique and meaningful questions that are sparked in the therapeutic process.

CHAPTER 3

Cognitive-Skills and Mood-Management Training: Changing Self-Defeating Thoughts and Promoting Self-Soothing

While we may not be able to control all that happens to us, we can control what happens inside us.

—Ben Franklin

SELF-HARMING ADOLESCENTS OFTEN REPORT grave difficulty in managing their oppressive self-defeating thoughts and painful angry and depressed feelings. It has been my clinical experience that simply altering the self-harming adolescent's unproductive and negative interactions with family members, peers, and involved helping professionals may have very little impact on improving her cognitive skills and self-soothing capacities. Therefore, it is critical that therapists devote some of the family treatment session time to meeting one-on-one with the adolescent. During this time the therapist can not only teach the adolescent about how her self-defeating thoughts, beliefs, and attitudes control her emotions and behavior, but also offer her a wide range of techniques for challenging these self-defeating thoughts and for soothing herself when experiencing emotional distress.

COGNITIVE-SKILLS TRAINING

When doing cognitive-skills training with self-harming adolescents, therapists first must teach them the A-B-C formula of cognitive therapy (Ellis, 1974, 1996). The letters represent the following:

A = activating event
B = cognitions, beliefs, and attitudes
C = emotional or behavioral response

It is helpful to provide the adolescent with some disguised case illustrations of how the A-B-C formula looks in action with real-life teenage situations. These examples help to normalize the client's experiences and demonstrate how to apply the formula to her own situation. As a therapeutic experiment, I have the self-harming adolescent take a week to come up with three examples in her life where her thoughts (B) caused her painful emotional distress (C). I then have her practice applying the A-B-C formula to each of the examples.

Linda, a Ukrainian 15-year-old high school junior, was referred to me by her school social worker for self-mutilating, getting poor grades, and family problems. Linda had confided in the school social worker that her mother had a drinking problem. Her parents had divorced 3 years ago. According to the school social worker, Linda's father was constantly pressuring her to get As in school. Another major stressor Linda was grappling with was her "rocky" relationship with her boyfriend Seth.

In my first family therapy session with Linda and her mother, I learned about the client's rocky relationship with Seth during our one-on-one time. I used some of this time to teach Linda the A-B-C formula and gave her the experiment of picking 3 recent examples in her life where her thoughts caused her emotional distress. These were the examples she gave:

Example 1
A = Linda's father told her she was a "loser" after she received a C on a math test. (This was an improvement for her.)
B = Linda told herself that she would "never be good enough" for her father.
C = Linda felt depressed and this led to cutting.

Example 2
A = Linda's alcohol-intoxicated mother started yelling at her after school for not cleaning her bedroom and not studying enough.
B = Linda told herself that her poor school performance was making her mother's drinking problem worse.
C = She felt depressed and this led to cutting.

Example 3
A = Seth told Linda at school one day that she was "getting fat."
B = Linda told herself that she was "not pretty enough."
C = Linda felt very depressed and this led to cutting.

With the help of the A-B-C model, Linda could clearly see how her irrational self-defeating thoughts drove her to feeling depressed and subsequently cutting herself as a form of self-punishment. Linda found that the cutting served a dual purpose for her: First, it was a form of self-punishment for "not being good enough" for others. Second, it gave her temporary relief from "feeling down."

Disputation Skills

Once the self-harming adolescent has developed more self-confidence and skill in using the A-B-C formula on a daily basis, the next step is to teach her a variety of ways to dispute or challenge her irrational self-defeating thoughts and beliefs. I like to teach adolescents how to use *self-talk* (Ellis, 1974), to *decatastrophize* (Seligman, 1995), and to *externalize the oppressive self-defeating thought* (White, 1995). As one way of practicing the use of self-talk (McMullin, 2000), I have the adolescent ask herself the following questions when an activating event triggers irrational beliefs or self-defeating thoughts:

- What belief or thought is pushing me around in this situation?
- What evidence exists to support this belief or thought?
- Does any evidence exist that challenges this belief or way of thinking?
- What is likely to happen if I think this way?
- What will I do differently when I stop thinking this way?

It is also advantageous to explore whether she has created her own self-talk that helps her to disrupt negative thought processes. If her own unique self-talk strategies have been successful, I will explore with her how she can utilize them more regularly. With adolescents who have not come up with their own self-talk, I tap their creative powers to come up with one or two self-talk "tapes" they can play whenever they are pushed around by frustrating or stressful events. These tapes may feature the adolescent's favorite tunes, lines she frequently uses with peers that bring about good cheer or laughs, or meaningful quotes from a musician, popular media celebrity, or book character.

When self-harming adolescents are highly stressed by an activating event, they often have a tendency to catastrophize (Seligman, 1995). One highly effective way to help adolescents to learn how to decatastrophize (Seligman, 1995) and challenge their irrational beliefs or self-defeating thoughts is to play "detective" and search for evidence to support their unhelpful beliefs or thoughts. I ask the adolescent to pretend to be a super sleuth, to pull out her imaginary magnifying glass and, in a week's time, try to find important clues or hard facts to support her irrational beliefs and self-defeating thoughts. Typically the adolescent will return to our next session without important clues and hard facts to support her unproductive ways of viewing and thinking about stressful situations.

THE CHILLING OUT ROOM

Another highly effective way to empower self-harming adolescents to disrupt their self-defeating thoughts and painful emotional patterns is the use of the *chilling out room*. The adolescent is to pick out a quiet room in her home that will serve as the designated chilling out room that she can immediately go to when experiencing emotional distress and the impulse to self-harm. In addition, to having a comfortable chair or couch to sit on, the room should contain a book shelf with a variety of colorful and interesting art and photography books (can be taken out from the library if does not own these types of books), regularly stocked with fragrant and colorful flowers, a CD player to play soothing classical, New Age, or Native American music, such as the music of Carlos Nakai (the adolescent also can use some soothing music that she finds relaxes her), and fresh clay. Most adolescents enjoy the sensation of running their fingers through fresh clay and making objects or sculptures with it. Some adolescents discover that they are talented sculptors and this becomes a new hobby for them.

The chilling out room strategy experientially teaches adolescents that they can rapidly get relief from emotional distress and experience pleasure through a variety of sensory means without having to self-harm. In fact, many self-harming adolescents discover that they gain a much a stronger dosage of pleasure from using the chilling out room then from the time-limited endorphin effect they got from self-injuring. Linehan (1993) has demonstrated in her research that the use of similar multi-sensory interventions can be quite effective with clients at risk for self-harming. Some of the adolescents in my research project found that the chilling out room strategy greatly contributed to their successfully conquering their self-harming difficulties (Selekman, 2005). Finally, I have found that the chilling out room strategy can be effective with other adolescent problem situations, particularly with youth that have difficulties with impulse control.

CHANGING FEELINGS

Self-harming adolescents often report that their typical emotional responses to stressful activating events have become rigid and have created additional problems for them. One way to help the adolescent build in more flexibility with experiencing a wide range of emotional states is to have her practice accessing each of her emotions and rapidly shifting from one to the next. The therapist can ask her to devote 10–15 minutes per day to practicing changing her thoughts to make herself feel happy, slightly sad, amused, proud, self-confident, safe, content, and so forth (McMullin, 2000).

CHANGING SENSATIONS

One reason why adolescents find self-harming behavior such an effective coping strategy for managing emotional distress is that they have gotten hooked on the endorphins released when they self-injure. Consequently, I ask clients who are being pushed around by self-defeating thoughts and intense emotional distress to do the following to counter the pleasurable endorphin effects: squeeze an ice cube or a popsicle, take a cold shower, bite into something with a strong flavor (a lemon, lime, grapefruit, a hot pepper, or gingerroot), rub Ben-Gay or Vick's Vapor Rub under her nose, or take a red lipstick with pressure and draw lines where she typically inflicts wounds on her body (Alderman, 1997). Most of these sensory-change strategies are adverse enough by themselves to disrupt the A-B-C chain and stop self-harming behavior.

CHANGING BEHAVIORS

Another way to break the A-B-C chain is to change the adolescent's behavioral response to her irrational self-defeating thoughts and intense emotional distress. I have had self-harming adolescents experiment with the following substitute behaviors: slash paint onto a canvas on an easel, hit a punching bag, punch a pillow or slam it against a wall, stomp on soda cans, slap a tabletop, and slash plastic bottles or containers and heavy cardboard. Alderman (1997) recommends that therapists have their clients experiment with pattern-intervention strategies such as:

changing what they typically do before they self-injure, varying the instruments used, changing the context of where the self-harming behavior occurs, varying the times and duration, adding some new element to the self-harming behavioral pattern, and changing the ways they typically nurture their wounds.

MOOD-MANAGEMENT TRAINING

In addition to teaching effective tools for challenging irrational beliefs and self-defeating thoughts, therapists also need to provide their clients with an arsenal of techniques and strategies for successfully managing any painful or debilitating emotional distress they may be experiencing. The more self-soothing techniques and strategies we can equip the self-harming adolescent with, the more able she will be to comfort herself confidently and effectively and not self-injure. Four highly effective mood-management tools and strategies are: *relaxation training, visualization, meditation,* and *aerobic exercise.*

Relaxation Training

A variety of relaxation strategies can be taught to the self-harming adolescent to help her soothe herself when she is faced with stressful events (Alderman, 1997; Davis, Eshelman, & McKay, 1994). I have found that *deep-breathing relaxation training* works particularly well for adolescents. This involves teaching the adolescent an alternative form of breathing. In preparing the adolescent for the relaxation training process, I ask her to identify the most recent stressful life event she experienced and reflect on her physiological response to it, particularly if she noticed that her breathing pattern became more rapid. Thinking of such an experience offers her the opportunity to see the connections between self-defeating thoughts triggered by an activating event, her emotional response of feeling anxious, depressed, or frustrated, and breathing patterns.

The first step with any form of relaxation training is to have the client place herself in a comfortable physical position. If the client decides to sit in a chair, she must sit in an erect position with an open chest. Sitting hunched over with shoulders and arms tilted inward will constrict the breathing process and defeat the purpose of this self-soothing strategy. Once the adolescent has assumed her most comfortable position, the therapist should have her place her hand on her abdomen, close her eyes, and take slow, deep breaths through her nose for about 5 minutes. I instruct her to notice carefully how her hand moves up and down. After clients have practiced deep breathing 15–20 minutes twice a day for a week, they usually become better skilled at learning how to control their breathing even in the face of stressful life events. They discover that by taking slow, deep breaths, they can rapidly decrease tension in their bodies and the initial emotional distress they may experience in response to stressful activating events.

Visualization

Most adolescents enjoy using visualization experiments to help combat irrational self-defeating thoughts and to soothe themselves when they grapple with emotional distress. To prepare her for the creative visualization experiment, the adolescent must identify a quiet place in her home to practice and select a comfortable sitting position on a chair or a large floor pillow. I like to recommend to the adolescent that she practice visualizing 2–3 times per day, with at least one practice session first thing in the morning when she wakes up. Finally, with any creative visualization experiment it is critical that the adolescent apply all of her senses to the experience and concentrate on color and motion, which will bring her visualization more to life (Alderman, 1997; Davis et al., 1994; Parnes, 1992). There are three types of creative visualization experiments I frequently employ with self-harming adolescents: *visiting your special place, creating your own guardian angel,* and *visualizing movies of success* (Selekman, 1997).

VISITING YOUR SPECIAL PLACE

With this creative visualization experiment, I have the adolescent try to access in her mind vivid images from a memorable past family vacation or a special trip with friends and then describe them using of all of her senses. Ideally, the visualization will be so detailed and crystal clear that the therapist can picture the described scene.

Monica, one of my Caucasian 16-year-old clients, cut her arms daily with a razor blade when she experienced emotional distress. When I suggested the visualization experiment, she decided to take a trip back to a family vacation on the Caribbean island of St. Lucia. The St. Lucia trip had occurred when she was 14 years old. At that time, Monica and her mother were much closer; they spent a lot of time together and they could talk about anything. A year later, the mother's highly successful clothing boutique opened additional locations in other cities, which required her to travel extensively. In Monica's eyes, her mother was putting her business before their relationship. When her mother was at home, she was either on the telephone doing business or always on the go. Monica had the self-defeating thought "She does not care about me" whenever her mother didn't listen to her. Feeling rebuffed, Monica would become depressed and turn toward self-harming behavior.

Regina, Monica's 8-year-old sister, her father, and the school social worker who had referred Monica to me were present at the first family interview. The parents had been divorced for 5 years. Evelyn, the mother, could not make the appointment because of an out-of-town business meeting. Earlier in the session, I had discovered that one of Monica's key intelligence areas was visual-spatial intelligence (Gardner, 1993). Not only did Monica paint and draw landscapes as a hobby but she also used such key words as "see" and "view" throughout the interview. Based on this information, I thought she would make an excellent candidate for creative visualization. While meeting alone with Monica, I had decided to propose the *visiting your special place* visualization experiment. Monica closed her eyes and began to describe in great detail a special beach area where she and her family had vacationed on the island of St. Lucia. Her description was so detailed that I could picture the white sand beach, the beautiful blue ocean, the tropical trees and flowers, the blue sky, and the birds flying overhead. Monica described the colors of each family member's bathing suit and how she and her mother tried to "dunk each other" in the ocean. While describing this special scene, Monica could feel the heat from the sun and an occasional tropical breeze on her skin. She also began to taste the salty water that she got in her mouth while splashing around and playing with her mother and sister in the water. Finally, she described for me how she could smell a combination of the ocean and the tropical flower scents in the air. It was clear that this family vacation was one of Monica's most special family vacation trips: She became quite elated and smiled while describing all of the images and sensory experiences of this magical place. We agreed that she would practice accessing this visualization 2–3 times per day for a week.

During her practice week, Monica found it quite easy to turn this visualization on and off. In fact, she met with success four times using this visualization to soothe herself after four negative encounters with her mother. Monica's mother was present at the second session and we spent some time identifying what was working in their relationship and specific areas needing intervention. For Monica, spending time together was highest on the list. Monica was quite courageous and took a risk with her mother by explaining how she felt that she "did not care about" her.

Evelyn appeared quite shocked and surprised to hear that Monica felt this way. She also shared with Monica for the first time her concerns about her cutting behavior. Regina had witnessed Monica cutting herself with a razor blade in the bathroom and told Evelyn about it. We were able to negotiate some designated times that would be considered "holy times" for them to spend together. Monica was put in charge of selecting how and where this time with her mother would be spent. She also shared with her mother her visualization of their past St. Lucia trip. This brought about a big smile and laughter, and Evelyn began to reminisce about this great trip.

During my one-on-one time in the session, Monica complained about still having the impulse to cut herself. She was worried that her mother would not follow through with her promise to spend time with her, and she wanted to learn some other helpful tools for comforting herself and avoiding the temptation to self-injure. I taught her how to use deep breathing to calm herself. Additionally, I decided to capitalize on her artistic abilities and instructed her to go into her basement studio when she was tempted to cut herself, put a canvas on her easel, and slash paint onto it. Monica thought this was a "cool" idea. I suggested that maybe the time was right for her to branch out from landscapes and try abstract expressionism. Before concluding our family session, I complimented the family and predicted that the "holy times" experiment would be a tough challenge for them due to their habit of relating like "ships passing in the night." We also reviewed the other new experiments that Monica would be implementing at home.

After five sessions with Monica and her family, she had totally stopped cutting and was no longer depressed. Evelyn had committed to the designated "holy times" that Monica had scheduled. Monica also brought in some examples of her slash art. I shared with Monica and her mother that she had made her mark in art history inventing her own unique style — slash art! They both laughed.

CREATING YOUR OWN GUARDIAN ANGEL

Another highly effective visualization experiment to employ with self-harming adolescents is to have them create their own inner guardian angels that can be accessed for self-protection when needed. The first step is to have the adolescent create in her mind an image of a door opening up to reveal her special guardian angel. It is critical that the therapist have the adolescent describe how the angel looks physically, how it moves, the color and appearance of its clothes, its facial expressions, and its tone of voice. I also ask the adolescent to come up with a name for her guardian angel. The next step is to have the adolescent imagine the various ways the guardian angel will protect her. I ask the adolescent the following questions to elicit this important information: "When you are seeking the guardian angel's help, what will she say to you to help comfort you?" "What specifically will she suggest you do to protect yourself?" Once the adolescent has been able to identify clearly what the guardian angel will say to her for support and recommend as helpful courses of action to pursue, the final step is to have her practice accessing her guardian angel 15–20 minutes 2–3 times a day.

VISUALIZING MOVIES OF SUCCESS

Most adolescents have experienced memorable sparkling moments in their lives. The sparkling moment may have occurred during a school play or band concert or during a school or community sports event. It may have been the time she received an A on a difficult class assignment or exam or when she prevailed over adversity during a stressful or traumatic life event. I begin this visualization experiment by having the adolescent close her eyes and picture a movie of a sparkling moment in her life. I have her apply all of her senses to the experience and detail the colors she sees and the movements of all of the participants. After she has accessed her movie of success, I like to ask about the various thoughts and feelings that came up for her while she relived this magical experience. Often adolescents derive a great deal of pleasure from visualizing their movies of success (Selekman, 1997).

Cindy, a Caucasian 16-year-old bulimic who was burning and cutting herself, had grave difficulty coping with family stressors and pressures at school. Her parents had a highly conflictual relationship and had threatened to divorce numerous times in the past in front of her. On many occasions, Cindy found herself comforting her mother after heated arguments with her father. Her father's beliefs were very traditional and he often used angry, out-of-control behavior such as yelling and slamming doors to silence family members. However, there were no reports by Cindy or other family members that the father had ever been physically abusive toward them.

In many ways, Cindy's behaviors were a metaphor for the family dynamics. There was a lot she "could not stomach." Frequently, she felt "burned" and let down by her father, who would promise her privileges and more freedom for good grades but often would not follow through on his promises. Cindy also felt "cut" up into pieces. There was the "academic wizard" Cindy, the "accomplished cellist" Cindy, the "mother's confidant" Cindy, and the "popular with the peers" Cindy. It appeared that the only way she could gain her father's approval was when she performed with excellence in those areas. The bingeing and purging typically occurred after her parents and her younger brother went to bed. She usually would burn and cut herself in her bedroom when her parents argued or when she was "let down" by her father.

During my one-on-one time with Cindy, I was able to teach her some thought-stopping techniques and pattern-intervention strategies to help her to stop bingeing and purging (Beck, et al., 1979; Ellis, 1974; O'Hanlon, 1987). To address the self-harming behaviors, I provided empathy and validation and reflected my ideas about the metaphorical nature of the behaviors. This did produce a shift in her thinking about her situation, which in turn decreased the frequency of her burning and cutting behaviors. However, the visualizing movies of success experiment had the biggest impact. The sparkling moment that Cindy selected was her 1999 performance of Bach's *Unaccompanied Cello Suite No. 4 in E-flat Major,* which she had played as part of a Christmas holiday program at her church. This was her all-time best performance in concert. I asked Cindy to access all of her senses and describe aloud this sparkling moment. Cindy's description was so detailed and crystal clear that I felt like I was sitting in the audience listening to her performance. She could hear the music playing in her ears while she visualized it. Because Cindy had found this experiment so enjoyable, we decided that whenever she was tempted to burn or cut herself, she was to go into her bedroom and access her special movie of success.

Three sessions later, Cindy not only had stopped burning and cutting herself completely, but also had begun building more fun time into her daily regime. As Cindy became increasingly more self-confident and better able to assert herself with her parents, she became less emotionally reactive to her parents' difficulties and stepped out of the confidant role. The parents were very pleased with all of Cindy's changes and agreed to work more directly with me on their longstanding marital difficulties.

Meditation

Many of my adolescent clients have found meditation exercises to be "cool" self-soothing strategies. The biggest challenge for the adolescent is to master the ability to focus all of her attention on one object without allowing other thoughts to interfere. The easiest way to enter a meditative state is to have the adolescent place her hand on her abdomen and focus on its rising and falling with every deep breath. This is called *grounding* (Davis et al., 1994).

THE SOUND MEDITATION

After the adolescent finds a quiet room and a comfortable chair to sit in, I have her close her eyes and focus all of her attention on different sounds she hears around her. The adolescent is to simply label silently to herself each sound she hears, and not get too attached to any one sound. She is not to ask herself questions about why she is hearing a particular sound or try and understand the meaning of it. Out of all of the different types of meditations I have used with adolescents, most of my clients have found this to be the most enjoyable and relaxing one to use. Some of my adolescent clients have entered such a relaxed state while doing this meditation that they have fallen asleep while practicing in my office and at home. The adolescent should do the meditation for 10-12 minutes

PRACTICING MINDFULNESS

Practicing mindfulness is a form of meditation that offers both deep relaxation and insight (Bennett-Goleman, 2001; Chodron, 1994, 2001; Davis et al., 1994; Goldstein & Kornfield, 1987; Kabat-Zinn, 1995). It cultivates a way of being in a harmonious relationship with "what is," whether that is parental yelling or nagging, unpleasant thoughts and feelings, school or peer stressors, or somatic discomfort. Through fully opening up one's mind to what is present and not fighting it or trying to push it away, one can cultivate a deep acceptance and ability to relax more fully in the present moment. Neurological and other medical research has indicated that daily meditation can decrease sympathetic activity in the autonomic nervous system, enhance right brain hemispheric functioning, help calm the amygdala (our mood centers), improve muscle relaxation, and reduce oxygen consumption (Bennett-Goleman, 2001; Bennett-Goleman & Goleman, 2001; Kabat-Zinn, 1990; Wallace, Benson, & Wilson, 1984). When having adolescents practice mindfulness, I have them focus on the rise and fall of their breath, certain sounds, or body sensations.

One simple mindfulness meditation I teach adolescents is a food meditation. I have the adolescent first assume a comfortable position in a chair or in a large floor pillow. I place a single raisin in her cupped hand. She is to spend a few minutes carefully studying the raisin's shape and texture and the shadowing around it. Next I have her slowly pick it up and feel its texture in her other hand. After a few minutes, I have her put the raisin in her mouth and pay attention to her salivating and her tongue and teeth touching the raisin. She is instructed to slowly bite into and chew the raisin, noticing its juices injecting into her mouth. Finally, she is to follow the chewed-up raisin mentally as it slides down her throat into her stomach (Bennett-Goleman & Goleman, 2001). Mindfulness meditations like these can help adolescents defuse their turbulent emotions and enhance their self-soothing capacities.

Aerobic Exercise

Another effective way self-harming adolescents can comfort themselves when experiencing emotional distress is to engage in some form of daily aerobic exercise. Any form of aerobic exercise will trigger the brain to secrete endorphins, help to reduce stress, build self-confidence, and improve one's general sense of well-being. I recommend that adolescents walk, run, swim, bike, and dance. Some self-harming adolescents I have worked with found yoga and martial arts the most beneficial. Both of these activities also involve special breathing techniques and greatly enhance concentration abilities.

Native American Shamanic Healing Methods and Teaching Tales

The healing methods and stories of Native American shaman and elders offer therapists and clients alike some valuable wisdom about how to manage life's challenges and stressors (Bear Heart, 1996; Hammerschlag, 1988; Kammen & Gold, 1998; Lee, 1998; Wall & Arden, 1990). These methods and stories can help some clients oppressed by repetitive self-defeating thoughts and difficulty managing their moods to challenge their irrational thought patterns and can provide them with valuable insight about their difficulties, strengthen their coping and self-soothing abilities, and alter their unproductive behavior patterns.

In his inspiring and fascinating 1996 book *The Wind Is My Mother: The Life and Teachings of a Native American Shaman*, Bear Heart, a Native American medicine man and elder, presents numerous principles and teaching tales he learned in his training to become a shaman and from the wise elders he encountered throughout his life. These principles and teaching tales have been quite effective with my clients in changing their unhelpful ways of viewing and trying to manage their problem situations:

- *"Coping with suffering gives meaning to life—it is what gives us our strength."* This important principle is derived from the Buddhist teaching that "life is suffering" (Chodron, 1994; Rinpoche, 1993). When we are faced with difficult situations or struggling to cope with a stressor, we need to look inward at our vast reservoir of strengths and resources, for "therein lies our peace" (Bear Heart, 1996, p. 138).

- *"In our struggles we may think we can't go any further, not realizing that it is merely a turning point."* Some of the difficulties we grapple with in life may feel so overwhelming that we have little faith that they can be resolved. Bear Heart recommends the following: "At times like that, go to the ocean and watch the waves come in. The tide has a steady rhythm, a tempo that is never affected by the storms at sea. When the tide hits the shore it goes as far inland as it can, and when it reaches its zenith it is not the end, it's merely a *turning point*. It then flows back out to sea, to where there is great power and strength" (p. 159). I have had some of my clients experiment with this task and they found it to be liberating and a source of strength.

- *"Be grateful for all of the difficult situations in life because you can learn something from each one."* Many of our hurts and struggles come from our irrational thoughts and attitudes. Bear Heart contends that we should "honor" the difficulties we experience and should say thank you to each one. Each difficulty we face in life is a teaching lesson and a source of wisdom. Therefore we have to move beyond our past hurts and present difficulties and pursue new "vistas and opportunities" (p. 114).

- *"Replace negatives with positives."* Bear Heart's tribe used to have a traditional ceremony for warriors returning from battle that helped to cleanse their minds of all of the death and bloodshed they had experienced in combat. This bathing ceremony washed away their negative feelings and sense of loss. The ritual is in line with the laws of physics that say no two things can occupy the same space at the same time: The negatives are replaced with more positive thoughts (Bear Heart, 1996).

- *"The best advice I can give to anyone at any time is: Never complete a negative statement."* Internal problems cannot be handled by external means. Bear Heart cautions us by saying, "You might start out thinking in a negative way but don't complete it because you're about to enter it into the computer up in your head and it could come true" (p. 118). In other words, what you expect is what you will get.

Bear Heart's healing principles and methods can be used with self-harming adolescents during one-on-one session time as part of the cognitive-skills and mood-management training process.

Native American Storytelling

In the Native American culture, parents and elders tell stories as an effective way to teach younger generations valuable life lessons about caring for and respecting others, nature, and the Creator, as well as about gaining the courage and self-confidence to resolve life's challenges. In fact, rather than being yelled at, grounded, or receiving some form of physical discipline when they misbehave, young people are "disciplined" by being told stories that help them to learn from their actions.

The following case example illustrates the effectiveness of Native American stories and healing methods. Courtney, a depressed Caucasian 14-year-old, was an eighth grader who turned to cutting as a form of self-punishment. Courtney's father recently had gotten a job transfer, and the family had moved into a new school district. The family move was traumatic for Courtney: She had been quite popular at her former school and was forced to say good-bye to two of her closest friends there. One of the biggest challenges Courtney experienced at her new school was cracking into already well-established peer cliques. Although peers showed some interest in wanting to socialize with her in and outside of school, they would not follow through on finalizing any formal plans with her. Combined with the loss of her two close friendships, this rejection propelled her into a state of depression. Courtney blamed herself for being rejected, believing that she wasn't "cool enough" or as dynamic as some of the popular peers she wanted to be friendly with were. As she became increasingly more depressed, Courtney started going to her bedroom to cut herself on her arms and legs with a razor "as a way to hurt [herself]" for "not being good enough." When Courtney had been pushed around by this self-defeating thought in the past, she would, at times, greatly reduce her food intake as a form of self-punishment. However, she found that the use of a razor on herself was much more effective.

Courtney had been referred to the school social worker by one of her teachers, who had noticed a series of deep cuts on one of her arms. Courtney opened up to the school social worker about "feeling depressed" and about her cutting behavior, which led to her referral to me for family therapy. In my first meeting with Courtney and her family, I gave her plenty of room to share her story about the loss of her friends and her grave difficulty with "making new friends," which she blamed herself for. When asked about her past successful strategies for making and sustaining friendships, Courtney could not remember any specific details about what had worked for her. However, one of her best coping strategies for dealing with peer disappointments was the use of a feelings journal. After hearing this, I made a mental note that two of Courtney's strong intelligence areas were written language and intrapersonal expression (Gardner, 1993), which could be utilized later with therapeutic experiment construction or selection. The parents were very supportive but didn't know how to help Courtney build new friendships.

When I met with Courtney alone, I adopted a therapeutic stance of curiosity and asked her, "I wonder if you are limiting your choices of potential friends by only selecting the cool and popular kids to become friendly with?" Courtney agreed that this could be part of the problem, but she quickly pointed out to me that in the past she had never had any difficulty being perceived as "cool" or fitting in with peers in general. I pointed out to Courtney that "each tough situation or disappointment we face offers us valuable wisdom, and that even when we suffer emotionally, these experiences make us more mentally tough and can teach us what to do differently in future interactions with peers." To further build on the theme of how suffering is the path to wisdom and inner strength, I decided to share with Courtney the following story about *Wisdom's Path*, as told by Uncle Frank Davis, a Pawnee Indian elder. Uncle Frank's mother had shared this story with him when he had asked her one day as a young child how one becomes wise like her.

> "Life is like a path," she said, smiling down at me, "and we all have to walk the path. If we lay down, we even lay down on that path. If we live through the night, we have to get up and start walking down that path again. As we walk down that path we'll find experiences like little scraps of paper in front of us along the way. We must pick up those pieces of scrap paper and put them in our pockets. Every single scrap of paper we come to should be put into that pocket. Then, one day we will have enough scraps of papers to put together and see what they say. Maybe we'll have enough to make some sense. Read the information and take it to heart. Then put the pieces

of paper back in that pocket and go on, because there will be more pieces to pick up. Later we can pull them out and study them and maybe learn a little more. If we do this all through life, we'll know when to pull out those scraps to read more of the message. The more we read, the more we'll learn the meaning of life. We become wise—or at least wiser than we were." (Wall & Arden, 1990, pp. 100–101)

After listening intently to Uncle Frank Davis's wonderful story, Courtney began to display brighter affect and started to question out loud if her own attitudes and expectations were getting in the way of her "making new friends." She also appeared to have shifted from a contemplative stage of readiness to change (Prochaska, 1999) to one of being ready to take action to resolve her challenging problem situation. I then asked Courtney to keep track of what she learned from each encounter she had with a peer both by pretending to watch herself from the vantage point of being in a bubble high above and through writing down on a scrap of paper what her reflections were after each encounter with a peer. The scraps of paper were then to be immediately placed in her pocket and read each night before she went to bed. When reviewing her scraps of paper, she was to look for both helpful and unproductive patterns in her behavior and thinking. Courtney then was to record in a daily journal what she had learned from each encounter with a peer. She was to save all of her scraps of paper and keep them in a lockbox.

After 3 weeks of doing this, Courtney had made two new friends with whom she was actively socializing after school and on the weekends. In reviewing her scraps of paper and her daily journal entries in our second and subsequent sessions, it was clear that Courtney was gaining some valuable insight into what was not working for her in terms of unrealistic expectations, self-defeating thoughts, and behaviors in social interactions. For example, on one of her scraps of paper she wrote, "Just because I'm dressing cooler to impress Sally and Jenny doesn't guarantee that they will want to be my friends."

Through the help of Uncle Frank Davis's story and this experiment, Courtney learned how to be a "better listener," "be patient" with trying to build new friendships, and to "catch" herself when she started to think in an "all-or-nothing" self-defeating way. By our fourth family session, Courtney's social life had greatly improved. She had stopped cutting herself and was no longer depressed. Clearly, Uncle Frank Davis's story had captivated her and offered her valuable wisdom about the importance of being patient and carefully examining one's part in relationship difficulty situations.

SOUL WORK

Soul work consists of engaging in unstructured activities that tap one's creative expression (Kammen & Gold, 1998). Soul work can take the form of making artwork, writing poetry, creating new music, singing, or dancing. In the Native American culture, tribe members stay connected to one another through sharing their creative art products, music, dreams, and dancing together. Before engaging in any of these activities, I recommend to the adolescent that she first create a quiet sacred space to express herself in. It is most important that the adolescent take the lead in determining the type of soul work she would like to engage in as a form of creative expression. The adolescent's key intelligence areas (Gardner, 1993) will dictate which type of soul work I recommend if she is looking for guidance with this experiment. For example, if the adolescent has talent in the visual-spatial intelligence area, it would make most sense for her to engage in art soul work. I recommend that artistic clients experiment with different mediums to help further expand their self-soothing options. Finally, I encourage my client to share her creative soul work with her families and friends.

CLEANSING RITUALS

In the Native American culture, cleansing rituals are regularly employed as a way to purify one's soul (Lee, 1998). For example, taking a long relaxing bath can be a form of renewal. As a way to further enhance the renewal experience for the adolescent, I recommend that she surround the bathtub with lit candles and use nice bath oils. I stress to self-harming adolescents the importance of their making room each day to pamper themselves in this way.

CENTERING STONES

Some ancient medicine men referred to stones as "stone people" because they believed that they contained living spirits with healing properties. Centering stones can be used when distressing thoughts or unpleasant emotions have led to an individual's becoming unbalanced (Kammen & Gold, 1998; Linn & Linn, 1997). A centering stone is like a friend "who takes the cares and concerns away on the winds of your breath" (Lee, 1998, p. 167). When giving advice on selecting a centering stone, I recommend to the adolescent that she pick one that is aesthetically pleasing to her in appearance and texture. Some of my clients have selected rocks they found in nature. Other teens have gotten their centering stones at rock and gem stores.

According to Linn and Linn (1997), the way to truly experience the living spirit with a centering stone is to hold it, carefully study it, and feel its various textures. The next step is to close your eyes, take a deep breath, and imagine yourself entering the center of the stone. As Alderman (1997) has pointed out, one way to disrupt the self-harming behavior pattern is by changing the sensations connected to this behavior. By replacing self-harming behavior with stroking the textured centering stone, the adolescent learns another effective self-soothing technique.

VISION QUESTS

In the Native American culture, when children reach puberty they are sent on a *vision quest*. The vision quest is an opportunity for young adolescents to seek their spiritual guides, find inner strength, and discover their life directions. On average, a vision quest lasts four days and nights. The adolescent remains in solitary confinement with the elements, ideally on top of a hill. Elevated spots are considered ideal because they allow one to see in all four directions, a metaphor for seeing all directions in your life (Bear Heart, 1996; Lee, 1998; Linn & Linn, 1997). The *sacred circle*, also known as the *medicine wheel*, consists of the four elements (earth, air, fire, water) and the four directions (east, south, west, north). The east direction represents the activation of ideas or new beginnings. In the south direction, new ideas are nurtured and the adolescent should tap his or her intuition. The west direction is the context for the experimentation of new ideas. It is a place for discovery and transformation. Finally, the north direction is a place for completion and the consolidation of ideas (Bear Heart, 1996; Bopp, Bopp, Brown, & Lane, 1985; Linn & Linn, 1997).

The spiritual guides often will come to the adolescent in a dream or a vision in the form of animals, which have symbolic meaning. For example, a snake represents transformation or the shedding of one's skin. The frog represents focus and direction. When the adolescent returns to the village with a vision, he or she is considered an adult. The vision quest benefits adolescents by helping them to: learn how to appreciate the healthful benefits of solitude, overcome their fears, increase their self-awareness, gain inner peace, have a break from commitments and schedules, and gain a sense of independence (Linn & Linn, 1997).

Because it is unrealistic to have an adolescent go on a vision quest during the regular school year, especially alone in unfamiliar territory, I suggest that clients take their spiritual journeys during the summer months or possibly over a long weekend with a parent, sibling, or a close friend. I have had a great deal of success using a family vision quest (father-daughter) experience as a powerful way to help foster a meaningful emotional connection between an adolescent and her father. The family vision quest experiment can also provide them with an ideal healing context for resolving past hurts and conflicts in their relationship.

I have adolescents prepare for their vision quest by finding a warm blanket or sleeping bag, a ceremonial offering (Native Americans take one or two small pouches of tobacco; however, the adolescent can take something else) to place on the periphery of her selected spot on the hill, and a sacred drum. The sacred drum represents the heartbeat and has the capability of altering one's level of consciousness. Drumming can literally transport the vision-seeker to a different spiritual realm (Lee, 1998; Linn & Linn, 1997). I have adolescents take some congas or another type of percussion instrument they can beat on.

Once the adolescent has selected an elevated spot, she needs to create a sacred circle six feet in circumference around the spot. She then has to select four stones or "stone people" to place equilaterally apart from one another on the sacred circle. The "stone people" not only serve as guardian angels for the vision-seeker but also represent the transition from one quadrant of your life to the next. Once she has finished setting up the sacred circle, the vision-seeker gives thanks to the earth and nature for providing her with a special place to have a vision quest and providing loving support during the vision quest process (Linn & Linn, 1997).

The final stage of the vision quest is the adolescent's calling for a vision. First the adolescent should pray and speak from the heart to the Great Spirit or the Creator. According to Linn and Linn (1997), the Creator answers prayers and provides visions through signs and symbols. When calling for his or her vision, the adolescent needs to carefully observe and listen for unusual animal behavior, sudden changes in the immediate area surrounding her sacred circle, changes in cloud formations and star constellations above her spot. As mentioned earlier, animals can be spirit keepers and deliver the vision. At times, visions can come in one's dreams (Lee, 1998). Once the vision has come to the adolescent, she can heal old emotional wounds, and gain inner peace and clarity about her future direction. I will add my interpretations of the adolescent's visions after she has first shared her thoughts. However, I am careful not to present my interpretations as if they are definitive explanations of the adolescent's visions. I try to avoid at all costs coming across as a privileged expert with my clients.

CHAPTER 4

Changing the Family Dance: Solution-Oriented Therapeutic Experiments and Strategies

On the human chessboard, all moves are possible.
—Miriam Schiff

ADOLESCENT SELF-HARMING PROBLEMS can be quite complex and challenging to resolve. Often the adolescent's, family members', concerned friends', and involved professionals' attempted solution patterns and outmoded problem views become rigidified. Thus, the problem life-support system (White, 1985) of the self-harming behavior remains intact and takes on a life of its own. This means that therapeutic experiments and solution strategies need to be targeted at all systems levels in which the self-harming behavior is occurring, is being communicated about, or inadvertently is being maintained despite all involved parties' best efforts to stabilize it.

Another important target area that may require therapeutic attention is the adolescent's disconnection from key family members, peers, and involved representatives from larger systems. Research indicates that adolescents who are emotionally disconnected from their parents are at greater risk for developing internalizing symptoms such as self-harming behavior, eating difficulties, and substance-abusing behavior (Papini & Roggman, 1992). Many self-harming adolescents have voiced their concerns about feeling emotionally disconnected and invalidated in the various social contexts in which they interface. In these clinical situations, the therapist can utilize connection-building strategies to bring key parental figures, siblings, peers, and involved helping professionals closer together in meaningful ways. Connection-building experiments and rituals can be used both in and out of therapy sessions depending on the unique needs and goals of the clients.

In this chapter I first discuss some major connection-building experiments and rituals that can help to foster a *sense of place* in key family and extrafamilial relationships for the self-harming adolescent. Some of the connection-building practices I present are derived from Native American healing methods and rituals. Next I present several in- and out-of-session therapeutic experiments and solution strategies that can effectively disrupt unproductive family interactions with the client as well as change family members' outmoded beliefs about her. Practical guidelines for when to select particular therapeutic experiments and rituals and how to implement them are provided.

CONNECTION-BUILDING PRACTICES

Connection is the positive outcome of time spent with others in a way that builds strong, supportive, meaningful relationships (J. Clarke, 1999). Adolescents that are engaged in solid, meaningful interpersonal relationships within the family and in other social contexts feel a strong *sense of place* in these relationships. Some self-harming adolescents long to connect with a distant or peripherally involved parent, a sibling that they may have a strained or conflictual relationship with, or a particular peer or peer group they wish to belong to. Within their family contexts, many self-harming adolescents have to contend with family members who are overscheduled, parents who are emotionally spent and work long hours, and a larger cultural context that encourages family members to put work, play, and television and computer screens ahead of spending time together as a family. According to J. B. Miller and Stiver (1997):

> Our fundamental notions of who we are are not formed in the process of separation from others. In short, the goal is not for the individual to grow out of relationships, but to grow into them. As the relationships grow, so grows the individual. (p. 22)

In case situations where I hear from the self-harming adolescent, the parent she is closest to, or from both that a troublesome disconnection with a more emotionally distant or peripherally involved parent or sibling exists, I propose connection-building experiments and rituals. As mentioned earlier, the connection-building process is not just limited to the family level but may include the contexts of self-harming adolescent's peers, extended family members, teachers, and other important adults in her life. There are six connection-building experiments and rituals that can serve as the catalyst for creating positive, meaningful relationships within the family and in other social contexts.

Family Storytelling

There is no better family connection-building activity than family members sharing excerpts and chapters from their personal stories with one another. This can include family members sharing with one another the key events of their days or parents or grandparents sharing memorable events from their childhood, difficult times in their lives, or how they prevailed over adversity and the wisdom they gained from these experiences. Stories serve as vehicles for maintaining family traditions: They impart valuable wisdom, make us more aware of our roots, keep the generations tightly linked together, and create a sense of community.

At a Thanksgiving Day dinner, my 8-year-old daughter, Hanna, was asking my parents a lot of questions about their own childhoods and what their parents were like. I was very pleased and moved by my parents' sharing their personal stories with Hanna. I could tell that she, too, was cherishing this sparkling moment of connecting in a meaningful way with my parents. My mother had spent a lot of time talking about her parents and all that she had appreciated about them. She also pointed out to Hanna that her Russian father expected that she and her sisters would always come to the dinner table nicely dressed with neatly combed hair. After hearing this Hanna replied, "What's so important about that?!" Both my wife and I were pleased to discover that we are raising a feminist who at an early age is already challenging patriarchal assumptions about how women should look and act!

Making room for the daily family ritual of storytelling is one highly positive way family members can stay connected to one another in a meaningful way. It has been my clinical experience that one of the best contexts for family storytelling is at the dinner table. Another useful time for parents to share their stories with their adolescents is during one-on-one times they may have scheduled together. I encourage parents to share both in and out of family sessions the trials and tribulations of their own adolescent years, particularly similar experiences they had as teenagers and how they managed to cope and prevail over adversity. This valuable parental wisdom may provide the self-harming adolescent with some useful ideas that she can begin implementing immediately to help her to resolve her difficulties.

Adolescents Mentoring Parents

Having adolescents mentor their parents—inviting them to share their expertise and wisdom with their parents—can accentuate the adolescents' strengths. This connection-building strategy is also particularly useful when the adolescent reports feeling disconnected from one or both parents or when they view or relate to her as if she is irresponsible, incompetent, or psychologically impaired. Empowering the adolescent in this way can challenge the parents' outmoded, problem-saturated views of her and help improve family communications.

Kathleen, a Caucasian 16-year-old who was self-harming by pulling out her body hair, had a highly strained relationship with her father. The only time Kathleen and her father interacted was around school-related problems or when she got into trouble with her mother. The father was much more actively involved in his 12-year-old son, Zack's, life because of their strong mutual interest in sports.

One of Kathleen's major strengths was her ability to design, sew, and knit her own clothes. In one of our family therapy sessions, I decided to propose the experiment of putting Kathleen in charge of teaching her father how to sew. Apparently, the father was constantly losing buttons on his shirts and pants and taking his clothes to the neighborhood dry cleaners to be mended. With grave doubts about his ability to master this skill, the father begrudgingly agreed to try the experiment. In a loving and supportive way, Kathleen confidently assured her father that he would learn how to sew in a week's time. In our next family session, the father eagerly reported that he had successfully mastered the sewing task and had found Kathleen to be a "superb teacher!" Both the father and Kathleen reported that they had had some great laughs while they were working together. With the help of this connection-building experiment, Kathleen and her father grew closer, their interactions became more positive, and the father found a balance in spending an equal amount of time alone with each child.

Solution-Oriented Family Sculpting and Choreography

Historically, family sculpting and choreography (Duhl, Duhl, & Kantor, 1973; Papp, 1983; Papp, Silverstein, & Carter, 1973; Satir, 1972) was employed by experientially oriented family therapists as a powerful and highly effective therapeutic tool for helping families to step outside themselves and gain a metaview of their destructive ways of interacting, their coalitions, and their rigid role behaviors. The most common family sculpting strategy is to have the self-harming adolescent place herself in the center of the room and guide the therapist in positioning each one of her family members in terms of emotional closeness and distance to her. I then have her use herself as an emotional barometer as I move her closer to each family member and instruct me to stop moving her if she starts to feel uncomfortable. At this point, it is helpful to explore with her why it was difficult to physically move closer to more distant family members. This may lead to the adolescent's revealing unresolved conflicts with particular family members or family secrets. Ample session time should be allotted for processing the self-harming adolescent's sculpture.

The next step is to have the adolescent sculpt the family the way she would want it to look in terms of closeness and distance. The therapist can ask the adolescent how this new physical arrangement would make a difference for her and other family members. This simple family sculpting format helps therapists to identify specific problem-maintaining interactions. It can be used as part of the goal-setting process, when the therapist is at an impasse with a family, or when the therapist picks up on innuendos that there may be family secrets. When using family sculpture or choreography as part of the goal-setting process, I have had adolescents dramatize how family members will look and interact differently in their ideal miracle pictures to help bring new solution sequences of interaction to life.

Family choreography (Papp, 1983; Satir, 1972) adds motion and more drama to a family member's sculpture. Props can be used as metaphors for relationship difficulties. With family choreography, the therapist's office becomes a Broadway theater house for the family dance. Family members often have a lot of fun with this exercise and gain valuable insight about their unproductive dance steps with one another.

For instance, Jaime, a Caucasian 14-year-old who was cutting and burning herself, did a family choreography in our third family therapy session. Up to this point, Jaime felt that the therapy was "not working" because her parents were "still not changing." Jaime had been cutting and burning herself for almost a year and blamed this problem on her parents' "never listening" to her and being "more married to their jobs" than to her and her 12-year-old sister, Jill. Jaime's first family choreography graphically depicted the major family problem of the parents' prioritizing their careers over their children. She positioned herself and Jill across the room from her parents. Jaime had me place two chairs at her parents' end of the room and instructed her parents each to pick a chair and run in circles around it. The chairs represented their careers. Needless to say, the parents were quite shocked by Jaime's family choreography and had not been aware that the family life/work situation had gotten that bad. After processing Jaime's first family choreography, I had her show us how she would like her family to look. Jaime had her parents run five circles together around her and Jill, then separately run one circle around each of their chairs, and then repeat the whole sequence. By the end of this highly productive family therapy session, the parents received the message that they needed to create firm boundaries between their family and work lives loud and clear. Two sessions later, not only had Jaime stopped cutting and burning herself but the parents also were asking Jaime and Jill what they would like to do as a family and consistently making themselves available for one-on-one time with each daughter.

The Compliment Box

In the hustle and bustle of family life, family members often forget to regularly acknowledge their appreciation for the small things they do for one another on a daily basis. Research on family strengths has indicated that showing appreciation is one of the six important characteristics of strong families (DeFrain & Stinnett, 1992; Stinnett & O' Donnell, 1996). Failure to acknowledge family members' efforts to be helpful, to reach out with support, to share appreciation for each other, and to take an interest in each others' lives can promote conflict and emotional distance and can sever relationship connections over time.

When I work with self-harming adolescents and families who report a lot of negative interactions such as blaming and criticizing, I propose the *compliment box* experiment as a way to improve family communication. I instruct the parents to find an old shoebox or another small box with a removable top. The next step is for the parents to cut a slit in the top of the box. Each day family members are to write down a compliment they have for one another and put them in the compliment box. The compliments are then read either right after dinner or at another designated time in the evening. Family members take turns reaching in the box and reading each other's compliments. If there are particular compliments that greatly surprised family members or moved them emotionally in a positive, powerful way, I have the family members put the compliment in a safe place in their bedrooms. This way family members can use the compliment slips as a constant reminder that they are connected to one another in a meaningful way, even in the midst of conflict. The following case example demonstrates how the compliment box experiment can create possibilities with a family struggling with chronic communication difficulties.

Karen, a Caucasian 16-year-old high-school junior, had been cutting herself and grappling with bulimia for 2 years. She had been in and out of individual therapy since eighth grade. Two of the major family stressors she was dealing with were her parents' chronic arguing and their constant blaming of her. According to Karen, her parents were constantly commenting on her poor grades and how she did not do her "chores good enough." They frequently reminded her about what a "wonderful student" her older brother, Jonathan, who attended an Ivy League school, was. In our first two family therapy sessions, the parents were quite pessimistic about the likelihood of Karen's changing and I experienced great difficulty establishing a small realistic treatment goal with them, even after using the miracle, coping, pessimistic, and subzero scaling questions. I also attempted to externalize (White, 1995) the "blaming pattern" that seemed to have a life of its own in the family. This also proved futile.

In our third family therapy session I decided to propose to the family the compliment box experiment. I first shared with the family that it was clear to me that they were all feeling demoralized by the lack of progress in our work together and the failure of past treatment to make a difference as well. When I explored with family members how often they compliment or acknowledge their appreciation for one another, not one family member could think of any specific time in the recent past that any of them had acknowledged each other. For the first time in our sessions together, the blaming stopped and the focus moved from Karen being the family problem to the family's problems with communication. I pointed out to the family how the use of the compliment box can help create a positive climate in the home, which in turn can change blaming and school performance problems. I also predicted that as a family they were about to venture into uncharted territory and that while they implemented the experiment there might be some flare-ups that normally occur when families are on the rocky road to change.

After a week's time, the family brought in their compliment box for me to see and hear some of the meaningful compliments they had received from one another. The family mood appeared to be much more positive. In fact, Karen appeared less depressed and more hopeful that things would continue to improve with her family. She had received a compliment from her father for getting a C on a difficult math test. In the past, he would have yelled at her for not getting a B on it. Karen's mother had given her a compliment for having a "better attitude" about school. Karen's mother observed her doing her homework several times. Karen had complimented her parents on "trying to argue less" over the past week. She took a risk with her parents and shared with them how this made her feel happier and less likely to cut or binge and purge to comfort herself. Following Karen's disclosure, the parents asked if I would be willing to see them for marital therapy. Once the parents made a commitment to improving their relationship, Karen stopped cutting and bingeing and purging.

The Talking Stick

In Native American culture, each tribe member's words were respected. While sitting around the sacred circle, the elders would pass the talking stick to one another like a microphone. The person who spoke would speak to the center of the circle. He or she would speak his or her truth without trying to influence or sell anyone on any particular idea. Each person represented his or her unique viewpoint. With an open heart and mind, those who listened looked into the fire ablaze in the center of the circle. Before each tribe member holding the talking stick spoke, he or she would say: "I am _____, and I will speak." When finished talking he or she would say, "I am _____, and I have spoken!" The talking stick taught tribal members about options and choices and that each member of the tribe had unique viewpoints that should be honored and respected (Lee, 1998).

The *talking stick* strategy is particularly useful with families in which a lot of blaming, interrupting, and mind reading is occurring. Some self-harming adolescents believe their voices are not heard and feel invalidated. The talking stick can help to teach family members how to listen to one another and respect each other's unique perspectives. When implementing this strategy, I explain to the family the purpose of the talking stick and how it can be beneficial to them. I then put our chairs in a circle and place a lit candle in the center of the circle on a small table. When a family member receives the talking stick, he or she is to speak to the center of the circle and share his or her issue or concern. The other family members are to gaze into the candle flame in silence, carefully listening to what the speaker is saying with an open heart and mind. After experimenting with this strategy in the office and processing it, I have the family go home and practice using the talking stick as a way to provide a structured and safe context for daily issues to be discussed when necessary.

Talking sticks can be purchased at Native American or other specialty shops. In some cases, I have had the adolescent create her own talking stick, particularly if I know that the she enjoys arts and crafts.

Building New Connections with Peers and Inspirational Others

Some self-harming adolescents have difficulty abstaining from cutting or burning because their closest friends are also engaging in this behavior and are very much a part of the problem life-support system (White, 1985). These adolescents argue that if they stop associating with their friends they will have no support system. When this is the case, I propose that I bring in some former clients who used to self-harm to serve as a new peer support group for her. The alumni peer consultants can provide the client with valuable wisdom, practical tips on how to stop self-harming, and effective, creative coping strategies for managing such stressors as emotional distress and family, school, and peer problems. Prior to bringing in the alumni peer consultants, I get written consent from the adolescent and her parents to contact my former clients. I also get approval from the former clients' parents to have them participate in the treatment process. I explain the rules of confidentiality to all parties involved.

In some cases, the self-harming adolescent may report feeling that she lacks a caring and responsive adult in her immediate and extended family to connect with for emotional support and guidance. One or both of her parents may be grappling with his or her own marital, mental health, substance, or physical health issues, which contributes to the disconnection. The adolescent may also feel like she lacks meaningful connections with adults at school or in her community. In these situations (and with parental consent), I may offer to connect the adolescent with an adult inspirational other (Anthony, 1987) with whom I have collaborated in the past. Besides offering valuable outside support and wisdom to the adolescent, the inspirational other can serve as an advocate for her at school if he or she is a teacher or coach.

IN-SESSION THERAPEUTIC EXPERIMENTS AND TREATMENT TEAM STRATEGIES

Several therapeutic experiments can be offered to families to encourage them to tap their imagination powers, creativity, and other strengths and resources. Similar to connection-building strategies, the therapeutic experiments presented here can help to strengthen family relationships, open the door for possibilities, and empower family members to achieve their goals. Therapeutic team strategies can be employed with stuck cases.

Imaginary Time Machine

The *imaginary time machine experiment* can be used at any stage of treatment (Selekman, 1997). I introduce the experiment by explaining: "Imagine I have a time machine sitting over here. You can go in it and take it anywhere in time you wish. Where would you go? Who would you meet up with? What would you be doing together? How would that person/people be dressed? What colors do you see? What do you hear? Are you touching anything? How does it feel? What do you smell? If you are eating something with this person/people, how does it taste?" To help bring this time-traveling experience to life for the self-harming adolescent, it is critical that the therapist have her apply all of her senses and include lots of detail about color and motion.

In clinical situations where an important connection has been severed between the self-harming adolescent and one of the parents, I will have her go back in time to a place (a specific one-on-one experience or a family event) where she experienced much more of a solid emotional connection with that particular parent. After having her detail this meaningful experience with all of her senses, I have her pick the most important actions, qualities, or ingredients that were occurring in that past relationship experience that she wishes to reinstate in her current relationship. The next step is to have the self-harming adolescent and this parent discuss alone or in the company of other family members how we can begin to implement what worked in the past in their relationship. Doing this in the company of the family can provide the therapist with the opportunity to tap other family members' expertise about how to maximize the potential for success in improving this troubled family relationship.

Dawn, a Caucasian 17-year-old, was referred to me for cutting and bulimia. The referral source also reported that Dawn had voiced to her for years that she felt emotionally disconnected from her father. The father was attending Alcoholics' Anonymous meetings daily and had been alcohol-free for 3 years. As a way to try to bring Dawn and her father closer together, I had her take a voyage in the imaginary time machine back to a time when she felt a strong sense of place in her relationship with her father. Once Dawn arrived at her destination, I had her describe in great detail everything she experienced using all of her senses. Dawn traveled back in time to the age of 10, when she was sitting in front of the fireplace snuggled up against her father listening to him reading her a story. According to Dawn, this was her favorite nighttime activity with her father throughout her childhood. When asked about why she selected this particular time in her life to travel back to, Dawn pointed out that her father had begun to drift away from her and the rest of the family a few weeks after this last special moment with him due to his "drinking problem's getting worse." Dawn went on to add that now A.A. meetings and his A.A. friends were monopolizing their family time together. The father appeared very troubled by Dawn's concerns and reached over to hug her. I first validated Dawn's feelings and then positively relabeled the father's dilemma by pointing out how "he was taking every possible measure now to protect his sobriety for the good of the family." Dawn and her mother found my new construction of the father's situation to be an acceptable explanation; however, they did voice a strong desire for him to set aside more time for both of them. They also requested that he reinstate his former positive quality of being "more affectionate" with each of them. After listening carefully to his family's requests, he made a strong commitment to remedy these problems.

Imaginary Feelings–X-Ray Machine

The *imaginary feelings–x-ray machine experiment* is particularly useful with self-harming adolescents who have somatic complaints or trouble expressing their thoughts and feelings (Selekman, 1997). I have also had quite a lot of success using this experiment in situations in which I sense the presence of untold family stories or secrets. Self-harming adolescents who are visual-spatial learners respond very well to this experiment. I begin the experiment by sharing with the family the following: "Imagine that I have sitting over here a special machine that can show us x-rays of what your feelings look like. Before I turn it on, I would like you (the self-harming adolescent) to select a family member to draw the outline of your body on this long sheet of paper lying on the floor. When I turn the x-ray machine on, I would like you to draw pictures of what you think your feelings look like. You can choose where to place your feelings in your body. After you draw your feelings, I would like you to tell a story about each feeling."

Once the adolescent has drawn her feelings and thoroughly reflected on her drawings, I invite family members to ask questions and offer their feedback to the client. The self-harming adolescent's drawings may have a profound impact on family members' problem views of her and the way they interact with her. Family members may learn things about the client that they never knew before. The therapist needs to reflect his or her own ideas from a position of *not knowing* and avoid giving definitive interpretations (Anderson & Goolishian, 1988).

Famous Guest Consultants

When I work with families that are feeling very stuck and appear to have lost their spontaneity and playfulness with one another, I introduce the *famous guest consultants experiment*. I ask each family member to come up with a list of three famous people he or she has always admired or really likes. The famous people can be historical figures, professional athletes, entertainment celebrities, writers, or spiritual leaders. Once the family members have generated their individual lists, I have them share the lists with one another. I then present the family with the hypothetical situation of imagining how their selected famous people would approach their presenting problem and influence their thinking in coming up with ideas for solving it. I have family members really try to place themselves in the heads of the famous people by thinking about each one's unique talents, metaphors related to their line of work, and areas of expertise. When fully engaged in this mental process, family members often generate some very creative problem-solving strategies. After they have come up with two or more strategies, I invite the family to choose which strategies they wish to implement at home as an experiment.

Tara, a Japanese 16-year-old, and her family were referred to me for her cutting and burning behavior. The parents were born and raised in the United States. Tara's father was a heart surgeon and rarely at home due to his demanding work schedule. When Tara did have contact with her father, they often clashed around her poor school grades, her Gothic dress, and her choice of friends. The mother was very concerned about Tara's cutting and burning problem. A month before our first family therapy session, Tara's father arranged for her to be psychiatrically hospitalized for what he believed was suicidal behavior. A week after getting out of the hospital, Tara started cutting and burning herself again. According to Tara, her father's style of interacting with her consisted of his yelling and taking away her privileges for long periods of time with no room for discussion. The family spent little time together as a group. When family members were at home, everyone typically did their own thing or an argument would erupt between Tara and her father, which often resulted in a self-injury episode.

By our second family therapy session, the mother and Tara pushed for improving the way family members interacted with one another and wanted to see the family spend more quality time together. The father agreed that he did not like the way things were with the family situation either. Because the family appeared to be plagued by negative interactions and problem-solving difficulties, I had them try the famous guest consultant experiment as a playful way for them to work together as a group. Tara selected Marilyn Manson as her main guest consultant. The father selected Clint Eastwood and his wife selected Michelle Pfeiffer. According to Tara, Marilyn Manson would recommend to her and her family that they take on their problems getting along "head on and not stop until they are resolved." Tara also believed that he would recommend to her father that he give her more of a voice in their relationship so they didn't end up with the "same kind of difficult relationship Marilyn still has with his parents" as an adult. Clint Eastwood recommended that the father have "better aim" with how and when he reprimanded and interacted with Tara. For the first time, the father made eye contact with Tara and shared how he, too, wanted things to change with their relationship. The father also shared with Tara that Clint would tell him that he has been using his "357 magnum pistol with her far too much," with the drastic consequences and lengthy grounding periods he had been giving her. The mother felt that Michelle Pfeiffer would push for more "family harmony, respect, and affection." Each family member agreed to test out the ideas they came up with over the next week. At the end of the session, I complimented the family on what an excellent job they had done with the experiment and at working so well together. The family returned a week later pleased with the positive results they had achieved with their creative self-generated solution strategies.

Family Collage Mural

When I work with families that lack spontaneity or playfulness or that spend very little time engaged in fun family activities, I propose the *family collage mural experiment*. As a group, the family is asked to create a mural depicting how they would like to look as a family in the future. Besides cutting pictures and letters out of magazines, they can also draw and paint on the mural sheet of paper. Once they have completed their family masterpiece, I have them reflect on their creation and on what they learned from the experience and from one another. At this point in the session, I introduce my imaginary crystal ball to the family and have each member gaze into it and describe the future steps he or she sees them taking as a group to make this future family picture a reality. I also recommend to the family that they find a place in their home to hang up their family masterpiece.

Interviewing the Problem and the Solution

Once the adolescent's presenting problem has been externalized, a playful and fun therapeutic option to pursue is to have her pretend to be the problem in the context of the family therapy session (Epston, 1998, 2000). The therapist plays the role of a *New York Times* reporter covering a story on the problem. The interview covers the following: What is the problem's reason for pushing this particular adolescent and her family around? What are its hopes and dreams? What are the tactics it uses on the adolescent and family members? Whom has it brainwashed to take its side both within and outside the family? The second part of the interview covers the following: At what times have the adolescent, family members, and involved helping professionals successfully stood up to the problem and not allowed it to push them around? What specific things do the adolescent and family members do to frustrate it? In what ways does the problem reassert itself to regain influence in the lives of the adolescent and her family? Throughout the interviewing process, family members are free to ask questions of the problem as well. Finally, I have the adolescent and her family process what unique insights they gained about the problem and their situation.

A nice twist to this in-session experiment is to have the adolescent play the role of her most potent solution strategy. In a similar fashion, I interview the personified solution strategy. I ask the following questions: In what ways are you putting Jane more in charge of herself versus her being at the mercy of the problem? Thanks to you, how is Jane looking at herself differently now? On a scale from 1 to 10, with 10 being highly confident, how confident are you that you will be able to withstand attempts on the problem's behalf to reassert its influence on Jane? Do you have any ideas for Jane of things she can do to increase your presence in her life? "Can you think of anything Jane, her parents, or involved helping professionals could do that would disempower or derail you?" This experiment is particularly useful for consolidating the adolescent's gains, for early identification of potential pitfalls or weaknesses of implemented solution strategies, and for relapse-prevention purposes.

Reflecting Team

The *reflecting team consultation method* was developed by Norwegian psychiatrist Tom Andersen as a respectful, collaborative way to work with families (Andersen, 1991, 1995). The nature of the family's problem situation dictates which reflecting team format I employ. The most common format entails having two or three colleagues first observe the session from an observation room with a one-way mirror and microphone that allows them to hear what is said in the therapy room. Then approximately 40 minutes into the hour, the team switches rooms with the therapist and the family so that the family and therapist can see and hear them engage in a 7-minute conversation in which they present their different views on the family's problem situation. The team members' reflections should be presented in a tentative way—that is, not as definitive explanations. Then the team and the family and therapist switch rooms again, and the therapist invites the family to reflect on the team's conversation. It is quite rare that a good team reflection fails to produce shifts in family members' problem views and unhelpful ways of interacting. The therapist is also liberated from feeling stuck by receiving fresh ideas from his or her colleagues. I find this team approach particularly useful when I work with parents that cling to negative fixed beliefs about the adolescent or in cases where I sense that there may be family secrets.

Another reflecting team format I like to use is to bring in the adolescent's close, concerned friends or invite former self-harming alumni to share their wisdom and expertise with the family and me (Selekman, 1993, 1995b). If the adolescent and her parents are deadlocked in intense conflict around certain issues, the friends observing the session behind a one-way mirror can switch rooms with the family and I and share how they have resolved similar difficulties with their parents. In situations in which the parents have a lot of questions about self-harming behavior in general and how to stop it, the adolescent alumni can provide the answers by sharing their unique stories and how they succeeded in stopping this problematic behavior. As a result of this powerful peer team intervention, parents have more compassion and empathy for their daughters' struggles and the clients learn some practical strategies for stabilizing the self-harming behavior.

For example, I had Rhonda, a depressed Caucasian 15-year-old who frequently cut herself, invite Paul, one of her closest friends to a family session as a peer consultant. Paul had also had problems with depression and had cut himself on a regular basis. Rhonda's parents asked Paul questions about the negative peer group they used to be involved in, why he used to cut himself, and any advice he had for them and their daughter. Paul pointed out that the whole peer group was "bugging out over depression." He used to cut himself for "stress management" and as a form of self-punishment. Paul also recommended that Rhonda should fill up her free time, take guitar lessons with him, and join a health club. Thanks to Paul's support, I finally was able to gain Rhonda's compliance in following through with my previous recommendations that she structure her afterschool hours with positive, healthy activities such as playing an instrument and joining a health club.

The Therapeutic Debate

With case situations in which I am feeling stuck in treatment, the family's interactions and beliefs are entrenched, and there appear to be secondary gains for the identified client's remaining symptomatic, the *therapeutic debate* (Papp, 1983) may offer solutions. The therapeutic debate team format entails having two observing team members enter the therapy room approximately 30–40 minutes into the hour. One team member takes the side of the parents while the other takes the side of the adolescent. The team members represent each party's position regarding the dilemmas around changing their problem views and ways of interacting. The therapist and family members are free to chime in at any point and join the debate. With the help of the therapeutic debate team, fixed family beliefs and rigid patterns of interaction can be altered, and family members may take important risks such as the disclosing family secrets.

A variation of the therapeutic debate team format is to have a third team member represent the presenting problem (the family's description of the problem) and join the debate process. This provides a unique inside-looking-out perspective through the eyes of the problem. Externalizing the problem (White, 1995) in this way helps to take the focus off of the adolescent as the family problem or scapegoat, disrupts unhelpful family beliefs and interactions, and unifies family members as a group to defeat the problem. The following case example illustrates how having a team member represent the presenting problem in the therapeutic debate can help dramatically to alter negative family interactions and problem-saturated views of the client.

Recently, in the context of a workshop I was giving for a family service agency, I participated in a live family therapy consultation session with Colleen, a 16-year-old who had been burning herself daily for the past 6 months. For the past 3 years, Colleen had been grappling with bulimia. Jim, the therapist, had been working with Colleen and her family for a year and a half and was feeling quite stuck. Prior to Jim, Colleen had seen two other therapists for her difficulties with bulimia and poor school performance. Tom and Kendra, Colleen's parents, were also in attendance at the consultation session. The parents were at their wits' end about how to manage Colleen's self-harming behavior. Billy, Colleen's 8-year-old brother, could not attend the session because he was still hospitalized after receiving spinal surgery. He had been born with spinal bifida and was described as being frail and sickly and requiring a great deal of the parents' attention. In fact, Colleen's biggest complaint with her parents was that they spent little time with her and they frequently failed to follow through with their promises, such as giving her privileges she had earned.

Rather than coleading the consultation session with Jim, I requested that I serve as the team member representing Colleen's burning behavior in the therapeutic debate. Two of Jim's agency staff volunteered to serve as team members supporting the parents' and Colleen's positions, respectively, in the debate. Midway through the therapeutic debate, I shared my thoughts as a representative of the burning behavior's views of Colleen and her family situation. I said to the family and my team members: "I represent Colleen's anger and frustration. I think she feels burned. She has little time with her parents and when they do talk, they make promises they can't keep. I might have to pack my bags and leave this family if the parents start delivering the attention and privileges Colleen is longing for." Colleen abruptly responded to my comments by saying: "Yes, he's got it! That's exactly how I feel." Her response appeared to indicate that I was right on target with my thoughts about her situation. The biggest breakthrough in the session following Colleen's response to my reflection was her parents' asking her how they could better meet her needs. They even asked Colleen what she would like to do for fun as a family over the upcoming weekend. When I followed up with Jim a month later, he indicated that Colleen had stopped burning herself, was no longer bingeing and purging, was earning more privileges, and that the parents were spending much more time with her.

OUT-OF-SESSION THERAPEUTIC EXPERIMENTS

Family members can implement a variety of experiments at home and in other social contexts. Here I discuss four major solution-focused therapeutic tasks that I frequently use with adolescents and their families. This is followed with a discussion of two connection-building therapeutic experiments that can open the door for family members to talk about the "not yet said" (Anderson & Goolishian, 1988) and can foster a deeper emotional connection between them.

The Secret Surprise

The *secret surprise experiment* is particularly useful in situations in which some exceptional behavior is already occurring with the adolescent (O'Hanlon & Weiner-Davis, 1989). While meeting alone with the adolescent, I have her come up with two positive surprises that she could pull off over the next week that would really blow her parents' minds. I like to have the adolescent do one surprise for each parent. She is not to let them know what the surprises are—they will have to guess. When I reconvene the family, I share with the parents that over the next week they will experience some pleasant surprises. I encourage them to pull out their imaginary magnifying glasses and, like Sherlock Holmes and Miss Marple, try to figure out what the surprises are. Family members are not to compare notes until our next appointment. Sometimes I reverse the process and have the parents surprise the adolescent.

Observation Tasks

I like to use *observation tasks* (Gingerich & de Shazer, 1991; Molnar & de Shazer, 1987) when I am working with parents that are in the contemplative stage of readiness to change (Prochaska, 1999) or constantly criticize one another's parenting abilities. I also ask parents who spend a lot of time complaining about their adolescent's behavior to step back and over a week's time, on a daily basis, keep track of any small signs of encouraging behavior on their daughter's behalf. This often helps them to make important discoveries.

Similarly, I have parents who are in conflict with each other each take a week to notice on a daily basis what the other parent does in relationship to the adolescent and with the other children that he or she thought was helpful, effective, or really clever. They are not to compare notes until our next appointment. This experiment is quite effective at resolving parental conflicts and unifying parents as a team.

Do Something Different

When I work with parents who have gotten into a "more of the same" rut with regard to their attempted solution strategies with their adolescent, I propose the *do-something-different experiment* (de Shazer, 1985; Gingerich & de Shazer, 1991). The most common problematic ways parents interact with their adolescent are: the parents take too much responsibility for the adolescent, the parents constantly get trapped in power struggles with the adolescent about who is in charge, and the parents are too emotionally disconnected. I present the following rationale to parents when introducing the idea of doing things differently around their adolescent: "Your kid's got your number. She can tell by the look on your face and the tone of your voice what's going to happen next. So over the next week, whenever your daughter invites you to take responsibility for her or pushes your buttons, I want you to do something off-the-wall or different than your usual course of action." Parents often have a lot of fun with this experiment and come up with highly creative behavioral responses. In addition to disrupting problem-maintaining patterns of interaction between the adolescent and her parents, this experiment helps parents to be more flexible and less reactive, and it strengthens their reflective skills.

A variation of this experiment is to have the adolescent experiment with responding differently to her parents when she is frustrated by them, invited to serve as a confidant, or urged to side with one parent against the other. In a school context, I have the adolescent blow a particular teacher's mind by responding differently to him or her when she is frustrated or angry. I have had teachers I am collaborating with experiment with doing things differently around my adolescent clients as a way to reduce conflict and improve their relationships.

Patricia, a Cuban 17-year-old who was cutting herself, was constantly getting pulled into her parents' marital arguments as a referee. Each parent would try to get her to take his or her side. This problem-maintaining pattern of interaction also occurred in our family therapy sessions. It was clear that Patricia was the family savior. While meeting alone with Patricia in our second family session, she disclosed her fears that her parents would divorce and explained how devastating that would be for her and her younger sisters. I provided support and commended Patricia on bringing her parents into therapy. I explored with Patricia if she felt okay with my taking over the responsibility of trying to help her parents with their marital difficulties. Patricia had no problem abdicating this long-standing family role. As an experiment, I recommended to Patricia that whenever one of her parents tried to pull her into one of their arguments or she was tempted to try to stop their arguing, she was to do something different. Patricia came up with the following three different responses: She would go up to her bedroom and blast her music so she would not have to listen to them, she would tell them that their marital issues were none of her business, or she would call a friend for support. With Patricia's help, I was able to get the parents to agree to work with me on their marital problems.

Pretend the Miracle Happened

The *pretend the miracle happened experiment* is particularly useful when very few or no exceptions at all are occurring (de Shazer, 1991; Gingerich & de Shazer, 1991). I meet alone with the adolescent and have her pick 2 days over the next week to pretend to engage in two to three of the parents' miracle behaviors for her. These behaviors were discussed earlier in the section on the miracle question inquiry (de Shazer, 1988). While pretending to engage in the parents' miracle behaviors for her, she is to notice how her parents respond to her. I also point out to the adolescent that doing this experiment could help put her in better graces with her parents and make it easier for us to negotiate the privileges she wants from them.

A variation of this experiment is to have the parents pretend to engage in the adolescent's identified miracle behaviors for them and then notice how she responds to them when they are pretending. I regularly use this variation of the experiment in my solution-oriented parenting groups (Selekman, 1999).

The Question Box

The *question box experiment* is particularly useful in situations in which there appear to be untold family stories or secrets that may be contributing to the maintenance of the adolescent's symptoms and the problem-maintaining patterns of interaction. When offering this experiment to families, I capture their curiosity by asking them if any family members have ever wondered if there were any untold family stories or things they were curious about with their family situations throughout the generations, with their present families, or with extended family members. I then instruct the parents to find an old shoebox or small box and cut a slit in the top of it. For a week's time and on a daily basis family members are to write down on a slip of paper any questions they have about the family drama or particular immediate or extended family members or relationships that they are troubled by or are seeking more information about. Family members have the option of either signing their names on the slips of paper or remaining anonymous.

The family brings the question box to the following session. I have each family member take turns blindly reaching into the question box and reading the question aloud. The power of this therapeutic experiment is that it violates the unspoken family rule that there are "certain things we will not talk about." Family members that have been harboring unspeakable, potent secrets are liberated from having to carry this tremendous emotional burden. Once a family secret is revealed, the family and I problem-solve together about how best to manage it.

For example, Gabriella, a Puerto Rican 14-year-old who was cutting and dissociating, had dropped into the family question box the following question: "Mom, why don't you ever let me visit Uncle Ricardo anymore?" After Maria, the mother, heard this question read off by her husband in our family session, she immediately requested to meet with me alone. Before doing this, I first wanted to see how the father, Gabriella, and her younger sister felt about my meeting alone with the mother. No family members had any objections to my meeting alone with Maria.

During this meeting, I made it clear to Maria that I would not harbor any secrets that had to do with her marital situation, with physical or sexual abuse of family members, or that were contributing to Gabriella's difficulties. The mother began to cry and disclosed that they did not have contact with Ricardo because he had sexually abused Gabriella when she was 5. Apparently, Gabriella did not remember this event. Maria had caught her brother in the act. The father also knew what had happened and had forbidden any family member to have contact with Ricardo. No report had been made to the police or the state child protection agency. I called the father in and shared with the parents that I was required to report any child abuse or sexual abuse of a minor and that I needed to call the child abuse hotline. After making the call and having the parents speak with the hotline worker, the parents agreed to answer Gabriella's question and reveal this family secret. Gabriella began to cry when her mother revealed the secret. I provided lots of support and empathy to Gabriella and her parents. I also pointed out to Gabriella and her parents that it is not uncommon for victims of abuse to cut and dissociate. In future sessions, I involved the family priest to support my efforts in helping this family heal and overcome their shame, and I actively collaborated with the child protection caseworker.

Family Vision Quests

With cases in which the adolescent is longing for a stronger emotional connection with her more peripherally involved parent, I propose the *family vision quest experiment*. The parent and adolescent first are to select a hilly or mountainous destination on which to have their vision quest experience. I have the family take sleeping bags, water, a set of Native American or conga drums, some extra clothes, an offering for the Creator, and a first-aid kit. The adolescent is to place four stone people or large stones equidistant to one another, forming a sacred circle. They are then to situate themselves at the center of the sacred circle between the stone people. After setting up the sacred circle, they are to give thanks to the earth and nature for providing them with a special place to have a vision quest (Linn & Linn, 1997).

The next stage of the family vision quest is for both the adolescent and the parent to call for a vision. They are to pray and speak from the heart to the Creator. While calling for their visions, they are to listen and look carefully for unusual animal behavior, sudden changes in the immediate area, or changes in cloud formations or star constellations above their sacred circle. At times, visions can come in their dreams (Lee, 1998). Once the adolescent and her parent have experienced their visions, they are free to share their unique, meaningful experiences with one another. The power in this wonderful family ritual is that it provides a perfect context for healing old emotional wounds and rebuilding parent-adolescent relationships.

CHAPTER 5

Untangling Family-Helping-System Knots: Facilitating Transformative Dialogues

Loyalty to a petrified opinion never yet broke a chain or freed a human soul.

—Mark Twain

A S NOTED EARLIER, SELF-HARMING adolescent cases are notorious for attracting helping professionals from larger systems like a magnet. Because of the provocative and extreme nature of the adolescents' self-injurious behaviors, it is not uncommon for concerned professionals to describe these youth as having borderline personality disorders, being clinically depressed or suicidal, or having been sexually abused. Once red-flagged by school personnel, these adolescents may be referred for a psychiatric evaluation with the district psychiatrist, have to participate in an emergency crisis intervention session with the school social worker or psychologist or be referred to agency or a community mental health center for an assessment, or, worse, be admitted to a local psychiatric hospital. Often the adolescent and her parents have little to no input in the assessments, treatment plans, or goal-setting process. To further complicate matters, the involved professionals may become polarized around their problem views and explanations and preferred treatment methods, becoming adversarial and sometimes inadvertently replicating a family's problem-maintaining interactions and role behaviors. I like to refer to these family-helping-system dilemmas as *knot* situations.

In this chapter, I present *transformative dialogue*: an innovative and highly respectful method of dialogical conversation with families, involved helping professionals from larger systems, and important members of families' social networks (Gergen & McNamee, 2000; McNamee & Gergen, 1999). With transformative dialogue, the main emphasis is on promoting a safe, respectful conversational context in which the members of the family-helping system can freely share their thoughts about the presenting problems, treatment planning, and goal-setting. Trying to change the behavior and interactions of the adolescent and her family is a secondary focus and often naturally evolves from the family's having a leading voice in their own treatment and the generation of new meanings and creative ideas during meetings with the family-helping system.

I also discuss important research findings on strong teams. In order to collaborate effectively with helpers from larger systems, it is critical that, throughout the treatment process, therapists carefully and continuously examine their interactions and thinking in relation to other members of the helping team. The chapter covers some important guidelines for hosting collaborative meetings with family-helping systems.

FROM PRIVILEGED MONOLOGICAL CONVERSATIONS TO TRANSFORMATIVE DIALOGUES

The therapist and treatment team hosting the collaborative meetings with the family-helping system must avoid at all costs adopting a privileged expert position. This entails avoiding premature enslavement to certain diagnostic labels and privileging one's problem explanations and treatment approaches or solution strategies. When therapists adopt a privileged expert position in the context of these meetings, they are capable of hearing only their voices and engaging in what I refer to as *monological conversation* or one-way conversation. In transformative dialogues, all participants in the conversation have a voice and coconstruct new meanings, new relationships, and possibilities together. Gergen and McNamee (2000) describe the process of transformative dialogue as follows:

> Through dialogic means, the range of participatory voices can be expanded and traditional forms of argumentation can be abandoned in favor of mutual exploration of options, assets, and limitations. The point of such dialogue is not to battle over the "correct" interpretation; all interpretations can be correct within a particular tradition. Rather, the hope would be to emerge with an expanded array of possibilities, an array that would sensitize professionals, clients, and the surrounding community to myriad factors possibly at play and a range of possible strategies, relational

forms, or institutional arrangements that can serve as resources. Finally, with multiple options on the table, moment-to-moment adjustments to changing circumstances could replace lock-step regimens that result from confident labeling. (p. 343)

One great example of transformative dialogue in clinical practice is the groundbreaking family therapy work of Jaakko Seikkula and his colleagues with psychotic clients in Finland (Seikkula et al., 1995; Seikkula, Alakare, & Aaltonen, 2000). Seikkula and his colleagues call their treatment approach *open dialogue*. Within 24 hours of their initial call to Seikkula's clinic, families are contacted by one of his staff to gather important intake information and to schedule appointments. In the initial telephone conversation, the family is asked what involved helping professionals, providers from community social-service and healthcare organizations, key members of their social-support system, and community and spiritual leaders they would like to invite to the first meeting. At the initial meeting, the family is respectfully given plenty of room to share their problem, concerns, expectations, and special needs with the attending helpers. The family also has the unique opportunity to listen to and respond to the helping professionals' and other concerned participants' thoughts about the presenting problems, treatment planning, coordination of services, and social-network-support plans they feel can best meet the family's needs. When it comes to case decision-making and concerns that arise outside of the meetings, the client and his or her family are always invited to these other meetings. No case-related decisions are made without the family's input in the treatment-planning process.

Seikkula and his colleagues have demonstrated through their treatment-outcome research that their open dialogue approach does reduce psychiatric admissions and can successfully stabilize at-risk psychotic clients in their homes (Seikkula et al., 2000). Using a similar method with self-harming adolescents and their families has helped me to prevent my clients from being psychiatrically hospitalized unnecessarily and more rapidly has fostered a cooperative climate among the professionals from larger systems, the concerned members of the family's social network, and me.

Guidelines for Hosting Collaborative Meetings with Family-Helping Systems

When hosting meetings with family-helping systems, therapists need to converse with all participants in a relationally responsible way—that is, they must engage in actions that sustain and enhance group interactions, which can lead to the generation of a multiplicity of new problem views and meaningful actions (McNamee & Gergen, 1999). How we converse with participants in these meetings can either help or hinder our relationships with them. By being respectful, patient, curious, and a good listener helps to create a climate where all participants feel safe to share their problem views, concerns, hopes, and expectations for the client, her family, and the hosting therapist. If we expect family members and participating helpers to be open about sharing their thoughts and abandoning their unhelpful problem views and patterns of behavior, we as hosting therapists should be equally willing to challenge our unhelpful assumptions about particular helpers, resist getting wedded prematurely to particular problem explanations and solution strategies, and change our unproductive ways of interacting with meeting participants. According to Kegan and Lahey (2001):

> Seeing that we may be wrong is the yang to the much accessible and hearty yin of our need to be (and belief that we are) right. If we productively doubt ourselves, we become learners about our own perspective as well as our colleagues'. Hearing how what we are saying makes sense and doesn't (where the gaps are, or what the other is confused about) allows us to test our own thinking, be clearer about what we mean—not to better ensure that the other gets it but rather to decide whether we think we should even change our mind about what we think. (pp. 139–140)

Renowned organizational consultants Peter Senge and Margaret Wheatley believe that "the first act of a great leader is having more faith in people than they do in each other, or in themselves" (McLeod, 2001, p. 32). The leader must be a "beacon of belief" in his or her colleagues' resourcefulness, creativity, and talents. According to Senge and Wheatley, "It's believing that human nature is the blessing, not the problem" (Mcleod, 2001, p. 32). When I mobilize the family, with key members of their social network, and with the professionals from larger systems, I adopt a mindset that each of these participants is a potential ally and brings to the table a vast reservoir of strengths, expertise, and wisdom that can help us as a group to disentangle any family-helping-system knots that have developed out of concern and from well-intended interventions. In addition, the hosting therapist should encourage family-helping-system participants to stay with, honor, and pursue further the transformative potential of their very *commitments* or concerns (Kegan & Lahey, 2001).

I am also sensitive to the fact that when you bring together family members with key members of the family's social network and helping professionals representing diverse cultural and organizational contexts, can greatly influence what each participant can see and hear. This can lead to conflict, adversarial relationships, and polarization around problem views and proposed actions. However, just as problem stories can be constructed and deconstructed in conversation, so can relationships. Therefore, what appears to be a strained or adversarial relationship can and will change over time. The same process is true with participants that are highly pessimistic or wedded to certain pathological explanations or *DSM-IV* labels: There is no need to challenge them, become defensive, or parade your views, because the problem story is in a constant state of evolutionary flux and there are a multiplicity of explanations for any identified "problem." McNamee and Gergen (1999) contend that relationships are byproducts of particular forms of talk. When reflecting on particular family members' or helpers' statements, I always try to incorporate their language, metaphors, and belief system materials as a way to help to foster a cooperative relationship with them. I also avoid presenting my ideas as if they are final explanations and instead offer my thoughts with a "suspension of disbelief" (Spence, 1982).

At times a particular helper's statements in our collaborative meetings might provoke in us a strong emotional reaction and negative mindset about this provider. One useful tool the hosting therapist can use in these situations is *suspension*. According to Isaacs (1999), suspension consists of placing our assumptions about a particular group member or the way a problem situation is being viewed or handled in an imaginary cloudlike shape over our heads (like the cloudlike shapes over cartoon characters' heads) and critically analyzing our assumptions so as to understand them better and learn new viewpoints about what we are thinking or saying. Bohm (1995) contends that when the roots of thoughts are observed, thought itself seems to change for the better.

THE KEY CHARACTERISTICS OF STRONG TEAMS

Some important research findings on the characteristics of strong teams can help to inform our collaborative practices with involved helping professionals from larger systems. Donnellon (1996) has identified six characteristics of strong teams:

1. Strong team identification
2. Members feel a common perception of interdependence

3. Low power differentiation among team members

4. Close social distance

5. Collaboration and confrontation used to manage conflicts

6. Win-win negotiation style

When team members identify strongly with their teams they have a shared identity and use inclusive pronouns like "we," "our," and "us." Even if they disagree about a particular issue, they know one another well enough that any of them can speak for the group as a whole on many subjects without having to check first. Strong team members can simultaneously maintain their identification with the team and their home agencies or the organizations they represent (Donnellon, 1996).

Indicators that mark interdependence among team members include acknowledgement of mutual interests and expressions of individual needs, proposals for group actions, and solicitation of team members' views, needs, and preferences (Maltz & Borker, 1982; Tannen, 1990). A sense of interdependence is not only reflected in team members' talk, but also manifests in the management of team tasks and in the process of goal attainment.

With strong teams, members strive to minimize power differences among one another. Team talk that actively minimizes power differences between speakers and listeners includes: making requests, giving disclaimers, showing politeness, not interrupting, not dominating the floor, inviting others to change the topic, and giving apologies when necessary (Donnellon, 1996).

Strong teams display a high degree of emotional and social closeness. Members freely share their admiration, empathy, and humor with one another. Linguistic indicators of social closeness are: an informal style of communicating, claims of common views, and displays of knowledge of or concern for other team members' desires (Donnellon, 1996).

Strong teams recognize that conflict is inevitable and desirable (Donnellon, 1996). The absence of conflict in a group may be more problematic than its presence (Janis, 1972). When conflict is avoided or driven underground, it can corrode teamwork (Kegan & Lahey, 2001). Team members are focused on integrating their different viewpoints on a particular issue and use collaboration and confrontation management tactics to redefine the problem in such a way that all members' views are taken into account (Follett, 1995).

The primary negotiation style of strong teams is win-win. When it comes to negotiating goals and tasks, team talk takes the form of the elaboration of members' varying ideas, exploration of the implications of these ideas, and the reevaluation of one's own interests in light of those of the others (Donnellon, 1996; Follett, 1995).

A seventh characteristic of strong teams that I would like to add to the list is a team's ability to self-reflect. As a group, they can step outside themselves and gain a metaperspective to identify what is working, where things are breaking down, and how the dynamics from members' home agencies, organizations, or the families they treat may be playing out in the team interactions.

These empirically based findings on the key characteristics of strong work teams can inform our thinking and therapeutic actions in the context of collaborative meetings with family-helping-systems. Donnellon (1996) encourages teams to conduct a *team talk audit* to help them to determine where they may be getting stuck in their work together. The team talk audit assesses six key dimensions: *identification, interdependence, power differentiation, social distance, conflict management,* and *negotiation process.* In our collaborative meetings, a team talk audit can be used as a helpful tool to assist us in getting unstuck as a group when our conversations drift, when we appear to be skirting important issues, or when we are experiencing a knot situation. It is also important for hosting therapists to include themselves when assessing the group across all six of the team talk audit dimensions. In fact, it may be helpful for hosting therapists to ask themselves: How are my assumptions or actions in our meetings silencing the voices of some group members or affecting what we talk about? What questions can I ask to bring forth new ideas and connections?

We can assess the quality of the team talk in the collaborative process by asking ourselves: Are participants in the meeting using inclusive pronouns like "we," "our," and "us"? Do participants express a shared need with phrases like "We need to . . ."? What is the power differential—are participants giving each other space to have a voice in the conversations or interrupting one another and trying to dominate the floor? How close is the group socially—do participants speak to one another in a relaxed, informal way and feel free to express their individual needs or feelings? How are participants addressing conflicts with one another? Do they converse in a nonthreatening and nonjudgmental way? Is it okay to debate with this group? Do participants attempt to integrate dissenting views into the common perspective? Finally, we can evaluate the negotiation process by listening carefully to how participants try to find objective criteria for resolving their differences: Do they try to understand and articulate the underlying interests of all parties? Is there a win-win negotiation style operating with this group?

In helping-system-knot situations it is also important to assess the role of group members' home agencies and how organizational dynamics are playing out in the collaborative meeting context. These dynamics may take the form of meeting participants' skirting important issues, communications getting stopped up, adversarial relationships being set up, and participants' not discussing specific aspects or concerns about the presenting problems. Organizational consultants Linda Ellinor and Glenna Gerard (1998) recommend that the group leader ask the following questions when they are faced with situations where missing pieces of the problem are not being revealed or there is a strong need for fresh, innovative ideas:

- "What questions have we not been asking?"
- "What have we not focused attention on that might make a difference if it were included in our conversations?"
- "Have we been able to express the kinds of thoughts that normally remain unspoken but that would have made a difference for the better here today?"

With the help of these types of questions, the participants can gain a better understanding of how their home agency or organizational dynamics may be blocking them from taking more risks with one another, such as sharing their true concerns, catastrophic fears, important pieces of information about the problem situation, and honest feelings about one another's thoughts and actions.

CASE EXAMPLES

The Bipolar Blues

Debbie, a Caucasian 15-year-old high school sophomore, was referred to me by the school social worker after a fellow student had reported her to a dean when she noticed "several crusty cut marks on Debbie's abdomen and arms in the girls' locker room." The school social worker and

Debbie's dean had been very involved with Debbie since she entered high school. Apparently, Debbie was running around with a negative peer group that was constantly getting into trouble for being late to school and cutting classes. There also were concerns that the group was using drugs and that each member was clinically depressed. Debbie was failing her English, math, and history classes. For some time, the school social worker had been trying to get Debbie's mother, Barbara, to have a psychiatrist assess Debbie for bipolar disorder due to her "constant mood swings." The school social worker suspected that the mother's failure to follow through with her request was related to her alleged drinking problem. Debbie had shared with the school social worker that she was worried about her mother because she "drank too much." She had also reported to the school social worker that her stepfather was an alcoholic and that her mother was planning to divorce him. Debbie's weekly visits with her biological father were often disappointing and resulted in arguments over how poorly she was doing in school.

In my first family therapy session, I gave both Debbie and Barbara plenty of space to share their concerns and problem stories. Barbara felt that her daughter was "lazy" and ran around with a "negative crowd of kids." Debbie was most upset about her "drunken" stepfather "always yelling" and her mother constantly being on her "case about doing homework and chores." We were able to establish some realistic treatment goals around the completion of homework assignments and chores and Barbara's giving her daughter more space to take responsibility. Because there were a lot of concerned school personnel involved with Debbie, I had strongly recommended to the family that we meet with these professionals as a group. After securing signed consent forms to collaborate with all of the involved school professionals the family had identified, I asked the family what key members of their social network they would like to have attend the meetings as well. Barbara wanted to invite her mother, who was very actively involved in their lives. She felt that her ex-husband should be invited but not her current husband because of his lack of involvement in Debbie's life. Debbie wanted to invite her close friend Steve. I told the family that we needed to get written consent from Steve's parents and explained the rules of confidentiality. When the family left, I contacted the school social worker to organize a collaborative meeting at the school with all of the staff that the family requested.

Present at the first meeting were the school social worker, Debbie's dean, Debbie's guidance counselor, the English teacher, the math teacher, the history teacher, Barbara, Debbie, the maternal grandmother, Lillian, the biological father, Robert, and Debbie's close friend, Steve. After introductions were made, the school social worker took the lead in stating the purpose of our meeting and sharing her concerns about Debbie's emotional and academic problems. She felt that Debbie was "self-mutilating" as a way to try to "manage her intense mood swings" due to "bipolar disorder." Before Debbie had an opportunity to respond, her guidance counselor chimed in with concerns about Debbie's being "potentially suicidal." This concern grew out of a recent conversation she had had with Debbie in which the latter said in passing "I don't like my life." Debbie agreed with her social worker about the mood swings but pointed out that she had never felt like killing herself. She described her down moods as "the blues." The school social worker shared her frustration with Debbie's mother about not taking her daughter for a psychiatric evaluation. The mother responded to the school social worker that it was difficult to get away from her job during the day to take Debbie for an appointment. Suddenly, the dean entered the conversation and made it very clear to the mother that "Debbie must be psychiatrically evaluated!" He shared his concerns about her self-mutilating and depression. The mother agreed to follow up with this request. Because it was clear to me that the school social worker and the dean were not going to back down from their position about the need for a psychiatric evaluation, I offered the name and telephone number of a systems-oriented psychiatrist that I liked to work with. Everyone agreed that seeing my psychiatrist would be fine. Debbie's friend, Steve, chimed in and said that seeing a "shrink" was "not a bad thing." He mentioned that he had been on Zoloft for a while and found that it had helped him when he was depressed.

The teachers had a different take on Debbie's behavior. Debbie's English teacher wondered if she might have attention-deficit disorder due to her "poor organizational skills, losing assignments, and not paying attention in class." Debbie stood up for herself and argued that she did not have A.D.D. Her math teacher thought Debbie was smoking marijuana because of her "lack of motivation" and she had "a pungent smoke smell on her clothes." Debbie admitted to smoking cigarettes but claimed she did not do drugs. Finally, the history teacher thought that Debbie had "an attitude problem." Robert, Debbie's father, also believed that his daughter had a "negative attitude about school." It appeared that we were in the midst of a family-helping-system knot situation.

While listening to the participants' formulations about Debbie's supposed pathological conditions and behavior, I used the tool of suspension as a way to not react defensively to their positions. In an effort to introduce an alternative perspective on Debbie's situation, I took a risk and wondered aloud with curiosity what the participants appreciated about Debbie and saw as her strengths. Barbara shared with the group that her daughter was a "good artist" and can be a "big help around the house." Steve said that Debbie could be a "real stitch" and often "cracked [him] up." The school social worker agreed with Steve about Debbie's having a good sense of humor and added that she was "quite dramatic." Lillian, the maternal grandmother, shared with the group that Debbie was a "very loving and caring person." By inviting group participants to share what they appreciated about Debbie, I dramatically altered the atmosphere in the room. There was more smiling and laughter, and the participants appeared to be more hopeful about Debbie's situation. Even Debbie's pessimistic teachers offered to work with her on catch-up plans if she agreed to put in some afterschool hours to meet with them and accept their guidance. Steve offered to help Debbie break ties with the negative peer group she was affiliated with. Before scheduling our next collaborative meeting, the group generated the following recommendations:

- Debbie will see the psychiatrist for an evaluation.
- The teachers will provide extra help and create catch-up plans.
- The school social worker will see Debbie one to two times per week.
- Steve will provide added support outside of school.
- I would provide ongoing family therapy.
- Monthly family-helping-system meetings will be held.

One month later, the same participants met as a group. The psychiatrist also joined us. Debbie had been diagnosed with bipolar disorder and placed on Depakote, a mood-stabilizing medication. The school social worker, the dean, and the guidance counselor were all very pleased that a diagnosis had been determined and Debbie was finally on medication. The psychiatrist shared with the group how he arrived at this diagnosis. He also pointed out to the mother and the school staff the importance of keeping things "emotionally low-key around Debbie so as not to set off mood cycling episodes." He based this advice on his familiarity with the "expressed emotion research." Apparently, the maternal grandmother had shared with him in the evaluation session that her husband and his father had struggled with bipolar disorder and alcoholism. For the first time, the mother disclosed to the group her personal difficulties with alcoholism and how this had been a source of stress for Debbie. We had begun addressing this problem area in our last family therapy session. I commended the mother on her tremendous courage to share this important information with the group. Debbie told the group that she was very pleased that her mother finally "admitted she had a drinking problem" and was getting help for it. Other participants in the group offered their support to the mother as well. I shared with the group that the psychiatrist, who was also an addictionologist, and I would be working closely together to detox and treat Barbara on an outpatient basis. We were both concerned about Barbara's potential for experiencing severe withdrawal symptoms and wanted to tightly monitor her.

Debbie's teachers gave the group a progress report. They noted that Debbie was completing her catch-up assignments, meeting with them after school on a regular basis, and displaying a "much better attitude." The dean was pleased to report to the group that Debbie had not once ended up in his office over the past month. The school social worker said that Debbie was less depressed and appeared happier.

Steve reported to the group that Debbie had broken ties with her negative peers. Debbie said that it was this group of kids that had "taught" her "how to cut when you feel down." She proudly shared with the group that she had not cut herself at all over the past month. As a group, we decided to meet one more time in 2 months.

Two months later, we had our final meeting as an entire group. Debbie had received glowing reports from both the school staff and her family. She had pulled her F grades up to a C level. All of her teachers felt like Debbie was much more invested in her schoolwork. Debbie's parents and her grandmother told her in front of the group how proud they were of her school turnaround. Steve added that he felt Debbie was doing much better. Before ending our meeting, the parents thanked the entire group for being so helpful with Debbie's situation.

The Helping System Becomes the Family

Dana, a Caucasian 17-year-old, was referred to me by Marjorie, her school social worker, for self-mutilating behavior. Dana's mother had contacted Marjorie for the name of a private therapist who specialized in "adolescent self-injury problems." Prior to Marjorie's involvement, Dana's pediatrician was the first to discover that Dana had several burn marks on both of her arms. It was the pediatrician who strongly recommended to Dana's mother that she get Dana specialized treatment for her self-mutilating behavior. This was the second time Dana's pediatrician had referred her for therapy in the past 3 years. Two years earlier, the pediatrician had referred Dana to Dr. Brown, a psychologist who specialized in eating disorders. Dr. Brown diagnosed Dana with bulimia nervosa and continued to see her one to two times per week for individual psychotherapy. Dana also was being seen for monthly medication management sessions with Dr. Smith, a psychiatrist. Dr. Smith had placed Dana on Prozac. Despite all of the treatment Dana had received from her doctors, the bulimia problem still was not stabilized. While on the telephone with the mother, I secured verbal consent from her to talk to the school social worker for collaboration purposes. We also scheduled our first family therapy session.

Marjorie, the school social worker, had been involved with Dana for most of her academic career. Her contact with Dana was often related to the Dana's being caught in the girls' bathroom making herself throw up, her relationship problems with adolescent males, and her devastation at receiving "anything less than an A on an exam." Marjorie was unaware that Dana had been burning herself. She described the parents as "high achievers" and "very perfectionistic." The father was a highly successful businessman and seldom at home. Her mother was a board member for a social service agency. I also discovered that Dana's 10-year-old sister Melinda had leukemia, which was a major stressor for her family.

Out of curiosity, I asked Marjorie if she had had any contact with Dr. Brown or Dr. Smith. Marjorie described both of them as being "difficult to reach" and resistant to giving her much information about Dana. She suspected that both of them had psychodynamic theoretical orientations. Marjorie agreed to participate in future collaborative meetings.

In my first meeting with the family, only Dana and her mother, Lydia, came to the session. Willard, the father, was out of town on business. Lydia spent a lot of session time voicing her concerns about Dana's bulimia and burning behavior. According to Dana, the burning helped her to "feel numb" when she felt "down" or stressed out by her father. Apparently, Willard was a screamer and constantly riding her about getting good grades. Lydia pointed out to Dana that her father could be "difficult at times" but was very pleased with how well she was doing academically.

I asked the family about their past and present treatment experiences. They said they had never been in family therapy before. Both the psychologist and the psychiatrist occasionally met with Dana's parents alone. Dana felt that the treatment she was receiving was "not working." When asked why, Dana said, "It doesn't help when therapists sit there and nod their heads or are silent." Lydia, on the other hand, felt that both of the doctors had "helped Dana a lot." I explained to the family that it might be in our best interest to schedule a collaborative meeting with all of the professionals that were involved with Dana in order to coordinate services. The family gave me written consent to contact the family physician, the psychologist, the psychiatrist, and the school social worker. When I asked them about which members of their social network they wished to have in attendance at our collaborative meetings, Dana requested that her art teacher, Mrs. Jackson, attend. According to Dana, Mrs. Jackson was "real cool" and "cared a lot" about her. After listening carefully to Dana's lengthy description of her relationship with Mrs. Jackson, it was quite clear that she was an important adult inspirational other in her life.

Making contact with Dr. Brown and Dr. Smith was quite an ordeal. We played telephone tag for days, and when I eventually reached them neither doctor would speak to me without having my signed consent forms from the family in their hands. They also wanted to secure their own signed consent forms from the family before talking to me. A week later, I received calls from both of them. When I posed the idea of having all of us collaborate with the pediatrician, the school social worker, the art teacher, and the family as a group, they both balked at the idea of having the family present at the meetings. I asked both doctors about their concerns regarding including the family in our collaborative meetings. They responded that it could interfere with their "therapeutic alliances," that Dana's conversations with them were confidential, and that they wanted to keep their work with Dana separate from what other helping professionals were doing with her. However, after my lengthy conversations with both doctors, they agreed to participate in future collaborative meetings with the other involved professionals and me as long as Dana and her family were excluded from these meetings. I still felt, out of respect for Dana and her family, that they should participate in these meetings. I realized I was facing a family-helping-system knot. The pediatrician, school social worker, and art teacher, on the other hand, strongly embraced the idea of including Dana and her family in our collaborative meetings. I contacted the mother to let her know Dana's doctors' concerns and our decision to begin meeting as a provider group to try to coordinate services.

After brief introductions, I stated the purpose of these collaborative meetings and opened the floor for the participants to share their stories of involvement with Dana and her family. I was met with a few long minutes of dead silence. Finally, Marjorie began sharing her views and concerns about Dana and her family situation. She felt that Dana was under a great deal of "parental pressure to achieve academically" and believed this family dynamic contributed to her bulimia and self-mutilating problems. Mrs. Jackson disclosed that Dana had confided in her that her father was "a tyrant" and only interested in her academic success. Dr. Stanley, the pediatrician, described the father as being "difficult" and not easy to warm up to. Apparently he once had become very "verbally abusive" toward one of her nurses in the waiting room. A half hour into our meeting, it appeared that Dr. Brown and Dr. Smith were listening intently but were not planning to contribute their thoughts about Dana's situation. I took a risk with my curiosity and wondered what the doctors' thoughts were about what was going on with Dana. Dr. Brown agreed with what the other participants had said about the parents. She believed that Dana's bingeing and self-injury behaviors were her way of soothing herself when experiencing emotional distress. Her contention was that the parents, particularly the father, "failed to provide this self-soothing function for Dana to internalize" when she was much younger and viewed her as an "extention" of them. Dr. Smith agreed with Dr. Brown's formulations about Dana and her parents. She felt that the Prozac was having a "positive effect" in reducing Dana's bulimic symptoms. I shared my thoughts about Dana's turning to food and burning herself as a way to cope with the stress she was experiencing both at home and at school. I also disclosed my frustrations in trying to engage the father for family therapy. Again, I was met with total silence in the room. I decided to break the silence and invite the group to share their thoughts about continuing to meet as a group and solicit their treatment recommendations. All of the group participants agreed to meet on a monthly basis. The group members had the following recommendations:

- Marjorie and Mrs. Jackson would provide support at school.
- I would try to engage the father for family therapy.
- Dr. Brown would see Dana for weekly psychotherapy sessions.

- Dr. Smith would see Dana only for medication management.
- Monthly collaborative meetings would be held.

One month later, we met as a group to assess Dana's progress and our teamwork. For this second collaborative meeting, I decided to lay low and allow another group participant to begin our conversation. We sat for 5 minutes in silence before both the school social worker and Mrs. Jackson began to talk. Apparently, they both had a few productive meetings with Dana during which they offered a lot of support. After they both shared what they had discussed with Dana, there was dead silence in the room. Because this pattern of silence continued to repeat itself, I decided to take a risk and reflect my thoughts about what it might represent. I wondered aloud with the group if we were inadvertently replicating a pervasive pattern of interaction that was occurring in Dana's family. I shared with the group that I had experienced a similar pattern of interaction in my two family therapy sessions with the father present. The father had a tendency to dominate the floor time in our conversations and silence Dana and Lydia's voices. I also felt that the father's need to dominate and control was influencing my behavior in our collaborative meetings in terms of my need to try to take a leadership role in prompting conversations. Dr. Brown chimed in that maybe we were experiencing the "old parallel process dynamic" in our helping system. The other participants also started to make this connection as well. From this point on the group participants more freely volunteered important case material and took risks with sharing their thoughts, feelings, and concerns about Dana's situation. I also found myself feeling less compelled to adopt a leadership role in our collaborative meetings.

We ended up meeting three more times as a group. In our last meeting together, the family was invited to evaluate our work together. The father could not attend our meeting because he was out of town on business. Dana was no longer bulimic or burning herself. In my family therapy sessions, I had successfully broken the destructive interactions that were maintaining Dana's problematic behavior. I had also gotten the father to relate to Lydia and Dana in a more respectful way. Dr. Smith planned to begin weaning Dana off of Prozac. Dr. Brown had done a great job teaching Dana more constructive ways to self-sooth and cope with stress. She announced to the group her plans of terminating with Dana, which she had discussed with her in their last session. Both the school social worker and Mrs. Jackson had also observed many changes with Dana. The family and I met two more times to further consolidate their gains.

Both of these case examples illustrate how mobilizing the family, the key members of the family's social network, and the involved helping professionals from larger systems in a collaborative context can produce rapid, dramatic changes with challenging case situations. Working this way frees therapists from working in isolation with nightmarish cases and allows them to gain access to multiple perspectives and potential solution strategies.

CHAPTER 6

Going at it Alone: One-Person Family Therapy

Don't compromise yourself. You are all you've got.

—Janis Joplin

WITH SOME SELF-HARMING ADOLESCENT cases, therapists may experience grave difficulties engaging all family members for treatment, encounter what appears to be parental sabotage between sessions, or find that the parents' own issues with mental health, substance abuse, or marital or postdivorce conflict are contributing to the maintenance of the adolescent's symptoms. In some cases, conjoint family therapy may prove to be counterproductive due to intense parent-adolescent conflicts, destructive interactions, and the presence of multiple-symptom bearers. Additionally, older adolescents who are developmentally preparing to launch from their families may benefit more from individual therapy because it better addresses their individual and family issues.

Treating individuals with a strong family focus is not a new concept. Family therapy pioneer Murray Bowen often worked with individual family members as agents of change for their families. He would have them *take a voyage home* as an adult and directly address problematic intergenerational patterns of interaction, conflicts, and triangles with key family members to gain better insight into their family dynamics. Bowen (1978) also had his clients engage in *reversals*—that is, they deliberately acted differently than usual with family members with whom they had conflicts or who tried to triangulate them into coalitions against other family members.

Szapocznik and Kurtines (1989) have demonstrated that one-person family therapy is as effective as conjoint brief strategic family therapy in stabilizing adolescent substance abusers' behavior and changing problem-maintaining family interactions, beliefs, and role behaviors. In their study, the substance-abusing adolescents served as the agents of change for their families. This important research demonstrates that it is possible to effectively treat an adolescent—as well as the entire family system—without having his or her family members involved in the treatment process. I have found that a modified solution-based, one-person family therapy approach is a successful way of treating self-harming adolescents.

ONE-PERSON FAMILY THERAPY WITH ADOLESCENTS: MAJOR THERAPEUTIC EXPERIMENTS AND STRATEGIES

The adolescent's treatment goal and the nature of her family problem should dictate what therapeutic experiments and strategies the therapist selects or coconstructs with her. The first step is to determine with her what target problem areas she wishes to address first. For example, the adolescent may establish an individual treatment goal for herself, such as learning how to manage her emotions or stressful situation better. She may also want to work on changing troublesome repetitive behaviors that her parents exhibit, such as incessant nagging or yelling at her. In discussing goals, the therapist can teach the adolescent cognitive and mood-management tools.

The second step is to conduct an *enactment analogue* (Szapocznik & Kurtines, 1989). This entails having the client guide the therapist in mapping out on a flip chart a detailed circular description of the parents' nagging and yelling behaviors and how she typically responds to them. Once a good visual map of the key problem-maintaining patterns of interaction is drawn, the adolescent and the therapist can determine together at what locus points to intervene. A wide range of pattern-intervention experiments and strategies can be employed to disrupt these problem-maintaining patterns of interaction. Many of the adolescent clients I have worked with have found the following therapeutic experiments to be quite effective in altering their parents' negative behaviors: the *do-something-different task* (de Shazer, 1985), *pretend-the-miracle-happened task* (de Shazer, 1991), and the *secret surprise* (O'Hanlon & Weiner-Davis, 1989). In situations in which the parents are extremely emotionally disconnected from the adolescent or do not respond to her interventions, the focus of treatment becomes learning coping strategies, life skills, and creating a life outside the family. In these clinical situations, I may also involve inspirational others, older siblings, and close friends for added support.

Some adolescents in one-person family therapy may voice a strong desire to confront a parent or sibling with whom they have had long-standing conflicts. As a way to constructively manage this anxiety-provoking task, I may recommend that these adolescents and I use role-playing or visualization to boost their self-confidence and mentally prepare them. I also conduct a premortem (Klein, 1998) evaluation with them to carefully assess how things could fall apart with their intervention efforts and to generate back-up plans if things happen to fall apart.

"I HAVE BPD"

One late afternoon at my office I received a frantic call from Stephanie, whose 18-year-old daughter, Natalie, was "cutting and burning herself." According to Stephanie, Natalie had been engaging in these forms of self-harming behavior since the ninth grade. Stephanie and her ex-husband, Walter, had also called "a few reputable hospital-based programs" that treated self-mutilators. One of the programs had given the parents my name. Stephanie described Natalie as not being "too thrilled" about pursuing therapy again. Apparently she had not liked the past therapists and psychiatrists she had seen. Stephanie was also quite concerned about Natalie's "failing her first year of college, being depressed, abusing cocaine and alcohol, overspending, and having relationship difficulties." Natalie had been an exceptional student throughout her academic career and had started college at the age of 17. There was "intense conflict" between Natalie and her father. Natalie reported that her mother was "weak" and "unable to stand up to" her father. Her 27-year-old brother Hal had a great job in a western state and usually saw her one or two times a year.

The First Session

Natalie and Stephanie were present for the first session. After spending a sufficient amount of time joining with each family member around their strengths and resources, I asked the family what the specific trigger for seeking therapy at this point was. The following transcript is taken from the beginning of our session when I was trying to elicit what the family viewed as the "right" problem to address first. I tried to renegotiate the problem into more solvable terms by redefining it as a relationship pattern problem, and I secured Natalie's theory of change and expectations from me as a therapist.

Stephanie: What did you diagnose yourself as sweetie?

Natalie: I have BPD.

Matthew: Excuse me, but what is BPD?

Natalie: Borderline personality disorder!

Matthew: Is that what you think is going on with you?

Natalie: It doesn't define who I am but it seems to fit my situation. Self-mutilation is a symptom of a problem. We have difficulty connecting past experiences to present experiences. . . . We don't learn from our mistakes. Emotional reactions are disproportionate to the actual stimuli. I knew there was something wrong and I was going through all of the books and looking on the Internet for a description that worked. And I kept coming back to it again and again. It was the only description that seemed to fit. I think it describes what I need to be treated for.

Matthew: I'm curious, before you stumbled upon this BPD label what would you have called what was going on with you?

Natalie: I knew I was depressed.

Matthew: To help me better understand what is going on in your life that depresses you, how about if we start with your family since I don't know much about your family situation. Is there anything that your mother does that depresses you?

Natalie: No . . . my mother and I get along pretty well.

Matthew: Does your father do anything that depresses you?

Natalie: He doesn't depress me . . . he makes me angry. We can't have a discussion like a human being. It has to be screaming and confrontation—in your face. He never listens to the other person. (*crying*) It's hard feeling that just you is never enough. If I was one thing, he wanted me to be another thing. If I got a B, I should have gotten an A. It's never enough!

Matthew: I imagine it has been quite difficult to cope with the way your father relates to you like that. When your mother first called here her biggest concern was that you were supposedly burning and cutting yourself. If this is so, what does the burning and cutting do for you? When and where do you usually do it?

Natalie: I have not cut myself since the ninth grade. Well, when I am real upset about something . . . I get into a different place and just start burning myself. When I try to become more aware of what I am doing, I can stop it.

Matthew: Your mother was telling me that you have been in therapy before and that you did not find it to be that helpful to you. So in order for me to be most helpful to you, I would like to know, if you were to work with the most perfect therapist, what would he or she do that you would find to be the most helpful?

Natalie: Well I don't need someone to just sit there and listen, I need someone to help!

Matthew: You mean like give you tools or things to do?

Natalie: Yeah, I wanted to work with someone who has worked with people who are borderline or have symptoms like mine. A lot of therapists who used to work with me thought I was this manipulative kid. The last psychiatrist I saw was the most nervous man alive! He put me on Prozac. I don't want drugs. I would rather be crazy than numb!

At this point in the session, I shifted gears and asked the miracle question. I was now interested in hearing how Natalie and her mother envisioned their ideal treatment outcome pictures and in having us begin establishing a well-formed treatment goal together. Both Natalie and her mother had very little to say in response to the miracle question. For Natalie, the first sign of a miracle occurring would be being "better at communicating about things that hurt me." The mother also felt that a real miracle would be Natalie's "being more communicative about things that bothered her" rather than "burning herself."

Matthew: I'm curious, are there any tiny pieces of the miracle already happening a little bit right now?

Natalie: I had a party a week ago and I was mad about something. I went into the kitchen and was about to burn myself and stopped myself.

Matthew: Are you aware of how you did that? I mean, did you tell yourself something that worked?

Natalie: I said to myself this is so stupid to burn yourself. I told myself that it was okay to be angry. It's okay to be this person.

Matthew: Wow! That's incredible that you were able to do that and gain that wisdom about your situation.

Natalie: I've been talking to my friends a little more about the things that bother me. Another thing that would be like a miracle would be my emotions not going over the top.

Matthew: Anything else you can think of that you have been doing that has been helping?

Natalie: I have been opening up to my mother about things that bother me.

Matthew: How has that been helpful?

Natalie: She has been very supportive.

Matthew: Stephanie, have you observed any pieces of the miracle happening with Natalie's situation?

Stephanie: Well, she has been talking with me more about her friends, school, and her father.

Matthew: Is that different for her to do that with you?

Stephanie: Yes, especially lately with everything that's going on with her. As far as I know, she has not burned herself in a few weeks.

Matthew: Is that so Natalie?

Natalie: I have not burned myself in 3 weeks.

Matthew: Wow, that's incredible! How have you been able to do that?

Natalie: I don't know. I guess I am talking more with friends. I have the type of friends that demand to know what's up with me. They won't accept "I don't know" with me. My friend Cecile is a very assertive person and cares a lot about me. She's good for me.

Matthew: How will you know that you have really succeeded here?

Natalie: I will be able to tell someone that I am angry.

Matthew: I would like to get a rating where things have been, with your ability to tell someone you are angry and not burning yourself a month before you came here and where you rate things now. On a scale from 1 to 10, with 10 being fairly consistent with telling others that you are angry instead of burning yourself and 1 being not saying a word to others and burning yourself, where would you have rated yourself a month ago?

Natalie: At a 5.

Matthew: How about you, Stephanie? Where would you have rated things a month ago?

Stephanie: I would have to say she was probably at a 4.

Matthew: What about now, Natalie? Where would you rate things today?

Natalie: At a 6 or a 7.

Matthew: Wow! Would you give yourself a 7− or a 6+?

Natalie: I would have to say that I'm probably at a 7−.

Matthew: What steps have you taken to get from a 5 to a 7−?

Natalie: I'm getting better at communicating to others about things that hurt me, telling myself that it is stupid to burn myself when I'm angry.

Matthew: Is there anything else you have been telling yourself that seems to help?

Natalie: Tell myself that it is okay to be angry.

Matthew: What about you, Stephanie? Where would you rate your daughter now?

Stephanie: I would have to say she is probably at a 7.

Matthew: What steps have you seen her take to get from a 4 to a 7?

Stephanie: She's been much more open with me lately. She stopped burning herself.

Matthew: Let's say, Natalie, I see you in a week's time and you come in here and precede to tell me that you made further progress and took some steps up to an 8−. What will you tell me you did?

Natalie: I would have gotten better at communicating things that hurt me to my mother or my friends.

At this point in the interview, I took an intersession break to write my editorial reflection and come up with a therapeutic experiment in line with Natalie's initial treatment goal for herself. When we reconvened, I shared my editorial reflection with the family, offered two therapeutic experiments, and invited the family's feedback on how they felt our initial meeting went and any helpful advice they had for me in terms of adjustments I could make in our work together. I began my reflection by sharing with the mother how impressed I was with how supportive and committed she had been to Natalie during these past rough periods in her life. I also complimented the mother on noticing that Natalie had already stopped burning herself. I complimented Natalie on how struck I was by her tremendous resourcefulness and insightfulness in trying to figure out what was going on with her and by how well she guided me in how I as a therapist could best help her. I also complimented her on the big steps she had already taken to stop burning herself—on her use of such helpful self-talk as telling herself: "It's stupid to burn myself" and "It's okay to be angry." Finally, I complimented Natalie on her new ability to communicate to her friends and her mother about things that hurt her. I pointed out how most adults struggle with this ability and can't assert themselves.

I offered Natalie and her mother two therapeutic experiments. Stephanie was asked to pretend over the next week to be a super sleuth like Miss Marple and pull out her imaginary magnifying glass. She was to notice on a daily basis further steps Natalie took to communicate to others about things that made her angry or hurt her and whatever else she saw her do to keep from burning herself. Natalie was asked to notice on a daily basis the various things she would be doing to avoid the temptation to allow her "emotions to go over the top" and to slip back into burning herself. To help cover the back door in the event of Natalie's having a burning slip over the next week, I shared with the family that there is often a hangover period once family members change, and the road can be rocky enough to cause some back sliding, but they needed to remember that they would not be back at square one if this happened.

To close the session, I invited the family to share with me how they felt the meeting went. Natalie was quick to say that she found it to be very helpful. What she appreciated most about the session was my being very active and underscoring what was already working with her situation. Stephanie shared how pleased she was with Natalie's progress and said this was the first time she had realized how angry her daughter had been with her father for years. This information had helped her to understand why Natalie had turned to burning, substance abuse, overspending, and underachieving in school. When I asked the family if there was anything they wanted me to change or adjust in how I was working with them, Natalie voiced a strong desire to see me "individually" for our future sessions. Stephanie agreed that it might be more helpful to Natalie at this time for her to have her own private time with me.

The Second Session

A week later, Natalie came in much more self-confident. She did not have one burning incident all week! Apparently she had come very close to having a self-harming episode when her father started to lecture her about her "not working over the summer" and "being irresponsible." Her "emotions were over the top" when she returned home from seeing her father; however, she called her good friend Cecile for support instead of burning herself. I gave Natalie a big high-five and showered her with compliments for constructively managing a stressful and emotionally charged situation with her father. According to Natalie, her father was "so busy listening to himself talk" that he hadn't heard her say that she had already applied for several jobs and was doing some babysitting in her neighborhood. I checked in with Natalie to see where she rated herself on her scale of goal attainment. She felt that she had made it up to an 8−.

I shared my concerns about how tenuous things were in her relationship with her father. When I offered the idea that she bring her father into our next session to address their relationship difficulties more directly, she felt that "it would be a waste of time."

In past family therapy sessions, she said, he had tended to blame her, dominated the floor, and challenged the therapists. At this point, I decided to do a U-turn and approach this problem area from a different direction. I decided to map out on the flip chart the repetitive problem-maintaining pattern of interaction that Natalie and her father typically fell prey to when they were together. It was clear while I mapped out how they communicated with one another that the father typically set Natalie off in their conversations. Her part in the maintenance of this problem interaction was pushing his buttons by swearing at him, talking over him, and walking away from him. As a therapeutic experiment, I proposed the do-something-different task (de Shazer, 1985) as a way to help navigate this repetitive family minefield with her father. Natalie was willing to do anything at this point to change her relationship with her father.

Besides complimenting Natalie on all of her great progress, I armed her with some additional tools she could use when her emotions went over the top. I taught her meditation techniques and encouraged her to engage in soul work (Kammen & Gold, 1998) over our break period. Natalie planned to get back into her creative writing and workout routines. As a vote of confidence, I gave Natalie the option of coming back in 3 or 4 weeks. She elected to come back in 3 weeks.

The Third Session

Three weeks later, Natalie returned with a glowing progress report. She rated herself at a 9−. Natalie had not burned herself once. She was writing daily, working out more regularly, and still babysitting. She also found meditating helpful. Natalie also had two opportunities to experiment with doing things differently in relationship to her father. The first time they were together after our previous session, he had started to lecture her about how she "should lead her life." Rather than swearing at and interrupting him, she took some deep breaths and thanked him for all of his suggestions. Natalie started to laugh while she shared this story with me. Apparently the father immediately stopped lecturing her when she responded this way and began to pay more attention to what she had to say.

To help consolidate her gains, I asked her what would she have to do at this point to go backwards. Natalie confidently stated that she could not see herself going backwards. However, she did point out that if she failed to take action to prevent her emotions from going over the top, she probably would start burning herself again. She also said that failing to communicate about what hurt to her friends and her mother would also be a problem. Finally, "fighting back" with her father would also be a lost cause. When I asked Natalie when she would like to come back, in 6 or 8 weeks, she confidently responded that she would see me in 8 weeks.

The Fourth Session

After a lengthy 2-month vacation from therapy, Natalie returned reporting considerable progress. There were no burning episodes. She had landed a fun job at a gas station. Natalie and her father were getting along much better. She was starting to make plans to get back into college again. Natalie rated herself at a 10− on the scale. When asked what she would need to do to get to a flat 10, Natalie made it clear to me that there was no such thing as a perfect 10! We decided to meet one more time before she went off to college in a month.

The Fifth and Final Session

I spent the bulk of Natalie's last session amplifying and consolidating her gains. I also tapped her wisdom as an expert consultant to see what ideas she could offer me to help other young women just like her. In this last session, I was quite impressed with Natalie's wisdom, great sense of humor, and eloquence. Finally, I inducted Natalie into my alumni association of former expert clients. Natalie expressed her desire to help me in the future with other young women that self-harm. The following transcript consists of some of the highlights from our last meeting together.

Matthew: If I were to invite you back as a guest consultant, what advice would you give a young woman just like yourself about how she could stop hurting herself?

Natalie: Start saying it. Start saying whatever is making you burn yourself. What we do is turn it all inwards. We are afraid of confrontation. We are afraid of letting our emotions all out. Someone in our lives has told us that it is not right to be angry and it's not right to say how you are feeling and that's a horrible way to raise a human being. So I would tell her you're a woman, you're amazing, and if you feel something, you have every right to say it!

Matthew: Wow! That was so eloquent and beautiful. Any other helpful advice you would have for this young woman?

Natalie: Find something that makes you happy. I work at a gas station and I love it. Get to a place where you decide that you are going to come first.

Matthew: What do you mean by that?

Natalie: Before, I would go out for dinner because my friends wanted me to. I would try to quit smoking because my friends wanted me to. Now, I am going to do things for me.

Matthew: I want to test the waters now. What would you have to do to go backwards at this point?

Natalie: When I'm with others and get depressed, I usually go home. If I started taking myself too seriously again . . . you know, reading too much into things, worrying too much about meanings, relationships, intimacy. You put too much pressure on yourself.

Matthew: How do you view yourself differently now as opposed to how you used to view yourself?

Natalie: I feel stronger. I don't worry as much about how other people perceive me. I now want to do things for me, not what others want for me. By flipping the whole focus it came out of her.

Matthew: You came out of an old shell . . . and now you are flapping your wings and are in charge of you and that's what counts right now. It's interesting the way women are perceived in our society and socialized in their families and through the generations, receiving messages all of the time—"you need to be pretty" or "you need to act like a lady." All of these unhelpful messages . . . it is no surprise why women hurt themselves or develop eating disorders.

Natalie: Yeah, I eat like a horse so I could never have an eating disorder. A lot of women have said, and I completely agree, that we wish we had the discipline to be anorexic!

Matthew: You know, when we first started—I will be quite honest with you, I'm not a big fan of labels because they become identities and self-fulfilling prophecies—I remember you tossed around the label of borderline personality disorder, which is a pretty harsh brand stamp and something I don't find to be a very helpful label. I was wondering, before when you were talking about shedding your old skin and how you are now different from the person you used to be, have you shedded that label?

Natalie: It's really funny . . . it frustrates me that therapists are so afraid to give me a label! They were not afraid to give me one of the depression labels, the manic depression label—anything you can medicate. But if you say borderline, everyone gets all scared because you can't medicate that!

Matthew: Let me just say that there isn't any hard-line research that has grounded what a borderline is in reality. It is like a gray-area label.

Natalie: I know it used to be like that but there are now a lot more clinics that only deal with the symptoms of borderlines. We are hard to diagnose because we come with so many other things. We suck up every disorder we can—mega-fucked up! And it was like I didn't mind being labeled, because the label was what I used to beat it. Because if you don't have a label and you don't know what it is, you can't beat it! If I had not found it and done all of the research, I would have not been able to recognize what was wrong . . . the reactions that were completely insane for everyone else. I had to start fighting me!

Matthew: Do you feel that you beat it?

Natalie: I don't think I could ever beat it. I conquered it, I guess!

The 6-Month Follow-up

I spoke with Natalie on the telephone 6 months after our last session. Natalie reported that she had had no burning episodes, no substance use, was getting along much better with her father, was managing her moods better, was in better physical health, and was working and attending college.

Natalie's case clearly demonstrates that it is possible to stabilize the identified client's symptoms without having all family members present in sessions. The case also illustrates that one family member can be helped to serve as the agent of change, possibly altering longstanding problem-maintaining interactions, beliefs, and role behaviors in the family. Finally, the use of a one-person family therapy approach helped to support Natalie's developmental needs.

CHAPTER 7

Riding the Waves of Change: Goal-Maintenance and Solution-Enhancement Strategies

In almost every bad situation, there is the possibility of a transformation by which the undesirable may be changed into the desirable.

—Nyanaponika Thera

ONCE THE ADOLESCENT HAS STOPPED engaging in self-harming behavior and family members' problem-saturated views and ways of interacting with her have changed, the therapist has to take the time to amplify and consolidate their gains and arm them with the necessary tools for constructively managing inevitable slips. As Prochaska and his colleagues (1994) have found in their extensive research on how people change, slips are very much a part of the change process and it is the responsibility of the therapist to prepare clients for them. Predicting hangover periods and the likelihood of slips helps to keep clients on their toes and not view setbacks as being disastrous events (Fisch, Weakland, & Segal, 1982; Selekman, 1993; Selekman & Todd, 1991; White, 1986). In addition, the therapist must collaborate with the adolescent, her family, key members of their social network, and professionals from larger systems to determine what specific goal-maintenance and solution-enhancement tools and strategies can best strengthen the adolescent's and family's abilities to stay on track and successfully ride the waves of change.

Active involvement on the part of the family, key members of their social network, and professionals from larger systems is an important part of helping the adolescent to stay on track, constructively manage slips, and cocreate compelling future realities. In this chapter, I present a variety of goal-maintenance and solution-enhancement tools and strategies that can be used to amplify and consolidate the adolescent's and family's gains/ I also give troubleshooting guidelines and effective treatment strategies for managing clients who are struggling to comply with the collaboratively planned treatment regimen and are experiencing frequent slips or major setbacks. Finally, I discuss how I like to celebrate the adolescent's and family's changes at the end family therapy.

GOAL-MAINTENANCE AND SOLUTION-ENHANCEMENT ARE A FAMILY AND INVOLVED-HELPERS AFFAIR

It has been my clinical experience that failing to actively involve self-harming adolescents' families, key members of their social networks, and involved professionals from larger systems in the goal-maintenance and solution-enhancement process can set the stage for these youth to continually relapse. I find it most beneficial to invite these individuals to take part in the dialogue about what the adolescent specifically identifies as her key triggers for self-harming episodes. These triggers can take many forms, including self-defeating, irrational thoughts; unpleasant feelings; negative family and extended family interactions; involved helping professionals' frequently sharing their concerns and putting too much pressure on her to address her "problems"; associating with other self-harming peers; rejection by peers; seeing a razor blade or other object she used to self-harm with; and flashbacks or other painful memories. I also invite the adolescent to share with family members and the involved helpers what specifically they are doing that helps her to stay on track. By having all participants present and actively participating in these goal-maintenance and solution-enhancement discussions, they can learn specific details from the adolescent not only about what they should avoid doing with her but also about what they should do more of.

Unlike in the addiction field, where relapse prevention mostly consists of having clients identify negative triggers that promote craving and the likelihood of slips occurring (Gorski, 1989; Marlatt & Gordon, 1985), I like to have self-harming clients keep track of their *positive triggers* as well. Positive triggers can take the form of the adolescent's participating in healthful activities that relax her and produce pleasant feelings or specific solution-maintaining patterns of the participants' behavior and thought that comfort her when she is experiencing emotional distress and help to support her efforts to stay on track. The following goal-maintenance and solution-enhancement tools and strategies can be used to help to amplify and consolidate the gains of the adolescent and her family.

Consolidating Questions

Consolidating questions invite all members of the solution-determined system to make distinctions between old and new patterns of behavior and describe in great detail the future reality they would like to have (de Shazer, 1991; O'Hanlon & Weiner-Davis, 1989; Selekman, 1993, 1997). I begin asking consolidating questions as early in treatment as the first family session as a positive way to amplify and solidify their self-generated pretreatment changes. In second and subsequent sessions, these questions can help to increase family members' awareness about what they are already doing that helps as well as what they are doing that is problematic. Finally, I like to invite family members to imagine and detail future pictures of themselves as a group and as individuals continuing to pioneer a positive new direction with their lives. Some examples of general consolidating questions I frequently use with families are:

- "What would you have to do to go backwards at this point?"
- "What steps will you take to prevent a major backslide?"
- "What will you tell yourself to help you quickly get back on track?"
- "What specific things are your parents and your grandmother (lives with the family) doing that help you the most right now?"
- "In what ways has Miss Sharpe's (the adolescent's inspirational other) involvement in your life made a difference?"
- "When they are not nagging or yelling (identified problem-maintaining parental behaviors), how do your parents relate to you in ways that make a difference in terms of how you think, feel, and want to respond to them?"
- "What kinds of things do your closest friends do that really help you to stay on track?"
- "How do you view yourself differently now as opposed to how you viewed yourself when cutting/burning was getting the best of you?"

- "How are your new ways of viewing yourself and your situation making a difference for you today? How about with your parents? What about with your teachers? How about with your friends?"

Future Vision Questions

Once clients have made considerable progress in treatment, one way to further empower them and consolidate their gains is to invite them to take a voyage into future places in their lives where things continue to go well. The videotape metaphor (O'Hanlon & Weiner-Davis, 1989) and the imaginary crystal ball (Selekman, 1993, 1997) are tools that therapists can use to initiate this future vision process with everyone attending the family sessions. Future vision questions help to create a therapeutic climate that is ripe for fostering positive self-fulfilling prophecies for families. Some examples of future vision questions are:

- "Let's say we gazed into my imaginary crystal ball. Six months down the road, what further changes will I see happening with this family that will most surprise me? What else?"
- "When you stop coming here, what fun or enjoyable activities will all of you be doing during this time?"
- "Let's say somebody handed me a videotape of you and your family one year from now. What will I see happening on the video that you think I will be the most pleased with? What else?"
- "What aspect of the client's improvement or change will surprise you (the school social worker, a concerned teacher, a close friend) the most a month from now? What else?"
- "Let's say that next year on this very same day you have a 1-year anniversary party celebrating your family's victory in conquering your problems and in no longer needing any further counseling. Who will you invite to the party? What will your guests say about you in their speeches? In what ways will their words make a difference to you? What new, positive things will each of you be eager to share about yourselves with your guests?"

Questions That Invite Client Expertise After Slips

As mentioned earlier, slips go with the territory of change. Therefore, it is helpful for therapists to educate their clients and the involved helping professionals about the inevitability of slips and positively relabel them as opportunities for comeback practice (Tomm & White, 1987), as teachers of valuable wisdom about where the client and her family need to work together better as a team or build in more structure, and as springboards for further changes. At all costs, therapists must maintain an optimistic stance and not become paralyzed by their clients' pessimism following a slip. If we expect our clients to get back on track rapidly, our expectancy for change will have a positive impact on their behavior and instill hope. Berg and Miller (1992) have created a number of useful questions they ask substance-abusing clients to normalize their slips, elicit their expertise, and empower them to get back on track quickly. Some examples of the types of questions therapists can ask their clients following slips are:

- "How did you manage not to cut yourself the rest of the days of the week after your slip on Monday?"
- "What did you tell yourself or do that helped you to get back on track quickly?"
- "After the slip, did your parents do anything differently that you found helpful?"
- "How was this slip different from the last one?"
- "Did you learn anything from this slip that you will immediately put into practice?"
- "What do you need to do more of to stay on track?"
- "What would your (parents/school social worker/grandmother/ psychiatrist) say you need to do more of to help you to stay on track?"

Fire Drill Training

Similar to students' performing fire drills at school, families and involved helpers can practice working together in intervening early to prevent slips that appear to be brewing, as well as rehearse what steps each will take to constructively manage a slip. The adolescent can present a current stressful situation she is grappling with that, if left unchecked, could lead to a cutting or burning episode. Taking the lead, the adolescent can educate family members and helpers about the steps they could take to help her to cope and manage this stressor. I usually have the adolescent direct a dramatization of a hypothetical scenario in which she slips back into cutting or burning herself. As the director, she can instruct family members and the involved helpers on what specific things each should do to help her out in this situation. The fire drill practice sessions strengthen families' problem-solving capacities and abilities to confidently and constructively manage any future slips that might occur.

Bringing in an Audience to Reflect on the Adolescent's and Family's Changes

Another powerful way therapists can highlight the changes and gains adolescents and their families have made is to recruit an audience of people they would like to invite to a session in which the client and her family share their new ways of viewing themselves and interacting with one another and any other important discoveries they have made (Epston, 1998, 2000; White, 1995). The audience can consist of relatives, close friends, inspirational others, and representatives from larger systems who may have been involved in the referral process at the beginning of treatment but did not regularly attend family or collaborative meetings with the therapist. After listening to family members reflect on their important discoveries and various changes, the audience can reflect with interest, respect, and a wish to understand on what they heard. They also can share how their views about the client and her family have changed by reflecting on how things used to be at the beginning of treatment and how things are different now. The process of retelling and rehearing helps thicken and enrich the family's new, evolving self-stories (Epston, 1998, 2000; White, 1995). This process also decentralizes the therapist's role in the family's life, allowing their relationships with key members of the invited audience to become the context for their self-discoveries and future gains.

My Positive Trigger Log

One way to help the adolescent to stay on track after she stops her self-harming behavior is to have her log her positive triggers daily. When introducing the positive trigger log to the adolescent, I first have her think about and write down a list of things she has done or is presently doing that contribute to her having *high-hope thoughts* (McDermott & Snyder, 1999), such as the self-talk statement "I feel confident," and to her feeling emotionally, physically, and socially strong. I then have her prepare lists of things her parents, close friends, relatives, and involved helpers from larger systems are doing that also contribute to her to staying on track. I then invite the adolescent to explain in great detail how each of these triggers specifically contributes to her self-confidence and self-effi-cacy. After processing her lists, I have her fill in a blank *My Positive Trigger Log* (see p. 172) form and give her a stack of forms to fill out on a daily basis over the next week or prior to our next scheduled appoint-ment. The positive trigger log provides daily structure for the adolescent, increases her self-awareness of what works, and serves as a valuable resource that helps her to constructively manage high levels of emotional distress or crisis situations.

Interviewing the Adolescent's Most Potent Solution

Another highly effective way to solidify the adolescent's gains and reduce the likelihood of future slips is to *interview the adolescent's most potent solution strategy*. In a similar fashion to interviewing the problem (Epston, 1998, 2000), I will play the part of a *New York Times* reporter covering a story on the adolescent's most potent solution strategy. The adolescent is instructed to pretend to be her most potent solution strategy. This strategy can consist of useful self-talk or other coping or problem-solving strategies that help her to stay on track. I have used this in-session therapeutic experiment both in the company of all members of the solu-tion-determined system and during my individual session time with the adolescent in the context of family therapy. When the family and other helpers are present, they are free to ask questions of the most potent solu-tion strategy throughout the interviewing process. The following case illustrates how effective this technique can be.

Rene, a depressed 17-year-old African American, used to cut herself several times a day as a form of self-punishment. Her parents were devout Baptists and highly strict with her. After her mother caught her having sex with her boyfriend, Tyrone, in her bedroom, the parents forced her to sever her relationship and took away all of her privileges for 2 months. In addition, they would remind Rene on a daily basis that she had "sinned" and tell her how ashamed of her they were. The guilt Rene was experi-encing became so overwhelming that she turned to cutting herself with a razor for "being bad."

By using cognitive therapy techniques like having her dispute her cen-tral irrational thought of "I am a bad person," creating internal self-talk tapes, and using visualization, we were able together to stop the cutting

MY POSITIVE TRIGGER LOG					
Date	What I Did	My Parents/ Siblings	Friends	Other Involved Helpers	How Specifically Helpful

behavior. Although the parents, still believing "Rene was the problem," pulled out of treatment by our third session, they granted me permission to continue working with their daughter alone. I had no problem with the parents dropping out of treatment because Rene was the true customer for change; the parents were still in the precontemplation stage of readiness to change (Prochaska, 1999).

Rene identified her self-generated internal self-talk tape "I made a mistake but I am not a bad person" as her most potent solution strategy. I then proceeded to interview Rene while she played the part of her most potent self-generated internal self-talk tape.

Matthew: In what ways are you helping Rene be more in charge of herself versus her being vulnerable to cutting again?

Rene: I talk to her and tell her she is not a bad person and don't take it out on yourself.

Matthew: It is clear that since you have been involved in Rene's life you have been instrumental in helping her turn things around. Are you aware if Rene views herself differently now?

Rene: Well, I know she no longer feels guilty about getting busted in her bedroom with Tyrone. She seems to be happier.

Matthew: Could you rate for me on a scale from 1 to 10, with 10 being totally confident, how confident are you today that you will be able to withstand attempts on cutting's behalf to reassert its influence on Rene again?

Rene: I would probably say things were at an 8. I am feeling pretty strong right now because Rene's confidence is helping me out. I mean, there have been some real tough times lately—her parents still have an attitude about her, you know, and she misses not seeing Tyrone as much. You know, she mostly sees him at school.

Matthew: Let's say I interview you again in a month. What will you tell me you did to move yourself up to a 9 on the confidence scale?

Rene: I would have her not only count on me, you know, but do other things to take care of herself.

Matthew: Like what?

Rene: Well, she's a good dancer. She'll go clubbing again. Hang out more with Anita. Anita always makes Rene feel good.

Longer Time Intervals Between Sessions

Therapists can give a vote of confidence to clients and begin to decentralize their position in clients' lives by offering them longer time intervals between sessions. I find it most useful and empowering to clients to begin this process as early as their second family therapy session, particularly if there has been a great deal of progress in a week's time. Some families self-generate a number of important pretreatment changes while they wait for an opening in the therapist's schedule or if there are a few weeks of lag time between their appointment and their initial call to the office. In these situations, I have found it most advantageous to spend the bulk of the initial sessions amplifying and consolidating their gains, assessing with them if their situations are good enough now to terminate therapy or if they wish to leave the therapy door open, in which case I schedule a check-up session 6–8 weeks down the road.

A cautionary note: It is important that the therapist talk with the family about how comfortable they feel with taking a vacation from therapy when it is offered as a treatment option. Some clients' theories of change and expectations of their therapists may dictate weekly visits for a period of time. This especially may be true of families that have experienced multiple treatment failures and feel that therapy should be weekly and long-term. As a rule of thumb, I typically ask families when they would like to come back for their next appointments. Before sending families off on their vacations from therapy, I always plant in their minds the possibility that a slip might occur while they are riding the waves of change.

TROUBLESHOOTING TREATMENT GUIDELINES FOR CONSTRUCTIVELY MANAGING ADOLESCENTS EXPERIENCING FREQUENT SLIPS

In some cases, the family, key members of their social network, and involved helping professionals may not adhere to the mutually planned treatment regimen, and the adolescent and her family may experience frequent slips. In these situations, therapists first should take a look at how they may be contributing to the maintenance of the problems. They also should assess the cultural roles and the power imbalances related to gender that may be getting played out among the adolescent's peers, other concerned members of her social network, and the larger systems professionals. The following troubleshooting treatment guidelines can be used to identify key areas that need to be addressed in the therapeutic process:

- Differing opinions regarding what constitutes change may exist between the therapist, the family, key members of their social network, and involved helping professionals.
- The adolescent and/or family may lack an adequate support system.
- There may be a mismatch between the therapist's approach and the adolescent and/or her family's present treatment needs.
- A piece of the presenting problem or an emotionally troubling family secret may not have been addressed.
- The therapist and/or involved helpers may be stuck doing "more of the same."
- Important cultural issues and gender power imbalances may not have been addressed.
- A longstanding antagonistic relationship may exist between the parents and/or the adolescent and an involved professional in a position of power who has been unwilling to participate in collaborative meetings or collaborate alone with the therapist.
- The therapist may have a weak therapeutic alliance with one or both parents.
- The family may have failed to inform the therapist of other key professionals from larger systems, therapists or psychiatrists, or members of their social network that are actively involved and part of the problem's life-support system.
- Behind-the-scenes parental or sibling sabotage may be undermining the adolescent's progress.
- Parents' marital or postdivorce conflicts, mental health issues or substance abuse, may be adversely affecting the adolescent's ability to abstain from self-harming behavior.
- The therapist may not have intervened in the adolescent's association with a negative peer group.
- The therapist may not have explored with the adolescent how her abuse of alcohol, drugs, and food affects her ability to abstain from self-injury.
- A lack of therapeutic progress may have had a demoralizing effect on family members' faith in the therapist and belief that change is possible.

- Environmental stressors or obstacles may preclude change and contribute to the maintenance of the family's and adolescent's difficulties.
- The therapist may not have explored with the family the possible negative consequences of changing, which the adolescent and other family members may have serious concerns about.

These troubleshooting guidelines can be broken down into four key areas: *therapist/treatment factors, adolescent factors, family factors,* and *social network/larger systems factors.*

Therapist/Treatment Factors

Although some adolescents are able to stop their self-harming behavior early in treatment, this change may not be *newsworthy* to the members of the solution-determined system because in their minds the adolescent is still exhibiting other difficulties such as poor academic performance, associating with negative peers, or violating the parents' rules. This is why it so crucial for therapists to try to negotiate well-formed, realistic behavioral goals at the beginning of treatment and to elicit from the parents and involved helpers their expectations of the therapist and their unique theories of change. The parents and involved helpers can be asked about what they think the therapy process looks like and how they will know that counseling has really been successful. As early as possible in treatment, I will ask what specific indicators the parents and involved helpers will need to see that will tell them that they have achieved their initial treatment goals, as well as how they will know when they are ready to terminate therapy. Even if these types of questions are not asked at the beginning of treatment, it is never too late to ask them as a way to cooperate better with what the parents and the helpers want. I may also use "Columbo tactics" like confusion and curiosity to temper their unrealistic expectations of the multiple changes they want the adolescent to make and to invite them to guide me to a more realistic and productive treatment path.

Some adolescents and parents may lack a strong support system and be highly vulnerable to slipping back into old problematic patterns of behavior. In some cases, the adolescent may have chosen to abandon her negative peer group as a way to help herself to abstain from cutting or burning; however, this, may have left her without any friends. In these clinical situations, I offer to construct for her a new peer group consisting of my former self-harming adolescent clients. These alumni peers can offer the adolescent valuable wisdom about constructive ways to cope with stressors in her life, assist her in finding jobs and completing tough school assignments, and hang out with her until she makes some new friends. Inspirational others (Anthony, 1987) can be employed in a similar fashion.

I invite parents who feel isolated to join one of my solution-oriented parenting groups (Selekman, 1993, 1999), which provide valuable problem-solving tools and a sense of community in a supportive climate. The active involvement of the family's spiritual leader both in and out of therapy sessions can help provide additional support for them while they try to maintain their changes.

Sometimes after families stabilize their presenting problems, their goals and treatment needs change as well. This is why it is so crucial for therapists throughout the course of therapy to check in with their clients about how well things are going for them and ask about any changes or adjustments they would like to make in the treatment process. This allows therapists to match their therapeutic actions better with the clients' unique needs at any given stage of treatment. Scaling questions also can be used to assess how satisfied the clients are with their progress in treatment and to determine with them what their next steps of improvement need to be for goal attainment (de Shazer, 1988, 1991). In some cases, the clients may wish to establish a new treatment goal, address a current crisis situation in their lives, or attend to the adolescent's or another family member's desire to address an emotionally charged family issue that has not been discussed earlier in treatment. It is important for therapists to invite their clients to take the lead in defining their new treatment goals and identifying the pressing issues they wish to address next in therapy.

In some cases, therapists may overlook or fail to address an important piece of the problem that subsequently causes problems in the maintenance stage of change (Prochaska, 1999). For instance, the therapist may not have attended to an adolescent's highly conflictual relationship with her father or a sibling. In these situations, I invite the clients to take the lead in deciding whether or not they wish to establish a treatment goal or a work plan for this problem area.

As noted earlier, if the therapist suspects the presence of a family secret, he or she should ask open-ended conversational questions (Andersen, 1991; Anderson & Goolishian, 1988). Other therapeutic options that could be pursued with the family are the use of the *question box* therapeutic experiment or with the client's permission, having colleagues serving as a reflecting consultation team (Andersen, 1991).

Sometimes the therapist's theoretical orientation and treatment approach downplay the importance of allowing the adolescent to talk about past traumatic events or conflicts she may be having with particular family members. This silencing also can occur when the therapist fails to consider the role intergenerational patterns may be playing in the adolescent's struggles with staying on track. It is important for therapists not to be slaves to their theories and fall into the "one-size fits all" mental trap (Lebow & Gurman, 1996). As noted earlier, I believe that solution-oriented clinical practice consists of doing what might work at any given moment in any given therapy session, regardless of the technique's theoretical origins, as long as it is purposive and in line with the client's goals or needs at the time. This position greatly expands the therapist's range of therapeutic options.

In some situations the therapist may have done a fabulous job of joining with the adolescent but have a weak therapeutic alliance with one or both parents. In these cases the therapist must critically self-reflect on what he or she has failed to address with the parents that might help to forge a connection. The therapist may need to: elicit the parents' expectations of the therapist and theories of change, clarify whether the "right" problem is being addressed, or ask the parents what about their situation they think he or she is overlooking and should address. After learning what to do differently with the parents, I make all of the necessary therapeutic adjustments to meet their needs better. Persistent outreach can be beneficial when parents do not attend sessions. I have offered to do home visits with nonattending parents, met them for coffee, or sent them letters indicating how valuable their wisdom and involvement in family therapy sessions would be.

Adolescent Factors

Research indicates that an adolescent's continued involvement with a negative peer group can have a deleterious effect on her ability to maintain her changes (Henggeler, Schoenwald, Borduin, Rowland, & Cunningham, 1998). Therefore, it is important that the therapist gain an inside view of the nature of the adolescent's peer group. It is helpful to find out if her peers are also self-harming, abusing alcohol or drugs, and/or experiencing eating difficulties. I also attempt to infiltrate the ado lescent's negative peer group by having her bring her closest friends into one or more of our sessions. This allows me to learn more about the culture of the peer group, to build relationships with the members, and to attempt to change their group behaviors. It has been my experience that most adolescent clients think it is "cool" that their therapist wants to meet their friends and involve them in the treatment process. Another option is to offer to construct a new temporary peer group made up of alumni, as previously noted.

Some adolescents may experience great difficulty staying on track because they substitute chemical substances and/or food for their self-injury habits. Like recovering cocaine addicts who start drinking and quickly return to cocaine use, these adolescents fail to achieve long-term abstinence from self-harming. Most self-harming adolescents get hooked on the soothing or numbing effect of the brain's secretion of endorphins following a self-injury episode. When adolescents abuse certain chemical substances or binge and purge, they may experience similar effects. It is important for the therapist to explore with the adolescent if she is abusing chemicals or bingeing and purging. The therapist should teach the adolescent healthier ways to soothe herself, such as meditation, visualization, cleansing rituals, and soul work (Davis et al., 1994; Kammen & Gold, 1998; Lee, 1998).

Family Factors

Cultural issues and gender power imbalances may greatly contribute to the adolescent's difficulty staying on track. If the adolescent or family is describing experiences of institutional racism occurring in social contexts they regularly interface with, the therapist should serve as an advocate for his or her clients. Spiritual leaders play a central role in the lives of some cultural groups and can be a valuable resource to include in family therapy sessions, particularly when the therapist is feeling stuck.

Gender power imbalances may continue to present major problems for the adolescent if they aren't addressed. Externalization of patriarchal assumptions and patterns of behavior and reframing are effective therapeutic options to pursue with traditional fathers or bullying older brothers (Philpot et al., 1997; White, 1989, 1995).

Environmental stressors or major obstacles like a parent's loss of a job, severe financial problems, serious illness, or intense sibling or intergenerational conflicts may contribute to the family and adolescent's inability to stay on track for an extended period of time. I have worked with a number of self-harming adolescents who felt that their chronically ill or seriously physically handicapped siblings had monopolized their parents' attention and love. To avoid further overburdening their parents, these adolescents bottled up their anger, frustration, and sadness and turned to self-injury as a way to self-soothe or to numb their painful feelings. In these situations it is important for the therapist to provide empathy, support, and validation to the adolescent. The therapist also needs to help the parents to figure out how to spend more time with their adolescent and can use connection-building experiments and rituals to bring them together. Finally, the therapist also may need to serve as an advocate for the family in negotiating with larger systems professionals to attain resources the family desperately may need but not have due to bureaucratic red tape.

Other environmental stressors, such as the parents' poor mental health, substance abuse, or marital or postdivorce conflicts, may adversely affect the adolescent's ability to abstain from self-harming behavior. Once the adolescent's behavior is stabilized, the parents may begin arguing more frequently or a parent's mental health or substance abuse difficulties may become more central in the family drama. Therefore, the therapist needs to be prepared to cross the bridge into relationship war zones to see if the parents are willing to address their issues. The same is true with trying to establish a contract with a parent to address their mental health or substance abuse problems. However, with both scenarios, the therapist must carefully assess what stage of readiness of change (Prochaska, 1999) each parent is at and match the most appropriate interventions with their unique stages. If all of these therapeutic strategies prove unsuccessful, the therapist may want to pursue the option of utilizing a one-person family therapy approach with the adolescent to meet her needs better.

Sometimes, the adolescent struggling to stay on track may tell the therapist that she feels like one of her parents or siblings is deliberately trying to sabotage her treatment gains. This parent or sibling may have refused to participate in family therapy at the beginning of treatment. As mentioned earlier, the therapist should make persistent outreach efforts to engage nonparticipating parents or siblings who are very much a part of the problem life-support system. Initially it is helpful to see this parent or siblings individually in an attempt to build a relationship with him or her and to elicit his or her concerns about the adolescent, the therapist, or the therapy, for that matter. This will help the therapist to gain the much-needed therapeutic leverage. Finally, the therapist can pursue one-person family therapy with the adolescent if his or her efforts in conjoint family therapy are being thwarted by multiple family saboteurs.

Some families that have been oppressed by their problems for a long time become acclimated to living with constant difficulties and crises. In fact, chronic problems may result in secondary gains for certain family members. The *negative consequences of change* (Fisch et al., 1982) can be a useful therapeutic experiment to employ for families like these. The therapist can be curious and wonder aloud about the disadvantages of the adolescent's discontinuing her self-harming behavior and changing their family interactions or problem-solving methods. I like to write down everything family members say about how they think things will be better with their family situation once the adolescent permanently stops cutting or burning herself and improves in other areas; this way, if problems do crop up later in therapy after the adolescent has changed, I can hold family members more accountable for their part in the adolescent's failure to maintain her changes. In some situations where family members have serious concerns about the main presenting problem's being resolved, the problem may be serving as a smoke screen for unspeakable family secrets or preventing emotionally charged conflicts between the parents from surfacing. The therapeutic debate-team strategy can also be quite effective in these clinical situations (Papp, 1983).

Finally, lack of therapeutic progress may have a demoralizing effect on the adolescent and her family. With these tough clinical situations, the therapist needs to figure out ways to instill hope, perhaps by establishing a smaller, more realistic treatment goal, a new treatment goal more in line with the client's present needs, or by using coping or pessimistic questions to better cooperate with their pessimism (Berg & Miller, 1992). I may also use conversational questions to find out if I have overlooked any important piece of the problem situation or invite them to tell me what I need to be doing differently as a therapist (Anderson & Goolishian, 1988). Another useful therapeutic option would be the use of a reflecting team to inject some fresh ideas into the stuck treatment system (Andersen, 1991).

Social Network/Larger Systems Factors

Throughout the course of therapy, the therapist, key members of the family's social network, and involved helping professionals need to critically examine what may or may not be working in their efforts to help the adolescent and her family. This is why therapists and the involved helpers need to keep track of their score as a team—not simply as individuals. The therapist and the involved helpers must abandon everything that isn't working or that is too similar to what the parents and former therapists have already tried and proved unsuccessful.

Some families have had longstanding problems with particular professionals from larger systems at school or in the community. For instance, if a school dean has had past problems with the adolescent's older siblings or with the parents, he or she may have adopted a negative mindset about this family in general. The dean may also balk at the idea of collaborating with the therapist alone or with other involved helping professionals. In this situation, I would continue my persistent outreach efforts with the dean. I also might use the leverage of teachers I am already collaborating with to influence the dean's willingness to work together as a group. I might suggest that we hold our collaborative meetings at the school if that is more convenient for the dean. If all these efforts proved to be futile, I would encourage the adolescent and the parent who usually speaks with the dean to experiment with doing things differently in relationship to him or her in an effort to indirectly alter his or her problem-saturated views and behavior in relationship to them.

Sometimes therapists do not discover until well into treatment that other professionals and concerned members of the family's social network are very much a part of the problem life-support system. Once I find out from the family what level of involvement these individuals have in the family drama, I secure signed consent forms from them to begin incorporating them into individual or collaborative meetings.

CELEBRATING THE ADOLESCENT'S AND FAMILY'S CHANGES

Once the adolescent and her family have successfully managed lengthy vacation periods from family therapy and indicate that they are at a place to stop counseling, I plan a celebration party in my office for them. This may include a cake, achievement certificates for conquering their problems, and speeches from them and invited guests that reflect on how things were with the situation at the beginning of treatment and how things are different now (White & Epston, 1990). Finally, I explore with them if they wish to serve as expert consultants in the future in assisting me with other adolescents and families that are struggling with the same kinds of problems.

CHAPTER 8

The Stress-Busters' Leadership Group

The work of seeing is done
Now practice heart work
Upon those images captive within you.

—Rainer Maria Rilke

THE STRESS-BUSTERS' LEADERSHIP GROUP originally grew out of a consultation experience I had at a junior high school plagued by a rash of 12- to 14-year-old women who were cutting and burning themselves, practicing witchcraft, and creating widespread panic among the school staff. Needless to say, the school principal and a number of the teachers were wondering if these students were suicidal, clinically depressed, or in need of psychiatric evaluations. However, the school principal was quite progressive and open to trying out whatever I thought might be most helpful in stabilizing this crisis situation. The biggest challenges for me were that the majority of these students had been in treatment before and were known to be "therapy savy" and their parents were described by the teachers and other school staff as being uncooperative and difficult to work with. Additionally, some of the young women had already balked at the idea of seeing the school social worker or being referred with their parents to agencies or private therapists in the community. It was clear that most of these young women were not even window-shoppers for any form of counseling.

One day while I was brainstorming about how to approach this challenging situation, an interesting idea popped into my head: What if the school social worker and I were to approach these young women as if they already possessed natural leadership abilities and were scholars on stress management in their own right? Would they warm up to the idea of helping other stressed-out kids in the school? In further developing this idea, I decided to put together an eight-session psychoeducational skill-building group that would expose these students to the most effective therapeutic tools for managing emotional, family, social, and school stressors in their lives. After completing the sessions, the participants would be encouraged to use their knowledge and expertise in stress management by serving as peer counselors at their schools and providing presentations on stress-management prevention to elementary schoolchildren and to other organizations and groups in the community.

In following up with some of the junior high kids that participated in the first stress-busters' leadership group, I was quite pleased to find out that not only had they abandoned self-harming and other problematic behaviors completely but they also were involved in teen-leadership programs at the high school level. Additionally, they were actively involved in other school extracurricular activities and performing well academically.

As Prochaska and his colleagues have discovered in their important research on how people change, individuals in the precontemplation stage of readiness for change tend to accept proposals to get involved in *social liberation projects*—that is, in projects which they help other people with similar problems—even when they are not ready to address their own bad habits or difficulties (Prochaska, 1999; Prochaska et al., 1994). It is my strong belief that by helping others we help ourselves in the process. Adolescents get excited about social causes and making a difference in their schools and communities. Many of the adolescents who have participated in my stress-busters' leadership groups and the other groups where I have channeled their problematic behaviors into meaningful, constructive social action have continued to soar as teen leaders in making an important difference in other people's lives.

ORGANIZING THE GROUP

When organizing a stress-busters' leadership group, it is very important to keep the group homogenous with regard to age and the existence of self-harming behavior as a major presenting problem. However, I also have had good results running this group with adolescents presenting with bulimia problems as well. I like to limit the group to no more than eight participants, and I always keep it a closed group. It can be run in school and outpatient and inpatient settings.

To market the group, my cotherapist and I put together flyers describing the purpose of the group, including the topics covered and the skills taught. These flyers are distributed to area schools, agencies, mental health clinics, hospitals, churches, synagogues, parent self-help groups, and family physician offices in the community. It is also helpful to market this group to managed care companies and private practitioners.

The group leaders must secure written consent from all of the prospective participants' parents before launching the group. We also like to meet individually with each prospective participant to reiterate the purpose of the group and to assess fit and chemistry with the adolescents already screened and admitted into the group.

ROLE OF THE GROUP LEADERS

Ideally, a male-female cotherapy team should run the group to provide gender balance. The group leaders are responsible for providing a safe, supportive therapeutic climate that is rich with information about therapeutic tools the group members can put into immediate use and that builds on the strengths and expertise of each participant to cocreate a context ripe for change. The leaders strive to connect in a meaningful way with each group member by using key language and belief-system material, metaphors, validation, empathy, positive relabeling, normalizing, humor, and compliments. Throughout the group process, the leaders use a variety of therapeutic questions to elicit the group members' expertise, to open up space for possibilities, and for goal-setting purposes.

One helpful teaching tool the leaders employ with stuck or struggling group members is role-play. After the stuck adolescent and other group members role-play her conflictual, stressful relationship with a particular family member, peer, teacher, or extended family member, the rest of the group can be invited to generate potential solution strategies that she can test out over the following week. A variation of role-playing is to have the stuck adolescent play the role of her identified oppressive problem (for instance, a critical self-defeating thought that haunts her or a specific behavior that pushes her around). The group participants play her and the other people involved with this problem situation. Depending on the number of group participants involved in the role-play, my cotherapist and I have a few of the remaining members of the group listening as if they were in the shoes of the participants in the role-play. This gives the stuck adolescent the opportunity to gain some unique and newsworthy constructions of or ideas about her problem situation.

GROUP SESSIONS

Each session is an hour in length. The format consists of 15–20 minutes of an upbeat, interesting didactic presentation by the leaders, a 15- to 20-minute in-session skill-building exercise, and a stress-busting experiment offered to the participants at the conclusion of the session. The group meets eight times, with longer intervals between the sixth, seventh, and eighth sessions as a vote of confidence to the participants' progress in the group. The eight session topic areas covered in the group are:

1. What are my strengths and protective shields?
2. Mindfulness skills
3. Relationship-effectiveness skills
4. Mood-management skills
5. Self-soothing stress-busting skills
6. Navigating family minefields successfully
7. Effective tools for mastering school stress
8. Celebrating change: Congratulations stress-busting experts!

Session 1. What Are My Strengths and Protective Shields?

In the first group meeting, the leaders begin the session by establishing rapport with each group member. To become better acquainted with one another and learn about the participants' strengths and talents, the leaders ask each group member to respond to the following question: "If someone were to stop you on the street and ask you what two of your strengths are, what would you tell that person?" After each group member has had an opportunity to answer this question, the leaders shift gears and with great enthusiasm and excitement share with the participants how pleased they are about their decision to participate in the group, which is a great social cause. We also share with the group some of the meaningful, exciting projects graduates of the group have been involved with at their schools and colleges.

It is important for the group leaders to take the time to ask the participants about their expectations of us, of the group, and any other concerns they may have. We explain the session format to the participants and express our wishes that they fully cooperate with and try out all of the in-session exercises and the stress-busting experiments given at the end of each meeting. The leaders invite the members to come up with group rules and goals. After eliciting their problem stories and thoughts about their referral to the group, we use the miracle, presuppositional, and scaling questions to help them to articulate their short- and long-term treatment goals for themselves (de Shazer, 1988, 1991; O'Hanlon & Weiner-Davis, 1989).

In the next portion of the meeting, the group leaders give a short presentation called Resiliency Protective Factors. We present some of the most common protective factors found with resilient children and adolescents, including their: being creative and effective problem-solvers, having inspirational others, having at least one supportive, responsible adult caretaker in their lives, and succeeding in school. We then ask the group members to share with the group what they think their main protective factors are and specifically how they have been helpful to them in coping with past and present stressors in their lives. We like to refer to these protective factors as *protective shields* that help us to cope with stressful events in our lives.

The in-session exercise for this session is *visualizing movies of success* (Selekman, 1997). This exercise consists of having the group members close their eyes and capture in their minds movies of past sparkling moments in their lives when they successfully coped with painful life events or performed with excellence in high-stress situations. While group members are attempting to access their movies of success, we have them apply all of their senses to the images they come up with, concentrating on color and motion. After 10–15 minutes of visualizing, we invite the group members to share their personal movies with one another. In the context of this discussion, the leaders ask group members the following questions:

- "Are you aware of how you did that?"
- "What did you tell yourself that helped you to manage that situation so well?"
- "What did you learn from this experience that you have already put into practice with similar types of situations?"

These types of questions can help to amplify and consolidate the group members' pretreatment changes. Finally, we share with the group the old adage "nothing succeeds like success," while pointing out how group members' past successes can serve as blueprints for future successes.

To close the session, the leaders compliment each group member on their past successes, creativity, and strengths and resources. The first stress-busting experiment they are given is the *victory box* (see chapter 1).

Session 2. Mindfulness Skills

The second group meeting begins with the participants showing their victory boxes to the group and sharing with us two of their most noteworthy personal victories over the past week. To further empower and create possibilities with the group members, the leaders use regular and future-vision consolidating questions such as:

- "Are you aware of how you did that?"
- "After taking those big steps, do you view yourself differently now, as opposed to how you used to view yourself?"
- "Let's say in our next group meeting you brought in a videotape of you taking further big steps with (peers, your parents, your sibling, your difficult teacher). What will we see you doing on the video?"
- "How will those changes make a difference for you in your relationships with (peers, your parents, your sibling, your difficult teacher)?"

The leaders give a short presentation on Practicing Mindfulness Meditation. Many adolescents find this topic fascinating and usually become quite skilled at meditation techniques. We begin our presentation by pointing out how mindfulness meditation has its roots in an ancient system of Buddhist psychology in which human nature is viewed in a positive way and emotional problems are seen as temporary and superficial. In addition, we share with the group that mindfulness meditation increases our ability to see things just as they are from moment to moment, which can alter how we relate to and perceive emotional distress. The group members learn that by cultivating a capacity to quiet our mind and self-observe, we can gain wisdom from even the most stressful and painful life experiences (Bennett-Goleman, 2001; Goldstein &

Kornfield, 1987). To help give the group participants an opportunity to experience the benefits of mindfulness meditation, we have them practice meditating for 10–12 minutes. We have the group members practice using the sound meditation described in Chapter 3. If any unpleasant thoughts or feelings enter their minds while meditating, they are simply to label them to acknowledge their presence and center themselves by returning back to focusing on their breath (Davis et al., 1994). After the group members have had an opportunity to practice mindfulness meditation, we like to process with them what their unique experiences were like.

We conclude the group with compliments for each participant, by checking in with each member about how well they are doing at achieving their personal goals, and by giving a stress-busting experiment to do over the next week. The stress-busting experiment is for group members to practice mindfulness meditation twice a day for 15–20 minutes. We recommend that they have their meditations first thing in the morning and either right after school or before they go to bed.

Session 3. Relationship-Effectiveness Skills

We begin the third group meeting by exploring with participants what their personal experiences experimenting with mindfulness meditation were like. Often group members report that this form of meditation helped them to "chill" when they were stressed out. Others may report that their minds were so cluttered with disturbing emotions and intrusive thoughts that they had difficulty entering a meditative state. We suggest that these group members try the following the next time they practice meditating: Label and acknowledge the painful emotion or intrusive thought they are experiencing and remind themselves that they can disempower painful emotions and intrusive thoughts by viewing them as temporary and as masking their essential goodness (Chodron, 2001). To illustrate the powerful effects of our emotional patterns and self-defeating thoughts, Bennett-Goleman (2001) likes to use the example of the scene from the *Wizard of Oz*. Up to this point in the story, they viewed the wizard as a powerful, terrifying entity—until Dorothy's dog Toto calmly pulls back the curtain to reveal a little old man stooped over the controls, manipulating a huge wizard image. Emotional patterns and self-defeating thoughts are like that—if you see them clearly for what they really are, you take the power away from them. Group participants have found this example from the *Wizard of Oz* to be most helpful to them in seeing the benefits of mindfulness meditation.

Finally, for the group members who found the sound meditation "boring" or not very useful, we recommend the raisin food meditation described in chapter 3. One of the group leaders demonstrates how to do this simple food meditation.

We strongly encourage group members to keep practicing and further honing their mindfulness meditation skills so that they can get into a relaxed state more quickly and disengage from their disturbing emotions, intrusive thoughts, and stressful life events.

The leaders give a short presentation on the Politics of Gender as part of their discussion on relationship-effectiveness tools. We use video clips from popular movies and TV shows and magazine photos to trigger group discussion and to graphically depict how the images in the media have a powerful effect on how young women view themselves and how males view and relate to them. Furthermore, we discuss the role of patriarchy in how women are socialized to act and look. Last, we like to use the Russian literary critic Bakhtin's metaphor of the ventriloquist and his dummy to illustrate how young women's thoughts, feelings, and actions cannot be separated from their audience or the patriarchal lens through which they are filtered (Brown, 1998). Bakhtin (1981) calls the process of one voice speaking through another voice *ventriloquation*. As part of our group discussion, we explore with the participants in what ways they already resist falling prey to the feminization process, challenge the patriarchal traditions imposed on them, and maintain their unique voices.

Some of the relationship-effectiveness tools we teach are: resisting, assertiveness, communication, and problem-solving skills. Using the real-life experiences of the group members, the leaders demonstrate through role-playing how they would apply each of these tools in their unique relationship difficulties.

The in-session exercise consists of having group members select a partner to practice these relationship-effectiveness skills. They are to give their partners constructive feedback on how well they did at applying their selected tools in the scenarios. Following the exercise, the leaders process with the group what they found most helpful, explore with them if they learned anything new about themselves or their situations, and ask them where they are feeling stuck.

Prior to concluding the group meeting, we compliment each participant on how she shined in the exercise and on any other important changes that have occurred with her situation. The group is given two stress-busting experiments that are geared to further strengthen their relationship-effectiveness skills. They first are encouraged to further experiment with the relationship-effectiveness skills they found most helpful in their role-plays. We then ask them to experiment with stepping outside of themselves and observing themselves in social situations from a bubble high above. From this vantage point, they are to pay close attention to what they are doing successfully in the social encounters, as well as what they are doing that is self-defeating. With each important or stressful social encounter, they are to document daily in pocket-sized notebooks what they learned from their experiences.

Session 4. Mood-Management Skills

The leaders begin the fourth group meeting processing with the participants their unique experiences with both of the prescribed stress-busting experiments. With every personal victory or positive step group members report, the leaders respond with cheerleading and amplify and consolidate their gains. Scaling questions can also be used to further elicit group members' news of a difference. At this stage of the group, participants often begin to spontaneously compliment one another.

The presentation in this group session is called Changing Your Self-Defeating Thoughts and Emotional Patterns. The leaders illustrate on a whiteboard the A-B-C formula of cognitive therapy to show how self-defeating or irrational thoughts trigger our emotional reactions and behaviors (Ellis, 1974). To bring the A-B-C formula to life for the group participants, we have one of the members of the group apply it to a stressful life event or situation they are struggling to cope with. As part of this discussion, we introduce the therapeutic tools they can use to break the chain connecting their thoughts, feelings, and actions.

We teach them the following cognitive tools: disputation skills, thought-stopping techniques, searching for evidence to support their self-defeating or irrational thoughts, and shifting their emotional states (Beck, 1995; Ellis, 1996; McMullen, 2000; Seligman, 1995).

In order to help the group members become more proficient in using these tools in the context of their unique problem situations, we have them find a partner and practice the tools for 15–20 minutes. After the exercise, we process with the group members what they found helpful and field any questions or concerns they still may have about managing their moods.

The leaders end the group by complimenting each group member and giving the next stress-busting experiment. The group members are asked to practice using the cognitive tools they found most interesting and helpful on a daily basis whenever they are faced with a stressful event or being pushed around by a self-defeating thought or a disturbing emotion.

Session 5. Self-Soothing Stress-Busting Skills

The leaders begin the fifth group session by inviting group members to share the sparkling moments they experienced as a result of the cognitive tools they experimented with over the past week. With every positive step the participants report, we cheerlead and amplify and consolidate their gains. One way we help to solidify participants' gains is by asking them questions like:

- "What would you have to do to go backwards?"
- "Let's say you have a slip over the next week. What steps will you take to get back on track quickly?"

We give the group a short presentation on Caring for Your Soul. In the context of this presentation, group members learn the following self-soothing strategies: visualization techniques, soul work, cleansing rituals, and relaxation training. After reviewing the visualizing-movies-of-success experiment, we teach the group the visiting-your-special-place and creating-your-guardian-angel visualization strategies. We stress to the group the importance of nurturing oneself daily by making time for free play, creative expression, and pleasurable, meaningful activities. In the context of this discussion, group members often spontaneously share with one another their unique soul work activities and their best methods for pampering themselves. Finally, we teach the group *deep breathing* techniques. As an in-session experiment, group members are asked to select one of the visualization strategies and spend 15–20 minutes practicing it. After they have completed their practice sessions, we spend ample time processing their experiences with the visualization exercise and offer pointers and support to the group members who had a difficult time visualizing.

After we compliment each group member, we give the group two stress-busting experiments to do over the next week. With the first experiment, the participants are to practice their favorite visualization strategies twice a day for 15–20 minutes. They are also asked to devote some daily time to engaging in some form of soul work.

Session 6. Navigating Family Minefields Successfully

In the sixth group meeting the leaders open by exploring with the participants how their experiments went and by finding out what further progress they are making in general at better managing stressors in their lives. We amplify and consolidate their gains and use scaling questions to secure a quantitative measurement of how satisfied group members are with their progress and what they envision as their next steps in reaching an even higher level on their scales (de Shazer, 1991).

The leaders give a short presentation on Family Politics. The topics covered in this presentation are: family roles, parenting styles, triangles, problem-maintaining patterns of interaction and beliefs, intergenerational patterns, cultural traditions, and gender power imbalances. We invite the participants to share with the group which aspects of their own family politics trouble them the most. As part of this discussion, we explore with group members what they do to avoid getting triangulated into coalitions and how they constructively manage their emotional reactions to their parents' troubling behaviors (such as nagging, yelling, or invalidating them). It is also helpful to elicit from them how they get trapped in family members' webs or by their ploys. Group members have an opportunity to compare notes, hear that their fellow participants are experiencing similar family difficulties, and learn from one another about how to get through family minefields unscathed. Finally, we teach the group members the *do-something-different task* (de Shazer, 1985, 1988, 1991) as an effective tool that will help them to successfully navigate family minefields.

The fun and illuminating experiential exercise we like to use in this group session is *family choreography* (see chapter 4). The amount of time left in the group meeting determines how many family choreographies we can do. Typically we can squeeze in at least two of the group members' family choreographies. The members that volunteer to do choreographies are free to use objects in the room as props and are to pick other participants in the group to represent family members. We encourage the choreographers to allow their creativity to run wild in terms of how they depict their families as moving sculptures. After showing the group how they currently see their families, the choreographers are to show the group how they would like their families to look in the future. When each choreographer is done, we invite the other group members to share their thoughts and insights. Sometimes we have a few of the nonparticipating group members listen and observe as if they were one of the family members portrayed in the volunteer's family choreography. These participants are asked to give their unique perspectives and possible new insights about the family situation. The leaders present their reflections on the volunteers' family choreographies as well.

To close the group meeting, the leaders compliment each participant and the next stress-busting experiment is given. The group members are asked to try the *do-something-different task* (de Shazer, 1985, 1988, 1991) whenever they feel like a family member is attempting to engage them in a coalition or a conflict or is using them as a confidant. They are to keep track of what they do that seems to help them successfully counter family members' ploys and record their creative strategies in their pocket-size notebooks. The group is given 2 weeks to test out this experiment and as a reward for their hard work both in and out of the group.

Session 7. Effective Tools for Mastering School Stress

My colleagues and I look forward to the seventh group meeting, during which the group members talk about all of the creative, positive steps they took when they were experimenting with the *do-something-different task* (de Shazer, 1985, 1988, 1991). With every positive and big step that group members report, we respond with cheerleading and amplify and consolidate their gains. For the participants who still found themselves getting triangulated into coalitions, clashing with particular family members, or being unable to step out of the confidant role, we use the brain power and creativity of the group to generate solution strategies. We first may do a dramatization of the stuck participant's problem situation. It is also helpful to explore with other group members what unique coping and problem-solving strategies they employ to manage similar situations in their families. After the group has generated a number of potential solution strategies on the whiteboard, the stuck participant is free to select which of the strategies she would like to experiment with.

If the stuck group member describes the problem situation as oppressive or having a life of its own, we may attempt to externalize it (White & Epston, 1990). Finally, if we are picking up on some strong affect with this stuck participant, we may ask conversational questions to give her more room to share her painful story or the "not yet said" (Anderson & Goolishian, 1988). Some examples of conversational questions we may ask in these situations are:

- "Just before you came to the group for the first time, was there something you told yourself that you would not talk about in the group?"

- "What is your greatest fear if you talk about it? How does not talking about this untold story allow it to continue presenting problems for you or others?"

- "Were there any aspects of our discussions about families either today or last week that you found to be most upsetting to you? What aspects?"

- "What can we do as leaders or as a group to best help you out with this upsetting situation?"

The short presentation given to the group is called Survival Tips for Managing School Stress. In this presentation, the leaders discuss strategies for resolving conflicts and difficulties with teachers and peers, how to stay on top of schoolwork, and effective ways to make a difference in school. Regarding the last topic, we discuss how group members can get involved in teen leadership, student empowerment activities, and peer counseling. We share our hope with the participants that they will take all of the knowledge and expertise they have gained from their group experience and provide prevention workshops on stress management both at their home schools and at other schools or public places in their communities.

The in-session experiential exercise offered to the group provides the participants with the opportunity to constructively manage peer harassment and rejection. We have the participants break up into groups of four. One of the group members dramatizes her problem situation of being harassed by a particular female peer at school. Another group member plays her. Another group member plays the role of harassment (Lewis & Cheshire, 1998). Finally, the last group member plays the role of the young woman who has been spreading nasty rumors around the school about the volunteer. By externalizing the problem in this way, all participants in the role-play have the opportunity to gain new insights about these types of problem situations. Harassment itself teaches them about all of its tricks and brainwashing methods and about how the harasser it has trained may also be a victim in this relationship drama. In addition, the volunteer may learn powerful countering tactics that she can use to stand up to harassment and not allow it to push her around (Lewis & Cheshire, 1998). When processing this exercise with the group, participants not only report having enjoyed doing it but also find that their views of their problem situations have changed. Group members often report feeling a sense of liberation from their peer problems as a result of this exercise.

We conclude the group with compliments for each participant and give the next stress-busting experiment. As a vote of confidence, the participants are given a 3-week vacation from the group. While on vacation, the group members are asked to experiment with some of the new ideas and tactics they learned from the peer-rejection and harassment exercise.

Session 8. Celebrating Change: Congratulations Stress-Busting Experts!

The leaders begin this meeting by exploring with group members what further progress they made while on vacation from the group. We check if any of the participants had the opportunity to stand up to peer rejection or harassment. After dialoging about the group members' experiences and amplifying and consolidating their gains, the leaders' launch a festive celebration party to honor the participants' outstanding work in the group. We present them with achievement certificates and a nicely decorated sheet cake that has on it: "Congratulations Stress-Busting Experts!" The group members are asked to give speeches reflecting on how things were for them individually, with their families and peers, and at school prior to their participation in the group and how things are different for them now. Often group members spontaneously cheerlead for one another and give each other compliments in response to their personal speeches. To further amplify and consolidate their gains, the leaders ask the following types of questions:

- "If we were to invite you to our next stress-busters' leadership group as expert consultants, what helpful pointers or words of wisdom would you share with this group?"
- "Let's say we had a 1-year anniversary party for this group. What further positive changes will each of you be eager to report to the group at the party?"

Following the group members' speeches, the participants are inducted into the Stress-Busters' Expert Consultants' Association. As members, they are expected to engage in some of the following activities: be available to provide presentations on stress management to schools and for other groups and organizations in their communities; offer consultation to school social work staff and other personnel and provide support to schoolmates who are grappling with self-harming and other stress-related problems; and contribute articles to a *Stress-Busters' Quarterly* publication that is circulated around their schools. At some of the more progressive schools, we have been able to secure some office space once or twice a week for the graduates to establish an onsite Stress-Busters' Leadership Institute to provide training and workshops on stress management for interested students and support services for stressed-out kids at school.

For the group members who wish to have further counseling at the conclusion of the group, the leaders carefully assess with them what their unique needs are and make themselves available to provide individual, couple (with their partners), or family therapy. They can decide how often they want to be seen and which combination of people they wish to have attend the sessions. Often this clinical work is not long-term due to the extensive positive gains they achieved during the group sessions.

CHAPTER 9
Coda

We are each angels with only one wing;
we fly only by embracing one another.

—Luciano de Crescenzo

IN THIS BOOK I HAVE PRESENTED a plethora of therapeutic strategies and techniques for efficient, effective therapeutic work with self-harming adolescents and their families. Many of the therapeutic ideas I have discussed are empirically supported by research on psychotherapy treatment outcomes and by important findings from studies on the characteristics of strong families and resilient children (Anthony, 1984, 1987; DeFrain & Stinnett, 1992; Duncan & Miller, 2000; Haggerty et al., 1994; Hubble et al., 1999; Lambert, 1992; Stinnett & O'Donnell, 1996; Werner & Smith, 1992). Following is a review of some of the major themes of the book.

Adolescent self-harming behavior is a multidetermined problem requiring an ecological collaborative family therapy approach that addresses multiple domains of functioning. Through close collaboration with the adolescent, her family, key members of their social network, and involved helping professionals from larger systems, we determine together at what systems levels to target interventions. When conducting a multisystemic family assessment, therapists must take into consideration the roles gender, culture, society, and the media influences play in the development and the maintenance of adolescent self-harming difficulties. To coconstruct solutions, the solution-oriented brief family therapy model not only takes into consideration these important factors, but also capitalizes on the strengths and resources of the adolescent, family members, concerned peers, other key members of their social network, and involved representatives from larger systems.

Throughout the book I have stressed the importance of connection-building practices. As illustrated by many of the case examples, the adolescents were feeling disconnected, invalidated, and lacking a "voice" in their families and in social contexts they interfaced with. In these situations, the therapist needs to be the catalyst for building meaningful connections between the adolescent and her parents, peers, teachers, key members of her social network, and involved helping professionals from larger systems. I have presented several therapeutic experiments and strategies for fostering connection-building with these adolescents in the treatment process.

Another important dimension of therapeutic work with self-harming adolescents is the use of cognitive and self-soothing skills training. Many of the adolescents I have worked with reported lacking the tools to challenge their self-defeating thoughts and to constructively manage high levels of emotional distress. Simply changing problem-maintaining family interactions may not alter or help improve the cognitive distortions or emotional turmoil these youth are experiencing. Therefore, as therapists we need to arm our clients with an arsenal of tools that they can employ at any given moment to challenge their irrational thoughts and to soothe themselves. If the therapist has difficulty engaging the parents and/or if the adolescent is amenable to participating in a group, the stress-busters' leadership group is a viable therapeutic option.

When collaborating with involved helping professionals from larger systems, therapists need to be respectful and appreciative of each helper's expertise and disparate views, no matter how pathological their diagnostic formulations about the adolescent and her family may be. What may appear to be helping-system knots occurring in collaborative meetings can be viewed instead as an opportunity to be less isolated with a challenging case situation and to dialogue about our unique perspectives, concerns, and expectations, which can help to spark new ideas and generate high-quality solutions.

Finally, I have stressed the importance of being integrative and therapeutically flexible. This clinical thinking is in line with empirically based research that indicates the importance of matching client and situational factors with different interventions (Beutler, 1991; Henggeler et al., 1998; Hubble et al., 1999; Lambert & Bergin, 1994; Prochaska, 1999). According to Lambert and Bergin (1994), "There is a major trend toward eclecticism or integration of diverse techniques and concepts into a broad, comprehensive, and pragmatic approach to treatment that avoids strong allegiances to narrow theories or schools of thought" (p. 143).

IMPLICATIONS FOR THE FUTURE

Although clients and professional colleagues across the United States and abroad have reported that the solution-oriented brief family therapy model has shown highly favorable clinical results with self-harming and other serious adolescent problems, no scientific, well-controlled outcome studies have been conducted to truly demonstrate its efficacy empirically. The unpublished qualitative research I have conducted on the model has been limited to my colleagues' random selection of sessions to interview clients and follow-up interviews with them to elicit their perceptions of and experiences with this treatment approach. Like Metcalf, Thomas, Duncan, Miller, and Hubble (1996), we have found that clients more often than not cite the therapists' relationship skills as being most important to them, not any specific strategies and techniques akin to this model.

However, my colleagues and I are finding that by interviewing families throughout the course of treatment we are learning more about which specific therapeutic strategies and techniques they found particularly useful. For example, one father who was a computer specialist reported that his therapist's use of scaling questions (de Shazer, 1988) was most beneficial to him and his family in establishing a treatment goal and later in knowing where they stood quantitatively in achieving their goals. The father reported that in previous treatment experiences there were no treatment goals, the therapeutic process drifted aimlessly, and his daughter did not change.

Gingerich and Eisengart (2000), in the most comprehensive critical analysis of solution-focused brief therapy research studies to date, found that there have been only five studies that were well-controlled and showed positive treatment outcomes. Only one of these studies, however, was with adolescents, and the overall solution-focused brief therapy outcomes appeared modest at best. In addition, it was difficult to assess in this study the specific effects of this treatment approach as compared to the standard institutional care the control groups received (Seagram, 1997).

Clearly, in order to demonstrate the efficacy of the solution-oriented brief family therapy approach with self-harming adolescents empirically, a well-controlled research design combining qualitative and quantitative methods is a must. Gingerich and Eisengart (2000) would recommend the following guidelines for a treatment outcome study on solution-oriented brief family therapy:

- Therapists participating in the study should be given treatment manuals and intensive training in solution-oriented brief family therapy.
- There should be a large enough sample size to generalize the treatment outcome results.
- A random assignment procedure should be used with the subjects.
- There should be some type of conventional diagnostic grouping with the subjects around presenting problems or symptoms in order to select the most appropriate outcome measures.
- The control group should receive an empirically valid family treatment approach for adolescents, such as functional family therapy (Alexander & Parsons, 1982 Henggeler & Alexander, 1999). This will help to balance the therapists' allegiance to both the experimental and control treatments offered in the study. In addition, it will provide an opportunity to see how well the outcome results of solution-oriented brief family therapy compare to an empirically validated family treatment model for adolescents.

I also would recommend that a qualitative component be added to future treatment outcome research on the solution-oriented brief family therapy model. Having researchers interview families randomly throughout the course of therapy can tell us a lot about what aspects of the treatment they are finding most useful or unhelpful. Hopefully, with the rigorous research efforts Gingerich and Eisengart (2000) and I propose, we can move beyond therapists' anecdotal reports of clinical success and truly demonstrate the effectiveness of solution-oriented brief family therapy with serious adolescent problems like self-injury. I invite readers to join me in my quest to further develop the solution-oriented brief family therapy model, to demonstrate its efficacy through rigorous research methods, and to further expand our knowledge base in better understanding and treating self-harming adolescents and their families.

To conclude this book, I felt it would be most fitting to give Rhiannon the last word. After several months of hard work in individual and family therapy sessions, and with ongoing consultation with her therapists, Rhiannon successfully "closed the door" on her awful past. She wrote the following poem after accomplishing this tremendous milestone in her life.

Changed Ways

The world works in mysterious ways
It makes me think back to the days
I used to slice my arms up pretty bad
I lied more than I ever had
I lost a lot of trust and friends
I cheated on all of my past boyfriends
I did more drugs than I can remember
Billy killed himself in the month of September.
I treated my mom with so much hate
I'd run away for three weeks straight
I realize now that those things aren't cool
And I was acting like a fool
I'm glad I changed my life around
My feet are finally on the ground.

References

Abudabbeh, N. (1996). Arab families. In M. McGoldrick, J. Giordano, & J. K. Pearce (Eds.), *Ethnicity and family therapy* (pp. 333–347). New York: Guilford.

Alderman, T. (1997). *The scarred soul: Understanding and ending self-inflicted violence.* Oakland, CA: New Harbinger.

Alexander, J. F., & Parsons, B. V. (1982). *Functional family therapy: Principles and procedures.* Carmel, CA: Brooks/Cole.

American Psychiatric Association. (1994). *Diagnostic and statistical manual of mental disorders* (4th ed.). Washington, DC.

Andersen, T. (1991). *The reflecting team: Dialogues and dialogues about the dialogues.* New York: Norton.

Andersen, T. (1995). Reflecting processes; acts of informing and forming: You can borrow my eyes, but you must not take them away from me. In S. Friedman (Ed.), *The reflecting team in action: Collaborative practice in family therapy* (pp. 11–38). New York: Guilford.

Andersen, T. (1998). One sentence of five lines about creating meaning: In perspective of relationship, prejudice, and bewitchment. *Human Systems: The Journal of Systemic Consultation and Management, 9*(2), 73–81.

Anderson, H. (1993). On a roller coaster: A collaborative language systems approach to therapy. In S. Friedman (Ed.), *The new language of change: Constructive collaboration in psychotherapy* (pp. 323–345). New York: Guilford.

Anderson, H., & Goolishian, H. (1988). Human systems as linguistic systems: Preliminary and evolving ideas about the implications of clinical theory. *Family Process, 27,* 371–394.

Anthony, E. J. (1984). The St. Louis risk research project. In N. F. Watt, E. J. Anthony, L. C. Wynne, & J. Roth (Eds.), *Children at risk for schizophrenia: A longitudinal perspective* (pp. 105–148). Cambridge, UK: Cambridge University.

Anthony, E. J. (1987). Risk, vulnerability, and resilience: An overview. In E. J. Anthony & B. J. Cohler (Eds.), *The invulnerable child* (pp. 3–48). New York: Guilford.

Anthony, E. J., & Cohler, B. J. (Eds.). (1987). *The invulnerable child.* New York: Guilford Press.

Applebome, P. (1999, May). Two words behind the massacre in Colorado. *New York Times,* section 4, p. 1.

Bakhtin, M. M. (1981). *The dialogic imagination.* Austin, TX: University of Texas.

Bear Heart (1996). *The wind is my mother: The life and teachings of a Native American Shaman.* New York: Berkley.

Beck, A. (1995). Cognitive therapy with personality disorders. In P. Salkovskis (Ed.), *Frontiers in cognitive therapy* (pp. 165–181). New York: Guilford.

Beck, A., Rush, A., & Emery, G. (1979). *Cognitive therapy of depression.* New York: Guilford.

Bennett-Goleman, T. (2001). *Emotional alchemy: How the mind can heal the heart.* New York: Harmony.

Bennett-Goleman, T., & Goleman, D. (2001, February). *Emotional alchemy: How the mind can heal the heart.* Workshop presented at Transitions Learning Center, Chicago, IL.

Benson, H. (1996). *Timeless healing: The power of biology and belief.* Accord, MA: Wheeler.

Berg, I. K. (1994). A wolf in disguise is not a grandmother. *Journal of Systemic Therapies, 13*(1), 5–13.

Berg, I. K., & de Shazer, S. (1993). Making numbers talk: Language in therapy. In S. Friedman (Ed.), *The new language of change: Constructive collaboration in psychotherapy* (pp. 5–24). New York: Guilford.

Berg, I. K., & Gallagher, D. (1991). Solution-focused brief treatment with adolescent substance abusers. In T. C. Todd & M. D. Selekman (Eds.), *Family therapy approaches with adolescent substance abusers* (pp. 93–111). Needham Heights, MA: Allyn & Bacon.

Berg, I. K., & Miller, S. D. (1992). *Working with the problem drinker: A solution-focused approach.* New York: Norton.

Beutler, L. (1991). Have all won and must all have prizes? Revisiting Luborsky's verdict. *Journal of Consulting and Clinical Psychology, 59,* 266–232.

Beyebach, M., & Carranza, V. E. (1997). Therapeutic interaction and dropout: Measuring relational communication in solution-focused therapy. *Journal of Family Therapy, 19*(2), 173–213.

Beyebach, M., & Morejon, A. R. (1999). Some thoughts on integration in solution-focused therapy. *Journal of Systemic Therapies, 18*(1), 24–43.

Beyebach, M., Morejon, A. R., Palenzuela, D. L., & Rodriguez-Arias, J. L. (1996). Research on the process of solution-focused therapy. In S. D. Miller, M. A. Hubble, & B. L. Duncan (Eds.), *Handbook of solution-focused brief therapy* (pp. 299–335). San Francisco: Jossey-Bass.

Bohm, D. (1995). *Unfolding meaning.* London: Routledge.

Bopp, J., Bopp, M., Brown, L., & Lane, P. (1985). *The sacred tree: Reflections on Native American spirituality.* Twin Lakes, WI: Lotus Light.

Bowen, M. (1978). *Family therapy in clinical practice.* Northvale, NJ: Jason Aronson.

Bowlby, J. (1988). *A secure base: Parent-child attachment and healthy human development.* New York: Basic.

Brazleton, T. B., & Greenspan, S. I. (2000). *The irreducible needs of children: What every child must have to grow, learn, and flourish.* Cambridge, MA: Perseus.

Breggin, P. R. (2000). *Reclaiming our children: A healing plan for a nation in crisis.* Cambridge, MA: Perseus.

Brodsky, B. S., Cliotre, M., & Dulit, R. A. (1995). Relationship of dissociation to self-mutilation and childhood abuse in borderline personality. *American Journal of Psychiatry, 152,* 1788–1792.

Brokenleg, M. (1998). Native wisdom on belonging. *Reclaiming Children and Youth: The Journal of Strength-Based Interventions, 7*(3), 130–133.

Bronfenbrenner, U. (1979). *The ecology of human development: Experiments by nature and design.* Cambridge, MA: Harvard.

Brown, L. L. (2000). Discomforts of the powerless: Feminist constructions of distress. In R. A. Neimeyer & J. D. Raskin (Eds.), *Constructions of disorder: Meaning-making frameworks for psychotherapy* (pp. 287–309). Washington, DC: American Psychological Association.

Brown, L. M. (1998). *Raising their voices: The politics of girls' anger.* Cambridge, MA: Harvard.

Califano, J. A. (1998, October 19). A weapon in the war on drugs: Dining in. *The Washington Post,* p. A21.

Caplan, P. J. (1995). *They say you're crazy: How the world's most powerful psychiatrists decide who's normal.* Reading, MA: Addison-Wesley.

Carlson, T. (2000, November). Marilyn Manson has a secret. *Talk Magazine, 2*(3), 75–77.

Catalano, R. (2005, April). *Applying the knowledge base for prevention Science.* Keynote address presented at the 3rd Las Vegas U.S. Journal Training Inc. Conference on Adolescents, Las Vegas, NV.

Chang, J., & Phillips, M. (1993). Michael White and Steve de Shazer: New directions in family therapy. In S. Gilligan & R. Price (Eds.), *Therapeutic conversations* (pp. 95–112). New York: Norton.

Chodron, P. (1994). *Start where you are: A guide to compassionate living.* Boston: Shambhala.

Chodron, P. (2001, March). Sitting in the middle of fire. *Shambhala Sun, 9*(4), 41.

Clarke, A. (1999). *Coping with self-mutilation: A helping book for teens who hurt themselves.* Center City, MN: Hazeldon.

Clarke, J. I. (1999). *Connections: The threads that strengthen families.* Center City, MN: Hazeldon.

Cloud, J. (1999, May 31). Just a routine school shooting. *Time*, 34.

Conoley, C. W., Ivey, D., Conoley, J. C., Schmeel, M., & Bishop, R. (1992). Enhancing consultation by matching the consultee's perspective. *Journal of Counseling Development*, 69, 546–549.

Conterio, K., & Lader, W. (1998). *Bodily harm: The breakthrough treatment program for self-injurers*. New York: Hyperion.

Crane, J. (1991). The epidemic theory of ghettos and neighborhood effects on dropping out and teenage childbearing. *American Journal of Sociology*, 96, 1226–1259.

Davis, M., Eshelman, E. R., & McKay, M. (1994). *The relaxation and stress reduction workbook* (3rd ed.). Oakland, CA: New Harbinger.

Dawes, R. M. (1994). *House of cards: Psychology and psychotherapy built on myth*. New York: Free Press.

DeFrain, J., & Stinnett, N. (1992). Building on inherent strengths of families: A positive approach for family psychologists and counselors. *Family Psychology and Counseling*, 1(1), 15–26.

de Shazer, S. (1985). *Keys to solution in brief therapy*. New York: Norton.

de Shazer, S. (1988). *Clues: Investigating solutions in brief therapy*. New York: Norton.

de Shazer, S. (1991). *Putting difference to work*. New York: Norton.

Doherty, W. J. (2000). *Take back your kids: Confident parenting in turbulent times*. Notre Dame, IN: Sorin.

Donnellon, A. (1996). *Team talk: Listening between the lines to improve team performance*. Boston: Harvard Business.

Duhl, F., Duhl, B., & Kantor, D. (1973). Learning, space, and action in family therapy. In D. Bloch (Ed.), *Techniques in family psychotherapy* (pp. 55–67). New York: Grune & Stratton.

Duncan, B. L. & Miller, S. D. (2000). *The heroic client: Doing client-directed, outcome-informed therapy*. San Francisco: Jossey-Bass.

Elkind, D. (1988). *The hurried child: Growing up too fast too soon*. Reading, MA: Addison.

Elkind, D. (1994). *Ties that stress: The new family imbalance*. Cambridge, MA: Harvard.

Ellinor, L., & Gerard, G. (1998). *Dialogue: Rediscover the transforming power of conversation*. New York: John Wiley.

Ellis, A. (1974). *Techniques for disputing irrational beliefs*. New York: Institute for Rational Living, Inc.

Ellis, A. (1996). *Reason and emotion in psychotherapy: A comprehensive method of treating human disturbance*. (Rev. ed.). New York: Citadel.

Epston, D. (1998). *Catching up with David Epston: Collection of narrative practice-based papers 1991–1996*. Adelaide, South Australia: Dulwich Centre Publications.

Epston, D. (2000, May). *Crafting questions in narrative therapy practice.* Workshop presented at the Evanston Family Therapy Institute, Evanston, IL.

Favazza, A. R. (1998). *Bodies under siege: Self-mutilation and body modification in culture and psychiatry.* (2nd ed.). Baltimore, MD: John Hopkins.

Favazza, A., & Selekman, M. D. (2003, April). *Self-injury in adolescents.* Annual Spring Conference of the Child and Adolescent Centre, Department of Psychiatry, University of Western Canada, London, Ontario, Canada.

Feldman, M. K. (2000, March-April). Rug rat rage. *Utne Reader,* 16–17.

Fisch, R., Weakland, J. H., & Segal, L. (1982). *The tactics of change: Doing therapy briefly.* San Francisco: Jossey-Bass.

Follett, M. P. (1995). Constructive conflict. In P. Graham (Ed.), *Mary Parker Follett: Prophet of management.* Boston: Harvard Business.

Frank, J. D. & Frank, J. B. (1991). *Persuasion and healing: A comparative study of psychotherapy* (3rd ed.). Baltimore, MD: John Hopkins.

Fredrickson, B. L. (2002). Positive emotion. In C. R. Snyder & S. J. Lopez (Eds.), *Handbook of positive psychology* (pp. 120–135). New York: Oxford University.

Garbarino, J. (1995). *Raising children in a socially toxic environment.* San Francisco: Jossey-Bass.

Gardner, H. (1993). *Multiple intelligences: The theory in practice.* New York: Basic.

Gardner, H. (1999). *Intelligence reframed: Multiple intelligences for the 21st century.* New York: Basic.

Garmezy, N. (1994). Reflections and commentary on risk, resilience, and development. In R. J. Haggerty, L. R. Sherrod, N. Garmezy, & M. Rutter (Eds.), *Stress, risk, and resilience in children and adolescents: Processes, mechanisms, and interventions* (pp. 1–19). Cambridge, UK: Cambridge University.

Gergen, K. J. & McNamee, S. (2000). From disordering discourse to transformative dialogue. In R. A. Neimeyer & J. D. Raskin (Eds.), *Constructions of disorder: Meaning-making frameworks for psychotherapy* (pp. 333-349). Washington, DC: American Psychological Association.

Gilbert, R. M. (1999). *Connecting with our children: Guiding principles for parents in a troubled world.* New York: John Wiley.

Gingerich, W. J., & de Shazer (1991). The BRIEFER project: Using expert systems as theory construction tools. *Family Process, 30,* 241–249.

Gingerich, W. J., & Eisengart, S. (2000). Solution-focused brief therapy: A review of the outcome research. *Family Process, 39*(4), 477–498.

Gladwell, M. (2002). *The tipping point: How little things can make a big difference* (second edition). New York: Back Bay.

Goldstein, J., & Kornfield, J. (1987). *Seeking the heart of wisdom.* Boston: Shambhala.

Gorski, T. T. (1989). *Passages through recovery: An action plan for preventing relapse.* Center City, MN: Hazeldon.

Greenberg, R. P. (1999). Common psychosocial factors in psychiatric drug therapy. In M. A. Hubble, B. L. Duncan, & S. D. Miller (Eds.), *The heart and soul of change: What works in therapy* (pp. 297-329). Washington, DC: American Psychological Association.

Greenberg, R. P., Bornstein, R. F., Zborowski, M. J., Fisher, S., & Greenberg, M. D. (1994). A meta-analysis of fluoxetine outcome in treatment of depression. *Journal of Nervous and Mental Disease, 182,* 547–551.

Grotevant, H. D., & Cooper, C. R. (Eds.). (1983). *Adolescent development in the family.* San Francisco: Jossey-Bass.

Haggerty, R. J., Sherrod, L. R., Garmezy, N., & Rutter, M. (Eds.). (1994). *Stress, risk, and resilience in children and adolescents: Processes, mechanisms, and interventions.* Cambridge, UK: Cambridge University.

Hammerschlag, C. (1988). *The dancing healers: A doctor's journey of healing with Native Americans.* New York: Harper & Row.

Henggeler, S. W., & Alexander, J. (1999, October). *Family therapy in the culture of violence.* General Session presentation at the fifty-seventh annual AAMFT Conference, Atlanta, GA.

Henggeler, S. W., Schoenwald, S. K., Borduin, C. M., Rowland, M. D., & Cunningham, P. B. (1998). *Multisystemic treatment of antisocial behavior in children and adolescents.* New York: Guilford.

Hoffman, L. (1988). A constructivist position for family therapy. *The Irish Journal of Psychology, 9,* 110–129.

Hubble, M. A., Duncan, B. L., & Miller, S. D. (Eds.). (1999). *The heart and soul of change: What works in therapy.* Washington, DC: American Psychological Association.

Huston, A. C., Donnerstein, E., Fairchild, H., Feshbach, N. D., Katz, P. A., Murray, J. P., Rubinstein, E. A., Wilcox, B. L., & Zuckerman, D. (1992). *Big world, small screen: The role of television in American society.* Lincoln, NE: University of Nebraska.

Isaacs, W. (1999). *Dialogue and the art of thinking together.* New York: Currency.

Janis, I. (1972). *Victims of groupthink.* Boston: Houghton-Mifflin.

Kabat-Zinn, J. (1990). *Full catastrophe living.* New York: Delacorte.

Kabat-Zinn, J. (1995). *Wherever you are there you are: Mindfulness meditation in everyday life.* New York: Hyperion.

Kammen, C., & Gold, J. (1998). *Call to connection: Bringing sacred tribal values into modern life.* Salt Lake City, UT: Commune-A-Key.

Kauffman, C., Grunebaum, H., Cohler, B. J., & Gamer, E. (1979). Superkids: Competent children of psychotic mothers. *American Journal of Psychiatry, 136,* 1398–1402.

Kegan, R. & Lahey, L.L. (2001). *How the way we talk can change the way we work: Seven languages for transformation.* San Francisco: Jossey-Bass.

Kernberg, O. (1975). *Borderline conditions and pathological narcissism.* New York: Aronson.

Kilbourne, J. (1999). *Deadly persuasion: Why women and girls must fight the addictive power of advertising.* New York: Free Press.

Kirsch, I., & Sapirstein, G. (1998). Listening to prozac but hearing placebo: A meta-analysis of antidepressant medication. *Prevention and Treatment, 1,* Article 0002a. Available at www.http://journals.apa.org/treatment/volume 1/pre 0010002a.html.

Klein, G. (1998). *Sources of power: How people make decisions.* Cambridge, MA: MIT.

Kutchins, H., & Kirk, S. A. (1997). *Making us crazy: DSM: The psychiatric bible and the creation of mental disorders.* New York: Free Press.

Laird, J. (2000). Culture and narrative as central metaphors for clinical practice with families. In D. H. Demo, K. R. Allen, & M. A. Fine (Eds.), *Handbook of family diversity* (pp. 338–359). New York: Oxford.

Lambert, M. J. (1992). Implications of outcome research for psychotherapy integration. In J. C. Norcross & M. R. Goldfried (Eds.), *Handbook of psychotherapy integration* (pp. 94–129). New York: Basic.

Lambert, M. J. & Bergin, A. E. (1994). The effectiveness of psychotherapy. In A. E. Bergin & S. L. Garfield (Eds.), *Handbook of psychotherapy and behavior change* (4th ed., pp. 143–189). New York: John Wiley.

Lammare, J., & Gregoire, A. (1999). Competence transfer in solution-focused therapy: Harnessing a natural resource. *Journal of Systemic Therapies, 18*(1), 43–58.

Lazarus, A. A. (1996). *Behavior therapy and beyond.* New York: Jason Aronson.

Lebow, J. & Gurman, A. S. (1996, January-February). Making a difference: A new research review offers good news to couples and family therapists. *Family Therapy Networker,* 69–76.

Lee, S. C. (1998). *The circle is sacred: A medicine book for women.* Tulsa, OK: Council Oak.

Lerman, H. (1996). *Pigeonholing women's misery: A history and critical analysis of the psychodiagnosis of women in the twentieth century.* New York: Basic.

Levenkron, S. (1998). *Cutting: Understanding and overcoming self-mutilation.* New York: Norton.

Lewis, D. & Cheshire, A. (1998). Taking the hassle out of school: The work of the anti-harassment team of selwyn college. *Dulwiche Centre Journal, (2 & 3),* 4–26.

Linehan, M. (1993). *Cognitive-behavioral treatment in borderline personality disorder.* New York: Guilford.

Linn, D., & Linn, M. (1997). *Quest: A guide for creating your own vision quest.* New York: Ballantine.

Main, M. (1995). Attachment: Overview with implications for clinical work. In S. Goldberg, R. Muir, & J. Kerr (Eds.), *Attachment theory: Social, developmental, and clinical perspectives*, (pp. 407–474). Hillsdale, NJ: Analytic.

Maltz, D. N. & Borker, R. A. (1982). A cultural approach to male-female miscommunication. In J. J. Gumperz (Ed.), *Language and social identity* (pp. 55–67). Cambridge, UK: Cambridge University.

Marlatt, G. A. & Gordon, J. (Eds.). (1985). *Relapse prevention: Maintenance strategies in the in the treatment of addictive behaviors.* New York: Guilford.

Masten, A., Best, K. M., & Garmezy, N. (1990). Resilience and development: Contributions from the study of children who overcome adversity. *Development and Psychopathology, 2,* 425–444.

Masterson, J. F. (1981). *The narcissistic and borderline disorders.* New York: Brunner/Mazel.

Mattox, W. R. (1991, Winter). The parent trap. *Policy Review, 55,* 10.

McDermott, D., & Snyder, C. R. (1999). *Making hope happen: A workbook for turning possibilities into reality.* Oakland, CA: New Harbinger.

McLeod, M. (2001, January). Changing how we work together. *Shambhala Sun, 9*(3), 28–34.

McMullin, R. E. (2000). *The new handbook of cognitive therapy techniques.* New York: Norton.

McNamee, S. & Gergen, K. J. (1999). *Relational responsibility: Resources for sustainable dialogue.* Thousand Oaks, CA: Sage.

Metcalf, L., Thomas, F. N., Duncan, B. L., Miller, S. D., & Hubble, M. A. (1996). What works in solution-focused brief therapy: A qualitative analysis of client and therapist perceptions. In S. D. Miller, M. A. Hubble, & B. L. Duncan (Eds.), *Handbook of solution-focused brief therapy* (pp. 335–351). San Francisco: Jossey-Bass.

Miller, D. (1994). *Women who hurt themselves: A book of hope and understanding.* New York: Basic.

Miller, J. B. (1976). *Toward a new psychology of women.* Boston: Beacon.

Miller, J. B. & Stiver, I. P. (1997). *The healing connection: How women form relationships in therapy and in life.* Boston: Beacon.

Miller, S. D., Hubble, M. A., & Duncan, B. L. (1995). No more bells and whistles. *Family Therapy Networker, 19*(2), 52–58, 62–63.

Minuchin, P., Colapinto, J., & Minuchin, S. (1998). *Working with families of the poor.* New York: Guilford.

Minuchin, S. (1974). *Families and family therapy.* Cambridge, MA: Harvard.

Minuchin, S., & Fishman, H. C. (1981). *Family therapy techniques.* Cambridge, MA: Harvard.

Molnar, A., & de Shazer, S. (1987). Solution-focused therapy: Toward the identification of therapeutic tasks. *Journal of Marital and Family Therapy, 13*(4), 349–358.

Moos, R. (1979). *Evalution of educational environments: Procedures, measures, findings, and policy implications.* San Francisco: Jossey-Bass.

Naisbitt, J., Naisbitt, N., & Philips, D. (1999). *High tech, high touch: Technology and our search for meaning.* New York: Broadway.

Nylund, D., & Corsiglia, V. (1994). Becoming solution-focused forced in brief therapy: Remembering something important we already know. *Journal of Systemic Therapies, 13,* 5–12.

O'Hanlon, W. H. (1987). *Taproots: Underlying principles of Milton H. Erickson's therapy and hypnosis.* New York: Norton.

O'Hanlon, W. H., & Weiner-Davis, M. (1989). *In search of solutions: A new direction in psychotherapy.* New York: Norton.

Papini, D. R. & Roggman, L. A. (1992). Adolescent perceived attachment to parents in relation to competence, depression, and anxiety: A longitudinal study. *Journal of Early Adolescence, 12,* 420–440.

Papp, P. (1983). *The process of change.* New York: Guilford.

Papp, P., Silverstein, O., & Carter, E. (1973). Family sculpting in preventative work with well families. *Family Process, 12*(2), 197–212.

Parnes, S. (1992). *Visionizing.* Buffalo, NY: Creative Education Foundation.

Philpot, C. L., Brooks, G. R., Lusterman, D. D., & Nutt, R. L. (1997). *Bridging separate gender worlds: Why men and women clash and how therapists can bring them together.* Washington, DC: American Psychological Association.

Pipher, M. (1994). *Reviving Ophelia: Saving the selves of adolescent girls.* New York: Ballantine.

Prochaska, J. O. (1999). How do people change and how can we change to help many more people? In M. A. Hubble, B. L. Duncan, & S. D. Miller (Eds.), *The heart and soul of change: What works in therapy* (pp. 227–259). Washington, DC: American Psychological Association.

Prochaska, J. O., Norcross, J. C., & Diclemente, C. C. (1994). *Changing for good: The revolutionary program that explains the six stages of change and teaches you how to free yourself from bad habits.* New York: William Morrow.

Raskin, J. D., & Lewandowski, A. M. (2000). The construction of disorder is human enterprise. In R. A. Neimeyer & J. D. Raskin (Eds.), *Constructions of disorder: Meaning-making frameworks for psychotherapy* (pp. 15–41). Washington, DC: American Psychological Association.

Reimer, M. S., Overton, W. F., Steidl, J., Rosenstein, D. S., & Horowitz, H. (1996). Familial responsiveness and behavioral control: Influences on adolescent psychopathology, attachment, and cognition. *Journal of Research on Adolescence, 6,* 87–112.

Reimers, T. M., Wacker, P., Cooper, L. J., & DeRaad, A. O. (1992). Acceptability for behavioral treatments for children: Analog and naturalistic evaluations by parents. *School Psychology Review, 21,* 628–643.

Rinpoche, L. Z. (1993). *Transforming problems into happiness.* Boston: Wisdom.

Rosenfeld, A., & Wise, N. (2000). *Hyper-parenting: Are you hurting your child by trying too hard?* New York: St. Martin's.

Satir, V. (1972). *Peoplemaking.* Palo Alto: Science & Behavioral.

Schon, D. A. (1983). *The reflective practitioner: How professionals think in action.* New York: Basic.

Seagram, B. C. (1997). *The efficacy of solution-focused therapy with young offenders.* Unpublished doctoral dissertation, York University, New York, Ontario, Canada.

Seikkula, J., Aaltonen, J., Alakare, B., Haarakangas, K., Keranen, J., & Sutela, M. (1995). Treating psychosis by means of open dialogue. In S. Friedman (Ed.), *The reflecting team in action: Collaborative practice in family therapy* (pp. 62–81). New York: Guilford.

Seikkula, J., Alakare, B., & Aaltonen, J. (2000). A two-year follow-up on open dialogue treatment in first episode psychosis: The need for hospitalization and neuroleptic medication decreases. *Social and Clinical Psychiatry, 10*(2), 20–29.

Selekman, M. D. (1991). With a little help from my friends: The use of peers in the family therapy of adolescent substance abusers. *Family Dynamics of Addiction Quarterly,1,* 69–77.

Selekman, M. D. (1993). *Pathways to change: Brief therapy solutions with difficult adolescents.* New York: Guilford.

Selekman, M. D. (1995a). "Help me out . . . I'm confused:" The Columbo approach with difficult youth. *Newsletter of the Brief Therapy Network, 1*(4), 1–4.

Selekman, M. D. (1995b). Rap music with wisdom: Peer reflecting teams with tough adolescents. In S. Friedman (Ed.), *The reflecting team in action: Collaborative practice in family therapy* (pp. 205–223). New York: Guilford.

Selekman, M. D. (1997). *Solution-focused therapy with children: Harnessing family strengths for systemic change.* New York: Guilford.

Selekman, M. D. (1999). The solution-oriented parenting group revisited. *Journal of Systemic Therapies, 18*(1), 5–24.

Selekman, M. D. (2005). *The self-harming adolescents as experts research project.* Unpublished manuscript.

Selekman, M. D., & Todd, T. C. (1991). Crucial issues in the treatment of adolescent substance abusers and their families. In T. C. Todd & M. D. Selekman (Eds.), *Family therapy approaches with adolescent substance abusers* (pp. 1–20). Needham Heights, MA: Allyn & Bacon.

Seligman, M. E. (1995). *The optimistic child: A revolutionary program that safeguards children against depression and builds lifelong resilience.* Boston: Houghton-Mifflin.

Siegel, D. J. (1999). *The developing mind.* New York: Guilford Press.

Siegel, D. J., & Hartzell, M. (2003). *Parenting from the inside out: How a deeper self-understanding can help you raise children who thrive.* New York: Jeremy P. Tarcher.

Simon, R. (1997, January-February). The family unplugged. *Family Therapy Networker*, 24–33.

Snyder, C. R., Michael, S. T., & Cheavens, J. S. (1999). Hope as a psychotherapeutic foundation of common factors, placebos, and expectancies. In M. A. Hubble, B. L. Duncan, & S. D. Miller (Eds.), *The heart and soul of change: What works in therapy* (pp. 179–201). Washington, DC: American Psychological Association.

Sparham, E., Roy, J., & Stratton, P. (1995). Youth: The voices of a lost generation. *Human Systems: The Journal of Systemic Consultation and Management, 6*(3), 295–308.

Spence, D. P. (1987). *The Freudian metaphor: Toward paradigm change in psychoanalysis.* New York: Norton.

Spence, D. P. (1982). *Narrative truth and historical truth.* New York: Norton.

Stinnett, N., & O'Donnell, M. (1996). *Good kids: How you and your kids can successfully navigate the teen years.* New York: Doubleday.

Strong, M. (1998). *A bright red scream: Self-mutilation and the language of pain.* New York: Penguin.

Szapocznik, J., & Kurtines, W. M. (1989). *Breakthroughs in family therapy with drug-abusing and problem youth.* New York: Springer.

Taffel, R., & Blau, M. (1999). *Nurturing good children now: 10 basic skills to protect and strengthen your child's core self.* New York: Golden.

Taffel, R., & Blau, M. (2001). *The second family: How adolescent power is challenging the American family.* New York: St. Martin's.

Tannen, D. (1990). *You just don't understand.* New York: William Morrow.

Tomm, K., & White, M. (1987, October) *Externalizing problems and internalizing directional choices.* Paper presented at the Annual American Association for Marriage and Family Therapy Conference, Chicago, IL.

Wall, S., & Arden, H. (1990). *Wisdomkeepers: Meetings with Native American spiritual elders.* Hillsboro, OR: Beyond Words.

Wallace, R. K., Benson, H., & Wilson, A. F. (1984). A wakeful hypometabolic physiologic state. In D. H. Shapiro & R. N. Walsh (Eds.), *Meditation: Classic and contemporary perspectives* (pp.417–431). New York: Aldine.

Walsh, B. W. & Rosen, P. M. (1988). *Self-mutilation: Theory, research, and treatment.* New York: Guilford.

Weiner-Davis, M., de Shazer, S., & Gingerich, W. (1987). Building on pretreatment change to construct the therapeutic solution: An exploratory study. *Journal of Marital and Family therapy, 13*(4), 359–363.

Werner, E. E., & Smith, R.S. (1992). *Overcoming the odds.* Ithaca, NY: Cornell University.

White, M. (1985). Fear-busting and monster taming: An approach to fears of young children. *Dulwich Centre Review,* 29–33.

White, M. (1986). Negative explanation, restraint, and double description: A template for family therapy. *Family Process, 25*(2), 169–184.

White, M. (1988, Winter). The process of questioning: A therapy of literary merit? *Dulwich Centre Newsletter*, 8–14.

White, M. (1989). *Selected papers of Michael White*. Adelaide, South Australia: Dulwich Centre Publications.

White, M. (1995). *Re-authoring lives: Interviews & essays*. Adelaide, South Australia: Dulwich Centre Publications.

White, M., & Epston, D. (1990). *Narrative means to therapeutic ends*. New York: Norton.

Wolin, S. J. & Wolin, S. (1993). *The resilient self: How survivors of troubled families rise above adversity*. New York: Villard.

Wylie, M. S. (2004, September/October). Mindsight. *Psychotherapy Networker*, 29–39.

Zweig-Frank, H., Paris, J., & Grizder, J. (1994). Psychological risk factors for dissociation and self-mutilation in female patients with borderline personality disorder. *Canadian Journal of Psychiatry, 39*, 259–264.

Index